D1412976

This item must b   **st date shown**

SEFTON PUBLIC LIBRARIES

A fine will be charged on any overdue item plus the cost of reminders sent

MARITIME BRITAIN

A Celebration of Britain's Maritime Heritage

PAUL HEINEY

ADLARD COLES NAUTICAL
London

Published by Adlard Coles Nautical
an imprint of A & C Black Publishers Ltd
37 Soho Square, London W1D 3QZ
www.adlardcoles.com

First edition 2005

ISBN 10: 0-7136-7091-6
ISBN 13: 978-0-7136-7091-2

A CIP catalogue record for this book is available from the
British Library.

A & C Black uses paper produced with elemental chlorine-free
pulp, harvested from managed sustainable forests.

Cover and text design by Susan McIntyre.
Photo research by Susan McIntyre and Margaret Brain.

Typeset in Rotis Serif and Dax Wide.

Printed and bound in Spain by Book Print, S.L.

Note: While all reasonable care has been taken in the production
of this publication, the publisher takes no responsibility for the
use of the methods or products described in the book.

ACKNOWLEDGEMENTS
The author and publisher would like to give sincere thanks to
all the museums, tourist offices and other organisations that
have helped with the compilation of the information supplied
in this book.

PHOTO PAGE I: *Thames sailing barge* Reminder.
COURTESY OF THE SAILING BARGE ASSOCIATION.
PHOTO PAGES II-III: *Alnmouth, Northumberland.*
COURTESY OF PETER WAKELY/ENGLISH NATURE.

CONTENTS

INTRODUCTION

What draws you to the coast? Is it to stroll along the beach and watch the boats go by, or perhaps to eat fish and chips while enjoying the salty tang of a drying harbour as the tide ebbs?

Or does the coastline mean more to you than that? Do you stand on the cliff edge and gaze across the waves, thinking of those who first ventured across them: the brave souls who sailed the oceans to explore the world? Perhaps you think of fish, and the men who went to catch them; or you may have thoughts of warfare as you imagine long forgotten fleets at anchor, ready to fight and defend in the great battles that have been fought off our shores. You spot a yacht, and think of the pioneer circumnavigators; you see a lifeboat and wonder what deeds of immense bravery have been enacted by local crews. Our coast is so rich in history that the difficulty is not in seeking it out, but making sense of it when you stumble across it.

Much of the glory of Britain's maritime history lies in the past, but that does not mean it is forgotten, or entirely lost to us. Through our maritime museums, both large and small, a greater understanding and appreciation of our maritime heritage is waiting for us. Some of these museums are professional establishments with all one would expect of a national collection. But others might be small, local affairs, a single room perhaps; built with dedication and a desire to make us all understand what the sea has meant to those who lived and worked thereabouts. They have one thing in common – there is not one of them which doesn't have a gripping tale to tell.

The coastal museums, historic ships, lifeboats and lighthouses open to the public, are there for you to visit, and this book will tell you where. But the real purpose of Maritime Britain is to show you how all the pieces of this maritime jigsaw fit together to make up the glorious picture that is our seafaring tradition.

Arbroath harbour. PHOTO COURTESY OF ANGUS AND DUNDEE TOURIST BOARD.

FAIR ISLE, CROMARTY, FORTH

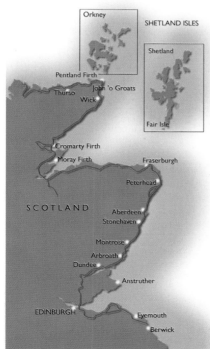

From Cape Wrath to Eyemouth, including Orkney and Shetland

- Shetland Isles
- Fair Isle ■ Orkney
- Pentland Firth
- North Coast of Scotland
- Wick ■ Cromarty Firth
- Moray Firth
- Fraserburgh
- Peterhead ■ Aberdeen
- Stonehaven ■ Montrose
- Arbroath ■ Dundee
- Anstruther ■ Leith
- Eyemouth

Rocks at Haroldswick. PHOTO © UNDISCOVERED SCOTLAND.

THE SHETLAND ISLES ━━━━━━━━━━━━━━━━━━━

Maritime Britain begins its journey on a windswept, rocky outcrop at the northern tip of Shetland, on which stands the **Muckle Flugga** lighthouse. Built by David Stevenson, this was one of 30 lighthouses he constructed in northern waters while engaged as engineer for the Northern Lighthouse Board. Muckle Flugga first showed its light in January 1858. It stands now at the heart of a world-famous reserve where 100,000 seabirds visit the rocks and cliffs hereabouts every season – guillemots, razor bills, kittiwakes and fulmars. For visitors to the northern shore of Unst, there are seals and otters to be seen at low tide, observed from the breath-taking cliff tops or the sandy strands.

This is a truly wild beginning to *Maritime Britain*, for around the coasts of these northern islands, winds can blow with a ferocity unmatched anywhere else in Britain making the local seafaring community as hardy as any you will find. Huge Atlantic swells pound the feet of these cliffs and these remote, windswept islands are often treeless. The prehistoric remains found hereabouts remind you that although much has changed in the rest of the world, the scenery of Shetland is as it was centuries ago.

■ Unst

There are 100 islands in the Shetland group, although only 15 are inhabited, and it is on the most northerly, Unst, that you will find the most remote maritime museum in Britain: the **Unst Boat Haven**.

Here, they have dedicated their museum to the preservation of the traditional craft of these waters by constructing, under cover, a typical Shetland beach scene. Even for such a small collection of islands as Shetland, it is difficult to describe any individual boat as being *the* traditional craft, but here you can learn the difference between the smaller 'whillies' and 'eela boats', the larger 'fourareen' or 'saithe' boats, and largest of all the 30-foot 'sixareen'. The overall impression of these boats, of whatever size, is the simplicity of construction which enabled them to be built with the limited materials (with little naturally- growing wood on Shetland and often imported from Norway) and using the simplest of tools. With its proximity to Norway and the Faroes, expect a strong Norse flavour.

One of the traditional craft displayed at the museum. PHOTO COURTESY OF THE UNST BOAT HAVEN.

■ Lerwick

Lerwick, originally a 17th century Dutch settlement, is the only town within the islands. It has a fine protected harbour which has found new prosperity since the coming of North Sea oil, making it a base for support vessels. Further north, at Sullom Voe, massive tankers take advantage of a rare, fjord-like sheltered stretch of water, in which to load oil brought ashore from the offshore fields by pipeline.

For a flavour of the Norse tradition that survives in these islands, the time to be in Shetland is the last Tuesday in January when the 'Up-Helly-Aa' is celebrated. This 18th century modernizing of a Norse

Oil tankers at Sullom Voe. PHOTO © UNDISCOVERED SCOTLAND.

feast, marking the end of Yule and lengthening of the days, involves the parading of a specially-built 30-foot galley through the streets of Lerwick, by 'guizers' wearing masks, before a ceremonial burning. The resulting party lasts for many hours after.

Lerwick has the **Shetland Museum** which reflects centuries of island life and houses an impressive collection of model boats, and early photographs.

■ Traditional fishing craft

THE SHETLAND YOLE This traditional craft of these islands displays its Viking influences. Built of overlapping planking, narrow and pointed at both ends, these little craft were the mainstay of the inshore fishing fleet. Built without reference to plans, or measurements, they were designed for simplicity of construction, and for seaworthiness. Not unique to Shetland, these craft are also found in Orkney, but all bearing the name 'yole'.

THE *SWAN* A Shetland Fifie LK 243, the *Swan* is a restored fishing vessel of the type common to Lerwick harbour and the northern waters in the 19th and early 20th centuries.

Having been built in Lerwick, (the *Shetland News* of May 5th 1900 reported '*She is the largest ever built in Lerwick, her dimensions being: length, 67 feet; length of keel, 60.5 feet; beam, 20 feet outside; depth, 9.5 feet from keelson. The timbers are mostly of oak, with larch and pitch pine skin, and in her whole construction practically no expense has been spared in order to secure strength.*') she spent much of her working life in Whalsay. She was discovered, a wreck, at the bottom of Hartlepool dock after being retired to Grimsby in 1960 and converted to a houseboat.

A major fund-raising campaign, and a great deal of local support, got her sailing again in 1996, and she now takes young-sters and trainees to sea to help to keep alive traditional seamanship. She has a place in hearts of all Shetland people, and has almost become their mascot.

The *Swan*. PHOTO COURTESY OF SHETLAND MUSEUM.

Böd of Gremista

In the 18th century, Gremista to the north of Lerwick, was an important fishing station. Small stone buildings, known as böds, were used for storing fishing equipment and dried fish – they were intentionally built to be draughty! An example of a larger form of böd with living accommodation still remains as a museum – the Böd of Gremista.

Interior of the Bod. PHOTO COURTESY OF SHETLAND MUSEUM.

Less immediately obvious is this böd's place in a wider maritime history. This was the birthplace of Arthur Anderson, the founder of what was to become the Peninsular and Oriental Steam Navigation Company, known as P & O. Born the son of fish curer, he served in the Navy before pursuing a career based on the belief that sailing the seas could be a pleasure as well as a commercial necessity. He tried, and failed, to persuade the British government to build a canal between the Mediterranean and the Red Sea. The French built the Suez canal a year after his death. Anderson's life is reflected in the museum housed in the Böd of Gremista.

■ The 'Shetland Bus'

These islands have always had a strategic, as well as a maritime significance, and despite their remoteness, were deeply touched by both World Wars. It was from here that the legendary 'Shetland Bus' ran during the Second World War, run by Norwegian resistance fighters with the help of the Royal Navy. These were daring voyages, often undertaken in appalling weather and with the constant fear of being spotted by German patrols or aircraft. Crossings were generally made at night, the ships unlit, but always with the risk of capture on arriving at the Norwegian coast.

In 1941, a secret base was set up at Lunna on the north east side of Mainland (the principal island) and from here radio sets, ammunition and secret agents were dispatched to Norway to help the resistance workers there. This base was later moved to Scalloway where the current Scalloway Museum tells the heroic tale of the Shetland Bus.

FAIR ISLE

This tiny island, owned by the National Trust for Scotland, is only four miles long and two wide. It gives its name to the shipping forecast area in which it lies, but it is probably more famous for its sweaters than its weather. It is edged with spectacular cliffs rising to 100 metres, on top of which live the population of 70 or so. It is a place of wildness, wildlife, and an eternal warm welcome.

The traditional local craft of Fair Isle, similar to the yoles, were rowed by three men who used a rapid chopping stroke of the oars which gave them great speed.

ORKNEY

Seventy islands make up Orkney, of which only 17 are inhabited. Wild, certainly, but not in the stark way that Shetland can present itself. On Orkney, the impression is of a more placid place with a greener landscape. Ancient history abounds, from the Skara Brae Neolithic site, to the tomb of Maeshowe and the standing circle of stones at Brodgar. But for maritime history, which is also in abundance, you must start at the **Stromness Museum**. Here you will learn of the recruitment of Orcadians by the Hudson's Bay Company in the 18th and 19th centuries to work in the fur trade in Canada. Orkney also became a centre for the stocking and replenishing of ships engaged in whaling who stopped there for food and water on their way northwards.

In the 18th century, Orkney had added importance when passage through the English Channel became hazardous due to the wars with France. Instead, ships chose to take the 'northern way round' passing from the Atlantic to the North Sea via Orkney. Waiting to take advantage of them was the notable pirate, John Gow. Gow's story was heard by Sir Walter Scott who visited in 1814 and it became the basis of his novel *The Pirate*. It is said that the plot of the book was given to him by Bessie Miller of Stromness who was in the dubious trade of 'selling' fair winds to sailors.

Part of Captain Cook's collection of harpoons left in Orkney during his return journey from the South Seas.
PHOTO COURTESY OF STROMNESS MUSEUM.

Victorian ship models and paintings. PHOTO COURTESY OF STROMNESS MUSEUM.

Despite it giving him the entire plot of a lengthy novel, Scott showed no affection for Orkney. He travelled, as a guest, aboard the lighthouse yacht, *Pharos*, as it went about its work of servicing buoys and lighthouses. He was suffering from a painful leg at the time, which might have coloured his view. He wrote:

'*We have been struggling with a very strong tide called the Rost of the Start which, like Sumburgh Rost, bodes no good to our roast and boiled. We are to weigh at two in the morning and hope to reach Kirkwall by breakfast tomorrow. I trust there are no rusts or rosts in the road. I shall detest that word even when used to signify antique or patina in one sense, or roast venison in the other.*'

Robert Garden's shop boat visiting Hoy. PHOTO COURTESY OF STROMNESS MUSEUM.

Home and Atlantic fleets in Scapa Flow 1909. PHOTO COURTESY OF STROMNESS MUSEUM.

SCAPA FLOW

This is one of the finest natural harbours in the world, and was of huge strategic significance in both World Wars as the Royal Navy's most northern base from where it had quick and easy access to the vital north Atlantic. It has witnessed many of the turning points in modern naval history. At the end of the first World War, the German fleet of 80 or so warships was effectively imprisoned in Scapa Flow as one of the terms of the treaty which brought the war to an end. Awaiting the final settlement, being argued over at Versaille, the German sailors led a miserable life in Scapa Flow, under-fed and bored, and beaten by the wild weather which sweeps through these islands.

Rangefinder from HMS Vanguard.
PHOTO COURTESY OF STROMNESS MUSEUM.

The eventual deal, to which the Germans were given a deadline of 21st June 1919 to agree, proved unacceptable to the German admirals who took into their own hands the decision about what should happen to the fleet, and the order was given for it to be scuttled. To the eyes of amazed onlookers, many of whom had been crowding the pleasure boats which took people on a tour of the fleet, one by one the ships sank. By the end of the day, 74 once proud warships were on the bottom of Scapa Flow.

LEFT: Items salvaged from the German fleet; ABOVE: wardroom china.
PHOTOS COURTESY OF STROMNESS MUSEUM.

The first major naval loss of the Second World War took place in Scapa Flow when HMS Royal Oak (31,200 tons) was sunk at her moorings by the German U boat, U-47 which crept in unnoticed via Holm Sound. 833 men were lost. To prevent further such attacks, Winston Churchill ordered the closure of the gaps between the islands by what became known as the 'Churchill Barriers'. These provide the current road links between islands.

Every year, on the 14th of October, a white ensign is placed on the hull of the Royal Oak by Royal Navy divers in memory of those who were lost.

The full story of Scapa Flow is told at the **Scapa Flow Visitor Centre** from Napoleonic times to WWII with much emphasis, of course, on the scuttling of the German fleet in 1919. Housed in a former pumphouse (one of which can be seen in action) this visitor centre is on the site of a former naval base, now removed. One large fuel tank remains which now houses major exhibits such as a bren-gun carrier and a small boat used in the dangerous wartime ferries between Orkney and Norway.

Scapa Flow Visitor Centre, Hoy.
PHOTO © UNDISCOVERED SCOTLAND.

THE PENTLAND FIRTH ━━━━━━━━━━━━━━━━

It is no easy step from Orkney to the mainland of Britain, for between the two lies the notorious Pentland Firth: a vicious stretch of water where mountainous and irregular seas can build (in even modest weather) which are capable of swallowing ships whole. It is said to be the second worst stretch of water in the world, after Cape Horn, and some captains passing from Europe to the Atlantic will still prefer the longer but safer passage north of Orkney.

The most severe part of the tide race is called 'The Merry Men of Mey' and the turbulence stems from the movement of the tide through the narrow gap between Orkney and the mainland. The entire North Sea, having filled itself on the flood tide, has little choice but to empty itself through the Pentland Firth which gives rise to currents in excess of 12 knots in places. This is so fast that most vessels would hardly make progress against it and, even on a calm day, causes the water to break and steep waves to form, known as 'Pentland Walls' over which ships have dropped. The losses over the centuries have been countless.

THE NORTH COAST OF SCOTLAND ━━━━━━━━━━

Despite its forbidding name and stark appearance, Cape Wrath, 360 feet high with its 70-foot lighthouse built by Robert Stevenson in 1827, has no anger about it, for 'wrath' is Norse for 'turning point'. One of the most

difficult and remote places to approach in the whole of maritime Britain, it requires a ferry ride across the Kyle of Durness and a 12-mile ride in a minibus. You then find yourself in the most remote and under-populated part of Britain. To the east lies Loch Eribol, know to all those who served in the North Atlantic convoys, who were required to spend many weeks here, as Loch 'Horrible'. Again, its name is misleading, for Eribol means 'home on a gravelly beach' although few who have waited there at anchor have found

Loch Eribol. PHOTO © UNDISCOVERED SCOTLAND.

anything domestic about the place. The island in the middle of the loch was used for target practice for bombers about to destroy the *Tirpitz*, moored in a Norwegian fjord.

But despite being less than ten degrees from the Arctic circle, the summers on this northern Scottish coast can be mild, with fine bathing from white sandy beaches. Many of the villages here were established as crofting communities after the Highland clearances of the 19th century, surviving on fishing and farming, gathering the plentiful seaweed for fertilizer.

The lighthouse at Dunnet Head.
PHOTO © UNDISCOVERED SCOTLAND.

John O' Groats (named after the Dutchman Jan de Groot, who was commissioned in 1496 to start a ferry service to Orkney after the islands had been won back from the Norwegians by the Scots) has the reputation as being the most northerly point of mainland Britain. But that honour, strictly-speaking, falls on Dunnet Head, where even at 300 feet above sea level, the windows of the lighthouse are splattered by the sea when storms rage in the Pentland Firth below. From here, on a clear day, are stunning views all the way from Cape Wrath to Duncansby Head, and north to Orkney.

WICK

This is the only major commercial centre in the north-eastern tip of Scotland. Once an early Viking settlement, it depended, like many of the fishing towns on this coast on the cod and salmon industry. Then came the herring boom which brought no less that 1700 boats to Wick during the 1860s for the six-week duration of the herring fishing season.

The **Wick Heritage Centre** tells the story of this town, which was once the largest herring

The herring smokehouse displayed at Wick Heritage Centre. PHOTO © BILL FERNIE.

ABOVE: Printing press and lighthouse lantern (RIGHT) from Wick Heritage Centre.
PHOTOS © BILL FERNIE.

port in Europe. Built and run by volunteers, this is the largest museum in north Scotland and winner of many awards. It contains as full a representation of a fishing town as could ever be achieved in a single museum, featuring the work of the coopers, net makers, the Wick radio station, the mechanism of the lighthouse on Noss Head to the north. The strongest reminder of the importance of the seasonal herring trade hereabouts lies in the fact that this town boasted no less than 47 inns which served 800 gallons of whisky a week at the peak of the season.

■ Whaligoe

As the coastline falls away to the south of Wick, it is littered with small, lonely and often remote fishing communities. It is worth pausing at **Whaligoe** to marvel at the 365 steep steps cut into the cliffs. Up and down these, baskets laden with herring were laboriously carried during the season from a now-ruined curing shed on the beach. The herring were bound for the market at Wick and were usually hauled by the women of the village.

The steps at Whaligoe. PHOTO © BILL FERNIE.

The Invergordon mutiny

Invergordon has provided a safe, secure, and deep water anchorage for the Naval fleets in both world wars, although it is more famous for its mutiny in 1931 than any other single event. An economic crisis, hard on the heels of the 1929 Wall Street crash, found Prime Minister Ramsay MacDonald imposing a 25 per cent pay cut on seamen, as well as cuts in benefits and pay for all public service workers. Half the Royal Navy – 12,000 sailors – went on strike at Invergordon in protest and refused to set sail. This made for dramatic national headlines. An Admiralty investigation led to the imprisoning of some strikers, and the dismissal of others.

THE CROMARTY FIRTH

One of the largest natural harbours in Europe, it is entered through a narrow gap between North Sutor and the Sutors of Cromarty. After the loneliness of the coastline so far, to see the North Sea oil construction site at Nigg Ferry, reminds us of the impact the discovery of oil has had on this coastline since the 1970s. The old traditional fishing economy has been replaced by one based on large investment, construction and maintenance on a grand scale. From here, southwards, oil has undoubtedly made its mark and established new maritime traditions.

With room for only two cars, the Cromarty to Nigg car ferry is the smallest in Scotland. PHOTO © UNDISCOVERED SCOTLAND.

North Sea oil

The oil fields stretch in a long line, following the oil-bearing strata in the sedimentary rock, from north of Shetland (the Magnus field) southwards till abreast Edinburgh (the Ekofisk field). The oil itself is formed from tiny decayed algae (plant material) and bacteria and is found in rocks 150 million years old. The first discovery was made in 1971 and the search continues as older wells close and new ones are brought on stream. The engineering effort is huge and major technological strides have been needed to reap this rich harvest.

The oil platforms are truly massive, and it is not unusual for them to operate in nearly 500 feet of water, have the height of an 80-storey office block, and withstand winds up to 120 miles per hour with the consequent seas.

Each platform might operate up to 40 individual wells from a single, main wellhead which could travel down as far as two miles through sea and rock before reaching the oil. In some strata, the oil will be under pressure and released as soon as it is 'hit' by the drills. In other cases, water or gas may have to be pumped down to create the pressure necessary for the oil to come to the surface.

Deep water is essential for the construction of these monster platforms, which is provided in the Cromarty Firth at Nigg Bay, and on the Firth of Forth.

The oil rig crews are the new workforce of the North Sea. Now the landscape is less peopled by oilskin-clad heroes who sailed the seas for fish, but are now replaced by the neoprene-suited divers who work in

these treacherous waters, and the 'rednecks' who provide the muscle to keep the precious oil flowing. This is a new industry, not yet mature enough to boast a museum of its own. But it is only a matter of time.

Oil rig platform in Cromarty Firth.
PHOTO © UNDISCOVERED SCOTLAND.

The sheltered waters of Findhorn Bay. PHOTO © UNDISCOVERED SCOTLAND.

THE MORAY FIRTH

The fishermen of the Moray Firth are well portrayed at the **Nairn Museum** which depicts the life of the fishing fleets of this coastline in its Fishertown Display Room. The earliest fishing in the Moray Firth was line fishing, usually for haddock, whiting and flounders. Longer lines were used for catching cod, ling and halibut. The construction of the larger harbour at Nairn shifted the emphasis, for larger boats could be operated which could fish as far away as Orkney, Shetland and Wick. It also meant that the town could harvest some of the prosperity brought by the annual migration of the shoals of herring.

The southern shores of the Moray Firth provide some of the most benign landscapes in the whole of Scotland with sandy beaches providing first class bathing. Sailing is centred on Findhorn – a village in its third incarnation, the first being buried beneath sand in a storm in the 17th century, then destroyed by floods in 1710. In the lee of the Highlands, the summers here can be warm.

■ Lossiemouth

Lossiemouth remains a busy fishing town with two sandy beaches. It was here that Ramsay MacDonald, the Prime Minister who sparked the Invergordon Mutiny of 1931 (see page 13), was born, and a reconstruction of his study can be seen in the town. The shipbuilding firm, Wood of Lossiemouth, were responsible for the creation of one of the most distinctive fishing vessels of these waters – the Zulu.

■ The Zulu

Before the 1870s, the fishing boats hereabouts were open-decked vessels of about 40 feet with a straight stem, raked stern and a short keel. This made it easier for boats to be hauled up the beach above the high water mark, avoiding the need to harbour the craft. In the event of needing to stay at sea for the night, the men would sleep in the open boat beneath only canvas and the stars.

The Zulu, designed by William Campbell, changed the face of the fleet. These classic fishing boats, driven by sail, were strong and fast and built in huge numbers. They ruled the roost in these waters till the coming of steam driven vessels, when the Zulu went quickly into extinction.

The fishing vessels of the north east of Scotland

Shetland yoles. PHOTO © CHARLES TAIT

YOLES: The early 19th century boats were based on the yoles of Orkney and Shetland; they were undecked, 30 feet long with a crew of 5 men and a boy.

SCAFFIES: Scaffies superseded the yoles, having a steeply-raked stern and bow which made for a short keel and a manoeuvrable boat.

FIFIES: By the 1850s, the fifie was the boat of choice, with a near vertical stem and stern making it better in heavier seas, and more close-winded than a scaffie.

ZULUS: The Zulu brought together the best of the scaffie and fifie, opting for a near vertical bow and a raked stern. Being a much larger and heavier boat, it allowed more sail to be carried, and hence had a greater speed. These survived till the 1890s when the first steam drifters appeared.

PHOTO COURTESY OF SHETLAND MUSEUM.

Crovie (ABOVE) and Gardenstown, typical of the fishing villages of this coast. PHOTOS COURTESY OF ABERDEEN AND GRAMPIAN TOURIST BOARD.

The spirit of the 'Drifter days' is best captured at the **Buckie Drifter Maritime Heritage Centre** where a reconstructed 1920s quayside sets the scene and a replica Buckie Drifter is there to give you a feel of the deck beneath your feet. The retired local lifeboat, *The Doctors* is here, and the finest collection of paintings of Buckie Drifters and their working environment by the artist Peter Anson.

Moving southwards to **Rattray Head** much of this coastline has a glorious past, but very much reduced fishing activity these days. Fraserburgh and Peterhead thrive as the busiest fishing ports in the north east.

FRASERBURGH ━━━━━

Housed in the former lighthouse at Kinnaird Head (the first lighthouse to be built on the top of a fortified castle), the **Museum of Scottish Lighthouses** now houses Britain's largest collection of lighthouse lenses and equipment. This was the site of Scotland's first ever light-house, built in 1787. The lighthouse in

The lighthouse museum at Kinnaird Head. PHOTO COURTESY OF MUSEUM OF SCOTTISH LIGHTHOUSES.

which the museum currently stands was decommissioned in 1991 and moved to a nearby prefabricated structure, but there is now a move to reinstate the light in the tower built at the original castle. This will bring together the original David Stevenson lens of 1902 with some of the latest light technology.

The Stevenson family

This most remarkable family of engineers was responsible for much of the lighthouse building in Scotland. Robert Stevenson (grandfather of Robert Louis) was born in 1772 and was entrusted with his first important commission: the building of the Pentland Skerries light in 1794. This was not his first lighthouse, having built Little Cumbrae on the Clyde in 1791. He was a determined man who 'distrusted literature and intellectuals'.

Between 1808 and 1842 he built 15 lighthouses, amongst them the legendary Bell Rock light, which was a major engineering achievement. The tradition of lighthouse building stayed with the family through Alan, David, Thomas, David A, and Charles

Lighthouse lantern. PHOTO COURTESY OF MUSEUM OF SCOTTISH LIGHTHOUSES.

Stevenson. The most recent Stevenson light, Torness, was built in 1937. There seemed to be no maritime engineering task that this family would not face. The last of the Stevenson family engineers, David A, deepened the Clyde for the newly built Queen Mary after her launch in 1934.

PETERHEAD

The sailors of Peterhead have a long association with more distant waters, having set out from here, in times past, for the whaling grounds of the north Atlantic and the Arctic. Even today, as the largest white fish landing port in Europe, it has the feel of a town which does business in distant seas. Its large harbour, begun in 1886 and finished in 1958, employed convicts from Peterhead jail to create what is known locally as the National Harbour of Refuge. It provides a safe base for not only the fishing fleet but also for oil industry support vessels.

At the **Arbuthnot Museum** and **Peterhead Maritime Heritage** you discover that seamen have voyaged far and wide from Peterhead, into wild arctic waters in pursuit of whales, hence the collection of Inuit (Eskimo) artifacts.

ABERDEEN

These days, Aberdeen is 'Oil City' and this is reflected in the busy commercial harbour from which massive support vessels steam daily to the oil fields to replenish and maintain them. Helicopters come and go, and the scent of heavy engineering is in the air. None of the traditional fishy smells of the east coast remain. This is reflected in the **Aberdeen Maritime Museum** which shows Aberdeen's traditional seafaring roots, but also the origins and influences of the new offshore gas and oil industry and the vast engineering infrastructures which support them.

South from Aberdeen are the fishing towns of Stonehaven, Montrose and Arbroath.

Aberdeen Maritime Museum.
BELOW: Tempting seafood from local waters. PHOTOS COURTESY OF ABERDEEN AND GRAMPIAN TOURIST BOARD.

STONEHAVEN

Stonehaven has been a fishing port since the 16th century, based around its natural harbour. It was around this time that the Tolbooth was built – one of the oldest buildings in the town which is now the **Tolbooth Museum**. Here, convicts were held before transportation to Gallows Hill half a mile away. Don't let this thought spoil your enjoyment of the fish restaurant housed on the upper floor.

Stonehaven and the harbour. PHOTO COURTESY OF ABERDEEN AND GRAMPIAN TOURIST BOARD.

The port of Stonehaven was never a major fishing harbour to rival those further north, and her breakwater was only completed as the herring boom was coming to an end. However, net repairing is still carried out on the green at Cowie Harbour as it has been for generations.

MONTROSE

For the landlubber, Montrose marks the start of serious golfing country, climaxing some miles south at St Andrews. But for the maritime enthusiast, Montrose presents itself as a thriving port with a new lease of life thanks to North Sea oil. What sets Montrose apart from other harbours on this coast is the remarkable Montrose Basin, a large contained tidal area of some 350 acres. The rise and fall of the tide creates a unique and changing habitat of salt marsh and reed beds providing habitat for a wide range of birds. It is designated a site of special scientific interest.

Montrose Basin. PHOTO COURTESY OF ANGUS AND DUNDEE TOURIST BOARD.

ARBROATH

At Arbroath, dominated by the ruins of a 12th century abbey, a signal tower stands overlooking the harbour. Built in the 19th century, it was erected to communicate with the Bell Rock lighthouse 11 miles offshore, built to warn sailors of the presence of the Inchcape Rock. The building of the Bell Rock light was yet another triumph for the master lighthouse builder Robert Stevenson. There was no doubt amongst mariners about the dangers of the Inchcape Rock – at high tide it vanished under water, and at low tide only the spiky tips showed.

The Signal Tower. PHOTO COURTESY OF ANGUS AND DUNDEE TOURIST BOARD.

Stevenson spent five years persuading the Northern Lighthouse Board that the project was feasible, only to see it taken away from him and given to another engineer. However, clever footwork by Stevenson, over no less than three years, brought the project back under his control. Progress could only be made in the summer months and it took a crew three years, working seven days a week, to construct the 110-foot light. To prove itself, on the night it was first lit, a storm blew up of sufficient strength to throw water over the top of the light itself. It continued to burn, much to Stevenson's satisfaction.

Arbroath harbour. PHOTO COURTESY OF ANGUS AND DUNDEE TOURIST BOARD.

The coastline near Arbroath.
PHOTO COURTESY OF ANGUS AND
DUNDEE TOURIST BOARD.

The first three verses of Robert Southey's
Ballad of the Inchcape Rock:

No stir in the air, no stir in the sea,
The Ship was still as she could be;
Her sails from heaven received no motion,
Her keel was steady in the ocean.

Without either sign or sound of their shock,
The waves flow'd over the Inchcape Rock;
So little they rose, so little they fell,
They did not move the Inchcape Bell.

The Abbot of Aberbrothok
Had placed that bell on the Inchcape Rock;
On a buoy in the storm it floated and swung,
And over the waves its warning rung.

On 30 July, 1814, Sir Walter Scott, journeying
on the lighthouse tender *Pharos* observed the
Bell Rock lighthouse, and wrote:

'*Its dimensions are well known; but no description can give the idea*
of this slight, solitary, round tower, trembling amid the billows, and fif-
teen miles from Arbroath, the nearest shore. The fitting up within is not
only handsome, but elegant. All work of wood (almost) is wainscot; all
hammer-work brass; in short, exquisitely fitted up.'

The Bell Rock is a fine monument to a legendary lighthouse builder,
but the rock itself remains a true hazard, best given a wide berth. R W
Munro in his book, *Scottish Lighthouses*, correctly remarked, '*... those who*
know it most intimately say that the best view of the Bell Rock is over the
stern of a ship.' The only ship to have fallen foul of the rock since the
lighthouse was built in 1811 was *HMS Argyll*, one of the Royal Navy's
largest battle cruisers which struck in 1915. On a wild night, Argyll was
steaming north with all haste to Rosyth, hoping to arrive before dawn
when the German submarines were thought to be active. The captain of
Argyll sent a signal requesting the Bell Rock to be lit – it was routinely
extinguished during the war. But due to the storm, the boats which set
out from the mainland were unable to get a message to the keepers. The
light was not lit, and neither was there any way of informing the captain
of the *Argyll*. Remarkably, there was no loss of life.

The Finnan haddie and the Arbroath smokie

South of Aberdeen is the village of Findon which gave its abbreviated name to the lightly-smoked haddock which was the village's speciality – Finnan haddie. It was made by a traditional method of smoking over open cottage fires, but this became illegal in the 19th century under the factory act. Aberdeen was quick to sieze the trade and took over the entire production leaving Findon haddockless. A writer, once spoke of the virtues of this lightly-smoked fish:

'Give me a platter of choice finnan haddie, freshly cooked in its bath of water and milk, add melted butter, a slice or two of hot toast, a pot of steaming Darjeling tea, and you may tell the butler to dispense with the caviar, truffles, and nightingales' tongues.'

Some, however, would argue that the joys of the Finnan haddie are more than matched, if not out-classed, by the Arbroath smokie, a native of some miles south. Smokies go through a slightly different process to the haddie. The smokie is first salted overnight which helps with the preservation of the fish and avoids the need for refrigeration. Next, the 'barrel' or smokehouse, is prepared. Any hardwood can be used to produce the smoke which gives the smokie its flavour. The fish are smoked for an hour or so until golden brown, when they are then ready to eat. The people of Arbroath will tell you that you need never ask direction to a smokie shop, you simply follow your nose.

DUNDEE

Dundee may have a reputation for jute and jam, but when it comes to maritime history it can offer a rich mix. You will find an evocation of the heroic and desperate days of the whaling fleets; also the world's most original wooden warship, the *Discovery*, the ship which took Scott to Antarctica. Originally built in Dundee, the *Discovery* has now been restored and placed on full display at **Discovery Point**, one of the major tourist attractions on this stretch of coast.

Verdant Works industrial museum, Discovery Point. PHOTO COURTESY OF ANGUS AND DUNDEE TOURIST BOARD.

The Discovery. PHOTO COURTESY OF ANGUS AND DUNDEE TOURIST BOARD.

■ Captain Scott and *Discovery*

Considered a 'delicate child', Scott was destined to take command of one of the most arduous of polar expeditions. He was born of naval blood but because of doubts over his health there was some uncertainty about whether he would ever join the family 'firm'. He came, however, to the attention of the President of the Royal Geographical Society who was impressed by the young Scott's naturally commanding manner and in 1900 he was appointed to lead the National Antarctic Expedition.

The *Discovery* was built especially for the trip by the Dundee Shipbuilders' Company and Scott was at her launching on 21 March 1901. Seeking a design suitable for the high, rough seas of the Southern Ocean, they decided a whaling ship offered the best pattern to follow and she was modelled on an earlier ship, also called *Discovery*, at the suggestion of the Arctic explorer, Nansen.

Her construction was massive, and she came equipped for everything that could befall a ship in icy waters – her prop and rudder could he hoisted out of the way to save them from damage by crushing ice. However, there were faults. The flat, shallow hull rolled in a seaway with an uneasy motion and Scott, sailing her for the first time in the English Channel, said she was 'sluggish, short-masted and under-canvassed'. He was later to find, in the roaring forties, that shortness of mast was no hindrance.

On arriving in Antarctica, *Discovery* spent the winters of 1902/3 and part of 1904 frozen in, conducting experiments and awaiting fresh supplies. She was eventually recalled to England and using explosives and muscle power, somehow broke through 20 miles of ice that lay between her winter base and the open sea. Scott, meanwhile, had trekked to within 480 miles of the south pole.

Discovery arrived back in Portsmouth on 10 September 1910 and was Scott's first choice of ship for his next expedition of 1910. The Admiralty, however, had sold her to the Hudson Bay Company, who would not part with her for any money!

HM Frigate *Unicorn*

This remarkable piece of British maritime history boasts of being not only the 'oldest British-built ship afloat' but also the 'last intact warship from the days of sail'. Her pedigree puts her amongst the best of the fighting ships of the Royal Navy: she was one of the 'Leda' class of frigate, containing such stirring names as *Shannon*, *Chesapeake* and *Trincomalee* (now *Foudroyant*).

However, she was destined to have no great naval career. She was built in a period of peace and was taken into service as a powder hulk at Woolwich. In the meantime, steam had finally eclipsed sail and her fighting days were done without a shot ever having been fired. She found use as a training ship for the RNVR in Dundee where she was berthed for almost a century in the Earl Grey dock.

Figurehead of the Unicorn. PHOTO COURTESY OF THE HERITAGE TRAIL.

Despite the neglect, it seemed she would never die. Throughout her life her timbers remained sound, but the filling-in of the dock (as part of the development of the Tay Road Bridge) forced a decision to have her scrapped. And she would have been, had it not been for the intervention of a former captain who got the decision reversed and had *Unicorn* moved down-river to her new berth.

Although in need of restoration, 90 per cent of her is the original structure. She served in the Royal Navy for 140 years and was only decommissioned in 1968.

Sailing on the Tay. PHOTO COURTESY OF ANGUS AND DUNDEE TOURIST BOARD.

The Reaper *sailing.* PHOTO COURTESY OF SCOTTISH FISHERIES MUSEUM.

ANSTRUTHER

At the heart of the East Neuk fishing villages of St Monans, Pittenweem, Cellardyke and Crail, can be found the **Scottish Fisheries Museum** at St Ayles Harbourhead, Anstruther. From these small, snug harbours the inshore fleets of the Firth of Forth set sail for crab, lobster, and herring. The Scottish fishing industry's ups and downs are well told in this fascinating museum.

It is thought that 1000 years ago, a herring export trade existed between Scotland and Scandinavia, but the major expansion in the east-coast herring trade did not take place till 1767 with the establishment of Wick as a major fishing centre. But by the end of that century, the east-coast fisheries were again in a sorry state due to the unpredictability of the arrival and departure of the shoals of herring. The early 1800s brought the real expansion with the building of gutting and curing sheds and the herring trade grew throughout the next 100 years, to peak in 1913 after the gradual introduction, over the previous 20 years of the steam drifters and trawlers.

Two world wars took their toll: fisherman served in the Navy, their craft were commandeered for naval duties, and by the time the Second World War came to a close, the herring industry was all but finished. The herring drifters have now virtually disappeared, although the sailing drifter, *Reaper* can be seen in Anstruther harbour.

The fisherwomen of Scotland

Packing herring in barrels. PHOTO COURTESY OF SCOTTISH FISHERIES MUSEUM.

They fell into two categories – those who stayed at home, called 'fishwives', and the ones who followed the shoals of herring as they migrated the entire east coast of the British Isles, gutting and packing the catch.

For those who followed the shoals, life had a pattern determined by the wandering herring. It was usual to start in the far north at the start of the season, which meant traveling to Shetland in June, carrying their clothes for their four or five months away from home in a wooden or tin chest, called a 'kist'.

They often worked in teams of three; two women gutting and one packing in barrels. It took just one slice of the knife to completely gut a herring which was taken from a wooden trough called a 'farlan'. She would be expected to gut 40 of these a minute, but some women managed 60. The gutted herring were inspected for size and quality, the best were called 'matties', which were fat and with no roe. Then came the 'fulls', the adult fish complete with roe and ready to spawn. The 'spents', which had spawned and lost their roe, were reckoned to be the poorest quality.

The packing of the barrels, also women's work, was as skilled a job as the gutting. The fish were arranged like a rosette, heads pointing inwards the first time, then outwards on the next layer to get as many in a barrel as possible; large quantities of salt kept the layers apart. This work continued from five in the morning till midnight, if the size of the catch demanded it. The weather would not be allowed to interfere with the work. A 19th century writer said of the herring workers: '*they acquired a self assurance and knowledge of the outside world that was rare in a woman of another sphere*'.

The women who stayed at home, the 'fishwives', had no easier a time of it. Apart from their domestic duties, they were expected to care for the nets, collect mussels for bait for long-line fishing, and bait the 1000 hooks that were attached to a line. They also played a part in the selling of the fish – helping to cart it to the fish markets. Even so, they were no slaves. An observer remarked, '*The women enslave the men to their will, and keep them chained under petticoat government*'.

Reconstruction of the living room in a fisherman's cottage. PHOTO COURTESY OF SCOTTISH FISHERIES MUSEUM.

But the **Scottish Fisheries Museum** is as much about the fishing communities as it is about the ships they sailed. The dangers of the work are clear. In the models of undecked boats, see how easily waves could sweep over them, sending little ships to the bottom, which was no uncommon occurrence. The museum also houses the 'Memorial to Scottish Fishermen Lost at Sea'.

The museum is the place to see a Zulu drifter, a Fifie drifter, a Montrose Salmon coble, yawls, yoles and long boats. Get a feel, too, for the domestic lives of the fishing families in reconstructed rooms, gutting and curing sheds.

LEITH

■ The SS *Explorer*

The SS *Explorer* is the last of the sea-going steam trawlers, built in 1955 and the final ship to leave Alexander Hall's shipyard in Aberdeen. Her career was in fishery research, working out of Aberdeen, and she boasts of being the first such ship to carry a computer which, at the time, occupied a substantial cabin. The other 30 cabins were occupied by scientists and crew. The officers lived in some luxury, their cabins even having fireplaces.

Like many such ships, she faced an uncertain future after decommissioning in 1984, and she has twice been saved from the breaker's yard. It is now the intention of dedicated enthusiasts and supporters that she will complement the former Royal Yacht *Britannia* by lying close by her in Leith. 'She's a similar age and size, but the opposite side of the coin – a real working ship'. Guided tours are available.

Britannia *at Leith.* PHOTO COURTESY OF ROYAL YACHT *BRITANNIA* TRUST.

■ The Royal Yacht *Britannia*

Now at rest in Edinburgh's port of Leith after 40 years service to the Royal Family, the Royal Yacht *Britannia* has undertaken 968 official voyages to some of the most remote parts of the world, including Antarctica. Her last voyage left from Portsmouth in January 1997.

No single voyage was conducted with the ship in anything other than perfect condition. Crew were chosen from men who saw perfection as their personal goal. For example, it was their job to ensure that the gangway was never steeper than 12 degrees. Crew dived daily as a security exercise to search the seabed beneath her when in harbour. The teak decks had to be scrubbed to perfection and all jobs conducted in silence, and completed by 8am when the Royal family woke. If a member of the ship's company should meet the Royal Family, they must stand as still as a statue and pretend they are not there. The running of the ship required 20 officers and 220 crew.

A decade ago it was unthinkable that the most famous royal yacht in the world might be open to the public, but here she is for all to see, and walk the decks, marveling at the polish in the state rooms, the engine rooms and the bridge. However, be prepared to find the state rooms grand rather than sumptuous, and the private rooms quite modest. The crew seemed to live like sardines.

Her final foreign mission was to convey the last British governor of Hong Kong, after the return of the British colony to the People's Republic of China on 30 June 1997.

Britannia's *sun-lounge.*
PHOTO COURTESY OF ROYAL YACHT *BRITANNIA* TRUST.

DOWN TO EYEMOUTH

South of the Firth of Forth, Scotland ebbs away and England takes charge of the coastline south of Berwick-upon-Tweed. And although the border between the two countries is a political one, there is little doubt that we are leaving behind one kind of coastline and entering another. True, there are still the stately cliffs of the Yorkshire coast to come, but we are now on a downward slope which takes us to the muddy, sandy flats of the Wash and the East Anglian coast.

Coming south, the last maritime museum in Scotland is at Eyemouth. Here the story is one of tragedy, for on the night of 14 October 1881, out of a clear sky, a gale sprang up which sank 23 boats and drowned 189 men. Here you can seen the stunning Eyemouth tapestry which was designed and made in the centenary year of the disaster.

The Rev. Daniel McIver wrote, 25 years after the disaster, and in memory of those lost:

'*Friday the 14 October 1818, should have a place in the calendar of calamities and disasters that have befallen our nation ... a storm of indescribable violence suddenly broke over the country ... great forests of trees were rooted up as easily as garden plants ... at 8 am the fishing fleet had sailed from the harbour ... sailing over a still sea. Without any visible warning from outside conditions, the sky suddenly thickened with dark heavy clouds; a fierce wind arose which was as wild in its fury as the calm was quiet; the sea began to heave its threatening bosom, like a man in whose heart passion was rising, and what between sudden darkness, the shrieking of the hurricane as it drove the creaking masts and ripping sails, and the thunderous roar of a boiling ocean, the poor fishermen thought that the Judgement day had come.*'

A visit to the **Eyemouth Museum** can only underline the words of Sir Walter Scott, who wrote, '*It's not fish ye're buying. It's men's lives*'.

Eyemouth harbour in calm weather.
PHOTO © UNDISCOVERED SCOTLAND.

Fair Isle, Cromarty, Forth Gazetteer

Unst Boat Haven
Haroldswick, Unst, Shetland
Isles, ZE2 9ED
☎ +44 (0)1957 711324
www.unst.shetland.co.uk/
frame.html
OPEN Every afternoon,
1 May–30 Sept or BA

Scalloway Museum
Main Street, Scalloway,
Shetland Islands
☎ +44 (0)1595 880256
www.shetlandheritage.
co.uk/shetlandbus
OPEN May–Sept (enquire)
or BA

Shetland Museum
Shetland Museum Service,
Lower Hillhead, Lerwick,
Shetland ZE1 0EL
☎ +44 (0)1595 695057
www.shetlandmuseum.
org.uk
OPEN Mon–Sat
DON'T MISS Sixareen: best
model of this type of craft
unique to Shetland. The
wooden leg from the man
who lost his leg in the
Arctic whaling. A flagon
discovered in the stomach
of a whale.

Böd of Gremista
Böd of Gremista, Lerwick,
Shetland
OPEN 1 Jun to mid Sep
Wed–Sun; 10:00–13:00
and 14:00–17:00
Free admission

North Ronaldsay Lighthouse
The Northern Lighthouse
Board working in partnership
with the North Ronaldsay
Trust have now opened
North Ronaldsay Lighthouse,
Orkney, for tours on Saturday
& Sundays (12 noon–17:30)
from May–Sept and at other
times by arrangement.
Contact Mr W Muir
☎ 01856 633257.
The lighthouse tower was
designed and built by Alan
Stevenson in 1854, and is
Britain's tallest land-based
lighthouse. The original
lighthouse beacon built by
Thomas Smith in 1789 is
still standing nearby.
PLEASE NOTE this tour is not
suitable for anyone suffering from heart, breathing or
balance difficulties and that
children under 1m in height
will not be allowed access,
this includes carried children.

Scapa Flow Visitor Centre and Museum
Pier Head, Lyness, Hoy,
Orkney Islands KW16 3NT
☎ +44 (0)1856 791300 or
873535 for Orkney Heritage
www.orkneyheritage.com
OPEN Daily, Mid-May–Oct;
Mon–Fri in winter

Stromness Museum
52 Alfred Street, Stromness,
Orkney Islands KW16 3DF
☎ +44 (0)1856 850025
www.orkney.org/museums/
stromness.htm
OPEN Daily, Apr–Sept;
Mon–Sat, Oct–March.

Wick Heritage Centre
19 Bank Row, Wick,
Caithness KW1 5EY, Scotland
☎ +44 (0)1955 605393
www.caithness.org/history/
wickheritagecentre/newwick
heritage/wickheritagecentre.
htm
OPEN Mon–Sat 10:00–15:45/
17:00 Jun–Sept

Nairn Museum
Viewfield House, Viewfield
Drive, Nairn IV12 4EE,
Scotland
☎ +44 (0)1667 456791
www.nairnmuseum.co.uk
OPEN Mon–Sat, Mar–Oct, or BA

Lossiemouth Fisheries and Community Museum
Pitgaveny Quay, Lossiemouth,
Moray, Scotland.
☎ 44 (0)1343 543221
www.moray.gov.uk/
museums/facilities/
lossiemouth.html
OPEN Enquire by telephone.
A small independent
museum displays the past
and present fishing industry
in the Moray Firth. Located
in a former net loft, other
local history exhibits include
a reconstruction of Labour
Prime Minister James
Ramsay MacDonald's
Lossiemouth study.

The Buckie Drifter
Freuchny Road, Buckie,
Moray AB56 1TT, Scotland
☎ +44 (0)1542 834646
www.moray.org/area/
bdrifter/intro.html
OPEN Daily, Easter–Oct. Sat &
Sun in winter; closed all Dec.

Museum of Scottish Lighthouses
Kinnaird Head, Fraserburgh, Aberdeenshire AB43 9DU, Scotland
☎ +44 (0)1346 511022
www.lighthousemuseum.co.uk
OPEN Daily

Arbuthnot Museum
St. Peter Street, Peterhead, Aberdeenshire, Scotland
☎ +44 (0)1779 477778
www.bbaf-arts.org.uk/sites/bbaf/arts/arbuthnot.asp
OPEN Mon–Sat except BH. Weds: am only

Peterhead Maritime Heritage
South Road, Lido, Peterhead, Aberdeenshire, Scotland
☎ +44 (0)1779 473000;
www.aberdeen-grampian.co.uk/thecoastaltrailpeterhead.htm
OPEN Daily, Jun–Aug (telephone for confirmation and times)

Aberdeen Maritime Museum
Shiprow, Aberdeen AB11 5BY (Aberdeenshire) Scotland
☎ +44 (0)1224 337700
www.aberdeencity.gov.uk/acc/default.asp
OPEN Mon–Sat,10:00–17:00; Sun 12:00–15:00

Tolbooth Museum
The Harbour, Stonehaven, Aberdeenshire, Scotland
☎ +44 (0)1771 622906
OPEN Daily ex Tues, Jun–Sept

Montrose Museum
Panmure Place, Montrose, Angus DD10 8HE, Scotland
☎ +44 (0)1674 673232
www.scottishmuseums.org.uk/museums
OPEN Mon–Sat 10:00–17:00

Tolbooth Museum, Stonehaven.
COURTESY OF ABERDEENSHIRE.GOV.UK.

Arbroath Museum
Signal Tower, Ladyloan, Arbroath, Angus, DD11 1PU Scotland
☎ +44 (0)1241 875598
www.scran.ac.uk
OPEN Mon–Sat; also Sun pm Jul & Aug

Broughty Castle Museum
Castle Approach, Broughty Ferry, Dundee DD5 2PE. Scotland
☎ +44 (0)1382 436916
www.dundeecity.gov.uk/broughtycastle
OPEN Daily, Apr–Sept; Tues–Sun, Oct–Mar

Discovery Point
Discovery Quay, Dundee DD1 4XA, Scotland
☎ +44 (0)1382 201245
www.rrsdiscovery.com
OPEN Daily, except Christmas & Jan 1 & 2

The Frigate Unicorn
Victoria Dock, Dundee DD1 3JA Scotland
☎ +44 (0)1382 200900
www.frigateunicorn.org
OPEN Daily

McManus Galleries
Albert Square, Dundee DD1 1DA Scotland
☎ +44 (0)1382 432084
www.dundeecity.gov.uk/
OPEN Daily

Scottish Fisheries Museum
St Ayles, Harbourhead, Anstruther, Fife KY10 3AB, Scotland
☎ +44 (0)1333 310628
www.scottish-fisheries-museum.org
OPEN Daily (except Christmas & New Year holidays)

Buckhaven Museum
Buckhaven Library, College Street, Buckhaven, Fife, Scotland
☎ +44 (0)1592 412860
www.scottishmuseums.org.uk
OPEN Tue, Thu–Sat (except BH). Times vary: library hours

The Royal Yacht Britannia
Ocean Terminal, Leith, Edinburgh, Scotland
☎ +44 (0)131 555 5566
www.royalyachtbritannia.co.uk
OPEN Daily except Christmas & New Year. Prebooking necessary in Aug

SS Explorer Fishery Research Vessel
SS Explorer Restoration Society, Catchpell House Business Centre, Carpet Lane, Leith, Edinburgh, EH6 6SP
☎ 0131 468 8500
www.leithhistory.co.uk/ssexplorer
OPEN Free guided tours available every Sat 14:00–16:00

Eyemouth Museum
Auld Kirk, Manse Road, Eyemouth, Scottish Borders TD14 5JE, Scotland
☎ +44 (0)1890 750678
www.scottishmuseums.org.uk/museums
OPEN Daily, Easter–end Oct; hours vary. Closed in winter

BA: By arrangement
BH: Bank holiday
GV: Group visits

TYNE,
HUMBER

From Berwick-on-Tweed to Great Yarmouth

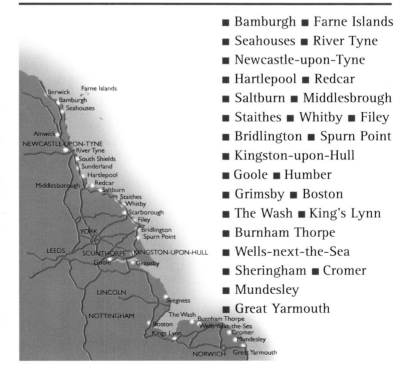

- Bamburgh ■ Farne Islands
- Seahouses ■ River Tyne
- Newcastle-upon-Tyne
- Hartlepool ■ Redcar
- Saltburn ■ Middlesbrough
- Staithes ■ Whitby ■ Filey
- Bridlington ■ Spurn Point
- Kingston-upon-Hull
- Goole ■ Humber
- Grimsby ■ Boston
- The Wash ■ King's Lynn
- Burnham Thorpe
- Wells-next-the-Sea
- Sheringham ■ Cromer
- Mundesley
- Great Yarmouth

Boulby Cliffs. PHOTO COURTESY OF CAPTAIN COOK COUNTRY.

The coastline of sea areas Tyne and Humber gradually crumbles from the craggy cliff faces of Yorkshire, past the swirling, shifting waters of the Humber estuary, to the flat, sandy shores of the Wash. From here, the coast wraps itself around Norfolk, depositing offshore sandbanks to trap unwary ships. This has never been an easy coast for navigators. The Yorkshire coast offers no shelter at all if the wind should blow onshore. The Humber would be treacherous to approach in an onshore gale without modern navigation aids, and the North Sea has never provided enough depth of water for the smaller harbours of Lincolnshire and Norfolk to be either safe or available at every state of tide.

Nevertheless, for all its lack of obvious suitability as the birthplace of maritime heroes, it can claim to have given to Britain the plucky Grace Darling, the intrepid James Cook, and the lauded Horatio Nelson. Also born and bred here was the most decorated lifeboatman in the history of the RNLI: Henry Blogg of Cromer. There is a quality about these waters that inspires greatness.

It is also a coastline which gave birth to distinct maritime tribes. There were inshore fisherman; always a law unto themselves and well represented here whether fishing for cod off Bridlington, or dredging mussels in the Wash. But other industries have bred new kinds of seamen. Between Whitby and the Tyne, the export of coal left its mark because the coal fields of the north of England played a large part in fuelling the Victorian industrial revolution; nearby maritime communities found themselves drawn into this frenzy of commercial advancement as the cry went out for more coal. In response, the colliers of the north-east set sail for London, or East Anglia, supplied by the Keel boats of the Tyne manned by crews described as a breed of sea gypsy who wore yellow waistcoats and black neckerchiefs. Further south, at Kings Lynn, lived the 'Northenders'. Thought of as rogues and vagabonds, they dressed in sealskin caps and moleskin trousers and were famous for their acrimonious disputes between families, often settled with fists.

All these tribes shared the common bond of the ever-changing, unforgiving and sometimes deceitful North Sea.

BAMBURGH

No seafaring tale captured the Victorian imagination like that of Grace Darling (1815–1842) the lighthouse keeper's daughter, who rowed through a storm to rescue shipwrecked souls. What greater image of courage could there be than of a plucky young woman, venturing into stormy waters that many a man would shun? No wonder she became

Bamburgh Castle. PHOTO © FREEFOTO.COM.

HULL & DUNDEE.

THE DUNDEE & HULL
STEAM-PACKET COMPANY'S
SPLENDID AND POWERFUL STEAM-VESSEL

FORFARSHIRE,

130 Tons Burden, and 200 Horsepower.

CAPTAIN JAMES MONCRIEFF,
IS APPOINTED TO SAIL AS UNDER, WEATHER, &c., PERMITTING.

FROM HULL.		FROM DUNDEE.	
WEDNESDAY, 6 December, 10 p.m.		SATURDAY, 2 December, 11 p.m.	
„ 13 „ 6 „		„ 9 „ 10 „	
„ 20 „ 9 „		„ 16 „ 17 „	
„ 27 „ 4 „		„ 23 „ 10 „	
1838.		„ 30 „ 11 „	
WEDNESDAY, 3 January, 9 „		1838.	
„ 10 „ 4 „		SATURDAY, 7 January, 10 „	
„ 17 „ 8 „		„ 14 „ 11 „	
„ 24 „ 2 „		„ 21 „ 10 „	
„ 31 „ 7 „		„ 28 „ 11 „	

FARES.

MAIN CABIN, ... £1, 1s.—FORE CABIN, . . . 15s.
DECK (Common Soldiers and Sailors), . . 7s. 6d.
Provisions, Wines, and Spirits, to be had on board, on very moderate terms.

Sailing times of the Forfarshire. PHOTO
COURTESY OF RNLI GRACE DARLING MUSEUM.

quickly elevated to the status of a national heroine. In recent years, it has been suggested that her story may have been embroidered, not by her but by over-zealous journalists and avid readers in search of a thrilling tale. It is not our business here to discuss whether this girl was an early victim of 'hype' but rather to pay tribute to what was, by any measure, an act of true heroism.

■ **The famous rescue**

The boat used in the famous rescue is on display in Bamburgh's **Grace Darling Museum**, and it is worth standing by this short, flat-bottomed coble and imagining the night of 7 September 1838. William Darling was keeper of the Longstone light and although he had six children, all but Grace were ashore that night. A storm raged and the air was filled with rain and spray through which Grace Darling saw a ship wrecked on the Harcar Rock, a mile away. She was the *Forfarshire*, a two-year-old passenger steamer bound from Hull to Dundee with 60 passengers on board. Boiler problems had forced the captain to shut down her engines. Although the Darlings didn't know it, before they even set out on their rescue more than 40 people had already drowned.

We cannot know what the row to the wreck was really like, although artists at the time allowed their imagination full reign in depicting it. But with a tide against them, as well as wind and wave, it effectively took two miles of hard rowing to travel the single mile from the lighthouse to the wreck.

They found nine survivors and five of them were taken back to the lighthouse by Grace's father – Grace remaining with the wreck. Then, two of the rescued men helped William Darling row back again to complete the rescue.

The first newspaper reports, which appeared four days after the rescue, focussed not on the rescue itself, but on debating if the *Forfarshire* had been seaworthy in the first place. It caused a major scandal, and only when that had died down did the story of Grace's courage emerge. It may have been some time in coming, but when the story finally arrived in the public prints, the writers let rip with emotion. For example: '*Surely, imagination in its loftiest creations never invested the female character with such a degree of fortitude as had been evinced by Miss Grace Horsley Darling on this occasion.*

■ The celebrity

As well as the writers, poets and artists were swift to capture the emotion of the moment and propelled Grace Darling to a status which in modern times would have elevated her to that of a superstar. Her biographer, Jessica Mitford, wrote, '*Grace Darling can be precisely and anachronistically described as the first media heroine.*' Of course, a lighthouse afforded her considerable privacy, but

Grace Darling by Henry Perlee Parker (1838). PHOTO COURTESY OF RNLI GRACE DARLING MUSEUM.

even so she was inundated with requests to make appearances, answer letters, give talks. There were even boat trips to the lighthouse, in calm weather, for tourists seeking merely a glimpse of the young woman, and Grace risked near baldness responding to repeated requests for locks of her hair. She was not released from the public torment until her early death, from influenza, just four years after the famous rescue.

Her premature death elevated her even higher, almost to sainthood. Even Queen Victoria was moved to send twenty pounds towards a memorial. The monument that stands in the churchyard at Bamburgh was designed to be seen by passing ships. Grace Darling was just 27 years old when she died.

The Royal Humane Society's annual report for 1839 posed the question: '*Is there in the whole field of history, or of fiction even, one instance of female heroism to compare for one moment with this?*'

The **Grace Darling Museum** contains not only the craft used by Grace and her father in the rescue, but relics from the *Forfarshire* and a collection of Victorian memorabilia which embraced the legend of the heroine of the Longstone light.

GRACE DARLING SONG (VICTORIAN BALLAD)

'Twas on the Longstone Lighthouse, there dwelt
an English maid;
Pure as the air around her, of danger
ne'er afraid;
One morning just at daybreak, a storm-tossed
wreck she spied;
And tho' to try seemed madness, 'I'll save the
crew!' she cried.
And she pull'd away, o'er the rolling sea,
Over the waters blue –
'Help! Help!' she could hear the cry of
the shipwreck'd crew –
But Grace had an English heart,
And the raging storm she brav'd –
She pull'd away, mid the dashing spray,
And the crew she saved!

The Longstone Lighthouse. PHOTO © CORPORATION OF TRINITY HOUSE.

THE FARNE ISLANDS ⸻

No group of islands could have been better placed to trap ships bound on the busy commercial route between Scotland and England. They lie midway between the fishing village of Seahouses, and Bamburgh, consisting of almost 30 islands (depending on how high the tide). Lindisfarne is the only inhabited island in the group and was once the home of two lifeboats although modern rescue craft operate from Seahouses and Berwick.

Feared for centuries by seafarers, the Farnes boast the Longstone Light which claims to be one of the brightest lighthouses in Europe. For trips to the Farnes, for watching birds or seals, the *Glad Tidings* runs daily from Seahouses, depending on the weather, occasionally making trips further north to Holy Island.

SEAHOUSES ⸻

For those not wishing to venture across the choppy, tidal waters to the islands themselves, then the Farne Islands Room at the **Marine Life and Fishing Heritage Centre**, Seahouses, will give a flavour. This museum celebrates Seahouses as a fishing town and its 'Time Tunnel' traces the

Upturned boats used as huts on the Farne Islands. PHOTO © FREEFOTO.COM.

history of the fishing fleets that worked from here. As in most east-coast museums, the herring, the herring-girls, and the fishermen who chased them (both fish and women) are well depicted. Also coopers (barrel makers) and smokers. The promise of marine life is fulfilled with seven tanks containing locally-found fish.

Don't be put off visiting Seahouses on the basis of a Northumberland guide book published in 1888 which described it as '*a malodorous place where fish-curing is extensively carried on*' for this town can lay claim to being the birthplace of the kipper, the result of an accident where some split herring were left overnight in shed in which a wood fire was burning. On discovery the next morning it was assumed that all the fish had been spoilt, but on tasting it was found that a delicacy had been created. There is only one remaining smokehouse in Seahouses today.

Long before the herring fleets brought prosperity to this town (the harbour was extended in the boom years of the 1880s to accommodate 300 craft) the geology of north Northumberland provided a unique opportunity. Developments in agriculture demanded lime be applied to the soil to provide the correct soil conditions in which crops could flourish. As limestone was the main rock found hereabouts, an industry arose in which the quarried limestone was 'burnt' in kilns together with coal (five parts limestone to one of coal) and the resulting lime residue shipped, often by sea, to agricultural parts of Britain, notably East Anglia. The remnants of the kilns are often confused with coastal defences.

Bridges over the River Tyne at Newcastle. PHOTO © FREEFOTO.COM.

RIVER TYNE

The fortunes of the River Tyne and the city of Newcastle are firmly built on coal which was being exported from here as far back as Elizabethan times. But it was the coming of the Industrial Revolution which elevated the Tyne into one of the most important rivers in Britain, second only to the Thames in terms of trade and shipping movements. So rich were the coalfields hereabouts (hence the pointless exercise of 'carrying coals to Newcastle') that when the cry went out from the expanding cities of the south of England for more coal to fuel industry, the miners and seamen of the Tyne area were more than ready to answer the call.

■ The keels and keelmen of the Tyne

The coal was transported to Newcastle from neighbouring coalfields using a distinctive craft called the 'keel'. The flat-bottomed keels have a noble parentage and are related to craft used by the Anglo-Saxons for their invasion in the 5th and 6th centuries. They called their craft 'ceols', and the Tyne keels are direct descendants of them, first used in the early 1300s. The word 'keel' is said to be the first English word ever to be written down by a Welsh chronicler in the 6th century, according to R J Charleton's *History of Newcastle Upon Tyne*. Driven by long oars, or sweeps, one at each end of the craft, a deep understanding of the tides and shifting sandbanks on the Tyne was required to safely transport the mountain of coal which was heaped amidships.

The keelmen who worked these craft regarded themselves as distinct from other sailors, preferring to live outside the town in Sandgate, where they became a law unto themselves. They were a hardworking but militant crowd and as tough as the next man, often wearing a uniform of blue jacket and yellow waistcoat to mark their clan identity.

They were not born Tynesiders but hardy men from the Scottish borders; and to preserve the special blood they were said to possess, it was common for keelmen's families to inter-marry.

The famous song, The Keel Row, is the only thing that remains of this unique tribe and its fleet of flat-bottomed boats. Rudyard Kipling once wrote of the song, *'The man who has never heard the 'Keel Row' rising high and shrill above the sound of the regiment... has something yet to hear and understand'.*

THE KEEL ROW

As I came thro' Sandgate,
Thro' Sandgate, thro' Sandgate
As I came thro' Sandgate,
I heard a lassie sing:

Weel may the keel row,
The keel row, the keel row
Weel may the keel row
That my laddie's in.

Oh, wha's like my Johnnie,
Sae leish, sae blithe, sae bonny?
He's foremost 'mang the
Mony keel lads o' coaly Tyne.

REFRAIN

He'll set and row sae tightly,
Or in the dance sae sprightly
He'll cut and shuffle sightly
'tis true – were he not mine.

REFRAIN

He wears a blue bonnet,
Blue bonnet, blue bonnet
He wears a blue bonnet,
A dimple in his chin.

REFRAIN

Detail from the 'Blacksmith's needle, a contemporary sculpture with a maritime theme, Newcastle quay.
PHOTO © FREEFOTO.COM.

NEWCASTLE-UPON-TYNE

Given that not far from here Stephenson was making huge engineering strides with his development of the steam locomotive, it is not surprising that minds should have turned to the use of steam as a motive power for ships. The **Discovery Museum**, in central Newcastle, is the north-east's biggest free museum and offers a major reflection on the lives and achievements of Tynesiders. From a maritime point of view, the museum's largest exhibit (at 30 metres long), the *Turbinia*, is of major interest and dominates the entrance hall of this museum.

Turbinia was built in 1894 to demonstrate the capability of the steam turbine engine. She boasted a three-stage axial-flow Parsons engine driving two 12 feet 6 inch outer shafts each with three 18 inch diameter, 24 inch pitch propellers. Despite her 45 tons, she could achieve a top speed of 34.5 knots.

The remarkable nature of this craft, and the astonishment that her appearance caused, is described by the photography pioneer Alfred John West who was amongst the first to take a still photograph of her while at top speed. He wrote: '*It was at this same (1897 Fleet Review at Spithead) Review that a wonderful little vessel named the "Turbinia" appeared, steaming through the Fleet at 35 knots, a speed never before achieved on water. She was the first ship to be fitted with the turbine machinery invented by her owner, the Hon C A Parsons of Newcastle-on-Tyne, and a great sensation was caused by her steaming through the lines at such a speed. Whilst she was at anchor in Portsmouth Harbour, I went aboard and told the owner that I would like to get a snap of his craft going at full speed. "No one has succeeded yet, although many have tried," replied Mr. Parsons. "I should like to have a shot at her," I persisted.*

"Alright, so you shall!" he said with a smile, "I will make another run through the fleet tomorrow, look out for me between lines A and B at noon. That should give you an opportunity." "I'll be there, opposite the Flagship," I told him.

Punctually at 12 o'clock there appeared between the leaders of the lines a smother of foam – it was the "Turbinia". As she raced past the

The famous photograph of Turbinia *by Alfred John West.*

Flagship, I was waiting in my launch and took a flying shot of her. When I developed the plate I was delighted to find that I had "got her", and the owner was so pleased with the result that he invited me to take a number of photographs and a cinematograph film of his craft on the Tyne.'

On what was later described as a 'gatecrashing' of the Spithead review, the designer Charles Parsons took the role of chief engineer. Parsons first started experimental work on marine stream turbines by building a two-foot model boat and progressing to the full-sized *Turbinia*. The importance of his development became instantly obvious to the Royal Navy who were somewhat embarrassed by the fact that the *Turbinia* could not be caught by even the fastest ship as she darted in and out of the fleet.

Charles Parsons was a supreme steam engineer whose motto was: '*If you believe in a principle, never damage it with a poor impression. You must go all the way.'* An Irishman, educated at Cambridge, he made a fundamental leap forward with his invention of the steam turbine. Before then, steam engines had been large and noisy and worked, in principle, by expanding high pressure steam in a piston. His novel idea was to harness the power of high pressure gases issuing from a jet and direct it at the blades of a turbine. He left Cambridge and established the Parsons Works in Newcastle-Upon-Tyne, taking advantage of the nearby coal and iron industries. To convince a sceptical world that his turbines had useful marine applications, he built the *Turbinia*.

Having forcefully established the turbine in marine propulsion, his reputation was made. It was a Parsons engine which drove the *Mauretania*, the *Titanic,* and many of the great ocean liners of the day. It is also, of course, by means of the steam turbine that most of the world's electricity is now generated.

Lighthouse and cannon on the Hartlepool headland. PHOTO SUPPLIED COURTESY OF THE DEPARTMENT OF ENVIRONMENT AND DEVELOPMENT, HARTLEPOOL BOROUGH COUNCIL.

HARTLEPOOL

There are really two Hartlepools – Old and West Hartlepool. The Old was first recorded in 647AD and the town's fine abbey of St Hilda's stands on the Hartlepool headland on a site first occupied by an abbey in 658. Later, John Wesley visited the town, and preached.

West Hartlepool, on the other hand, can hardly go back a couple of centuries. In fact, were it not for the railway, the town would never have existed in the first place. Local businessmen, notably Ralph Ward Jackson, established a new harbour to rival the one at 'old' Hartlepool. Its success was immediate. With the coalfields of Durham on the doorstep, and the iron ore mines of North Yorkshire within reach, West Hartlepool developed into a major heavy industrial centre making steel and building ships. By the First World War, there were no less than 42 ship-owning companies based here. So strategically important was the place that the very first shot fired against the British by the Germans was the bombardment of Hartlepool from the sea. West Hartlepool was a rough and ready town as gangs of labourers moved in and out seeking work. Some have likened the atmosphere in its heyday to that of America's Wild West.

Much of that heavy industry has now left, and government restructuring has brought together the old town and the new, but the flavour of the 18th century can be recaptured in the newly-built **Hartlepool Historic Quay**, where you also find the **Museum of Hartlepool**. By the quay is the chandler, gunsmith, swordsmith and 'the Admiral and the prisoner' in what is described as a '*taste of Nelson's time*'. All of this, of course, is reconstruction.

ABOVE AND RIGHT: Lots of interest for visitors to Hartlepool Historic Quay. PHOTOS SUPPLIED COURTESY OF THE DEPARTMENT OF ENVIRONMENT AND DEVELOPMENT, HARTLEPOOL BOROUGH COUNCIL.

■ The historic ships of Hartlepool

For a real slice of maritime history you must visit HMS *Trincomalee*. Hartlepool has won itself a well deserved reputation in the restoration of some of the most elderly ships afloat. Amongst them HMS *Warrior*, the Navy's first iron-clad warship now to be found in Portsmouth. Also *Trincomalee* which spent many years laid up in Portsmouth Harbour under the name *Foudroyant*, and now resides here as proof of the excellence of modern conservation work when coupled with enthusiasm and determination.

HMS *TRINCOMALEE*

A frigate of the Leda class, she was one of 47 built between 1800 and 1830. Frigates were light, fast ships which didn't have the fire power to take on enemy ships of the line, but were certainly faster and able to manoeuvre in ways that larger ships couldn't. They were at their handiest when chasing pirates, hostile merchantmen, or slavers. They were dashing little ships – message-carriers around the globe. *Trincomalee* was the twelth of these frigates to be built in India due to a lack of domestic oak; Indian teak being in greater supply.

HMS Trincomalee *afloat at Hartlepool Historic Quay where the ship is open to the public throughout the year. She was restored at Hartlepool between 1990 and 2001 in a project that won the World Ship Trust's Maritime Heritage Award. In 2004 the Trust won a Silver Award in the Excellence in England Tourism 'Oscars'. HMS* Trincomalee *is also a popular venue for weddings, functions and filming.*
PHOTO © THE HMS *TRINCOMALEE* TRUST.

She had no glorious start to her career and, removed of her masts, was laid up in Portsmouth harbour in 1819, the Napoleonic wars being over. Not till 1845 was she re-commissioned and spent time in places as far apart as the West Indies, Bermuda, Newfoundland, and patrolling the St Lawrence seaway on 'iceberg watch'. After refitting, she sailed for Vancouver in 1852, and to Alaska in 1854 (then Russian territory) to celebrate the crowning of Tsar Nicholas I. Celebration soon turned to aggression and afterwards she found herself joining an Anglo-French fleet in the north Pacific, ordered to destroy the Russian fleet. Later she guarded the Pacific islands of Pitcairn, Tahiti and Hawaii.

She docked at Chatham on 5 September 1857 where her masts were removed. It was 150 years later that they were replaced. She now awaits your salute in Hartlepool where she can boast of being the oldest British ship afloat.

THE PADDLE SHIP *WINGFIELD CASTLE*

Less distinguished than *Trincomalee* is the paddle steamer *Wingfield Castle* (1934), although she can claim to be Hartlepool born and bred and is once again a fine testament to the restorative powers of Hartlepool when it comes to rescuing elderly ships. By the standards of *Trincomalee*, of course, the paddle steamer *Wingfield Castle* is a mere child having been built here in 1934 alongside her sisters the *Tattershall Castle* and the *Lincoln Castle* which were commissioned for the London and North Eastern Railway Company to provide a passenger ferry across the River Humber between Hull and New Holland. Because of the shallow and shifting nature of the Humber, a shallow-draft ship, like a paddle steamer, was thought ideal.

PS *Wingfield Castle*. PHOTO SUPPLIED COURTESY OF THE DEPARTMENT OF ENVIRONMENT AND DEVELOPMENT, HARTLEPOOL BOROUGH COUNCIL.

Although built for foot passengers, the *Wingfield Castle* had deck space for a few cars, and pens for the transportation of livestock. A cow once managed to escape from its confinement and find its way into the crew quarters. Another cow didn't fancy the trip at all and jumped overboard and swam back to shore. Those incidents apart, these paddle steamers gave faithful service till the opening of the Humber bridge sealed their fate.

Wingfield Castle, since retirement, has served as a restaurant ship, a focus for lengthy legal disputes over ownership and now, thankfully, another centre piece to the growing collection on display in Hartlepool. The *Tattershall Castle* is moored on the River Thames, at London, and the *Lincoln Castle* is at the National Fishing Heritage Centre in Grimsby (see page 70), again serving as a restaurant.

REDCAR

The lifeboat *Zetland* came to Redcar on 7 October 1802, and was the eleventh of Henry Greathead's lifeboats to be built. Greathead has been called the 'inventor' of the lifeboat. His first, the *Original*, was built in 1790 and first tested at South Shields. She was 30 feet long, self-righting and carried seven hundredweight of cork to provide buoyancy. However, despite Greathead's fame, the original design was by William Wouldhave, the parish clerk of South Shields who entered a competition launched by a group of Newcastle businessmen known as The Gentlemen of Lawe

The Zetland. PHOTO COURTESY OF ZETLAND LIFEBOAT MUSEUM.

House, prompted by a tragedy in May 1789 at the mouth of the Tyne when eight were lost. The *Original* cost £91 and served for 40 years before being lost on rocks in a storm. Despite their innovation, and reputations, both Wouldhave and Greathead died penniless.

The *Zetland* is their monument. Constructed of seasoned English oak, she was of unusual design – double ended so that she could be rowed in either direction without having to make a turn. She carried no sail but was powered by oars, the crew consisting of coxswain, second coxswain, the bowman and ten oarsmen. Five of her oars were painted white, and five blue and the coxswain gave orders to 'pull on the blue' as appropriate.

Her arrival was cause of great celebration: '...*in the evening the fishermen were regaled with ale to drink success to the boat and the health of the builder*'. It was also declared by the men of Redcar that '*in the most voluntary and heartfelt manner the lifeboat would never want for hands to man her*'. Two months later she carried out her first rescue saving 15 souls.

The crew were summoned by the sounding of a lone drum (on display in the museum) which beat out the rhythm '*Come along, brave boys, come along*'. Horses from a local farm hauled the craft to the water. In all her years of service, only one lifeboat man lost his life from the *Zetland*.

She was replaced in 1864 as being 'no longer fit for service' and the order was given for her to be destroyed. The man charged with the job met a hostile crowd and her death was postponed. After some years in a barn, forgotten, she found a safe haven at the **Zetland Lifeboat Museum**, beautifully preserved and now under the wing of the RNLI.

THE SALTBURN SMUGGLERS

No stretch of coast has been without its smugglers, but few places lend themselves better to this dark trade than the town of Saltburn, which presented itself as a fishing community but locals were in no doubt that smuggling was the main trade here. Next door to the Ship Inn (one of the few survivors of 19th century Saltburn) you find the **Saltburn Smugglers Heritage Centre** where the star of the 'Smugglers Experience' is undoubtedly the Scotsman John Andrew, the Ship Inn's landlord in the late 1700s. Andrew was a master smuggler, although you would never have guessed because he appeared a gentleman: a wealthy and respected member of the community and no less than master of the local foxhounds. In truth, he ran a smuggling empire employing his own lugger, the *Morgan Rutter.* Taxes on imports were

Saltburn Smugglers Heritage Centre.
PHOTO COURTESY OF CAPTAIN COOK COUNTRY.

high at the time and so his trade was in alcohol, tea and coffee, using what was said to be a concealed tunnel which ran between the Ship Inn and his private home. He evaded capture for many years but was finally arrested in 1827 and served two years in York Castle.

Saltburn pier and cliff railway. PHOTO COURTESY OF CAPTAIN COOK COUNTRY.

CAPTAIN COOK COUNTRY

There is no avoiding the Captain Cook story hereabouts. His birthplace is commemorated, also his school and the port from which he set sail. Conveniently, for those who want to follow his life, you can work your way from his birthplace, at Marton, south of Middlesbrough, and move southwards to Great Ayton where he went to school. Onwards then to the small coastal community at Staithes where he was apprenticed to a haberdasher, and finally to Whitby from where he set sail on his remarkable voyages of discovery. It takes few miles to cover his early years, but each place represents a major stepping stone in the life of this supreme sailor and navigator

The Middlesbrough 'Bottle of Notes'

Before becoming too immersed in the traditional maritime history of Cook, it is worth a look at the remarkable 'Bottle of Notes' to be found in the Central Gardens, Middlesbrough, and erected as a public sculpture in 1993 as a tribute to Cook, their most famous son. Built and conceived by two Dutch sculptors, Claes Oldenburg and Coosje van Bruggen, both with international reputations, they first thought their work might take the form of a sailing ship. However, an Edgar Allen Poe story about the symbolism of the message in a bottle sent their thoughts hurtling in the direction of this amazing piece.

Built of steel – a tribute to the district's engineering, mining and metal working traditions – it consists of two steel bottle shapes, an inner and outer, painted blue and white. The sculpture leans, rather than being set upright, making it appear as if it has been washed up on the shore. The outside of the bottle is constructed of letters which made up the journal entry: *'we had every advantage we could desire in observing the whole of the passage of the planet Venus over the Sun's disc'* – a reference to one of the aims of Cook's voyages to the Pacific.

The Bottle of Notes. PHOTO COURTESY OF CAPTAIN COOK COUNTRY.

■ Birthplace Museum, Marton

You can visit this museum, but you will find no house in which the baby Cook was born – it is long gone. However, a granite vase marks the location in Stewart Park, Marton, Middlesbrough where James Cook was born on 27 October, 1728, in a thatched cottage built by his father who worked as a farm labourer, and eventually overseer at Aireyholme Farm near Great Ayton (which still exists as a farm and can be seen from a nearby footpath). The nearest you will get to Cook's birthplace will be a faithful reconstruction of the interior built in the award-winning **Birthplace Museum**.

Captain James Cook, by Nathaniel Dance. COURTESY OF THE NATIONAL MARITIME MUSEUM.

This museum takes Cook's youthful years as its theme, from birth to school at Great Ayton, his time in nearby Staithes, to the start of his seafaring career in Whitby, where he joined the Royal Navy. You will be greeted by a traditionally-carved Nootka totem pole (a tribute to Cook's mapping of Canadian waters) and join the *Endeavour Shuttle* to propel you back in time to join Cook on his great voyages of discovery. All the modern advances in audiovisual and computer techniques combine to make Cook's adventurous life ever more vivid. There are even the clubs, reputed to have been used to kill him, to remind you how such a spectacular career was brought to a premature conclusion in a fight with Sandwich Island natives in 1779.

The village of Great Ayton, home of the Captain Cook Schoolroom Museum. PHOTO COURTESY OF CAPTAIN COOK COUNTRY.

The life of Captain James Cook

1728 Born in Marton in Yorkshire.

1746 Accepted as a sea apprentice by John Walker, Quaker head of a Whitby shipping firm.

1755 He volunteers for the Royal Navy.

1763–1766 Surveys the coast of Newfoundland.

Summer 1768 Sails for Tahiti on *HMS Endeavour* to record observations of the Transit of Venus.

June 1769 On Admiralty order, he sets sail in a search for Terra Australis Incognita and also an exploration of New Zealand.

Autumn 1769 Circumnavigates New Zealand and concludes that it is not part of a great southern continent.

Spring 1770 Lands in Botany Bay and confronts the first aborigines.

Oct 1770 The *Endeavour* lands at Batavia for a much-needed refit where many of Cook's men suffer and die from malaria and dysentery.

July 1772 Cook sets sail with two converted colliers *Resolution* and *Adventure*.

Jan 1773 He becomes the first navigator to cross the Antarctic Circle.

Jan 1774 Cook's travels in the South Pacific have now proved that there is no habitable continent. Instead of returning home, he continues to explore.

Spring 1774 Explores and accurately charts Easter Island, and the Marquesas Islands.

Nov 1774 *Resolution* heads for home.

Summer 1776 Cook sets off again with the *Resolution* and *Discovery* in search of the North West passage.

Summer 1778 The two ships head north, charting the southern coast of Alaska but ice halts their progress and they return to the Sandwich Islands where they had stopped on the way north. Relations between the sailors and the islanders soon deteriorate.

Feb 1779 Cook and his men depart but are forced back two days later with rigging problems. Cook is attacked, overpowered and stabbed to death.

■ Captain Cook Schoolroom Museum, Great Ayton

The village school which he first attended in 1736 still stands and now houses a museum commemorating Cook's younger days. His was an unremarkable education, although Mr Pullen, the headmaster, noted that Cook had some ability at mathematics, and was inclined to follow his own plans rather than be led astray by others.

The young Cook, in sculpture form, looks out across the Great Ayton village green in a work created by Nicholas Dimbleby and unveiled in 1997.

■ Staithes Heritage Centre

Other than being by the sea, Staithes did not have much to offer young James Cook. Here, as a 17-year-old, he was apprenticed to a haberdasher, which was not the career for which he was destined. The shop where he worked has been long since lost to the North Sea storms, but Staithes itself is a remarkable fishing village and worth a visit other than for a retracing of Cook's youthful footsteps.

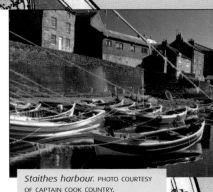

Staithes harbour. PHOTO COURTESY OF CAPTAIN COOK COUNTRY.

In essence, Staithes is no more than a convenient cleft in the rocky shoreline providing some shelter from the North Sea. Its roads are steep, narrow and twisting. The turn of every corner provides a surprise and the sea does not come into full view till you have worked your way along narrow alleys between houses, shops, chapels and workshops. Remarkably, in the early 1800s this was the largest fishing port north of the Wash, and home to a thriving boatbuilding industry based along the banks of the beck – the stream which runs from the surrounding hills into the sea. Steam brought about the village's demise as a fishing port when the coming of the railway meant fresh fish could be carried far inland putting the Staithes fish curers out of work. Also, the coming of Scottish steam trawlers made the traditional inshore cobles inefficient by comparison.

Smuggling, as in many of the coastal communities hereabouts, kept the village alive in the 19th century, and then the arrival of artists seeking new inspiration gave the place new life. For 30 years, from 1880 onwards, the Staithes Group of artists became influential as they progressed from realism to impressionism. There is a collection of their work in the **Whitby Museum**.

■ Staithes to Whitby

The next step for those following in Cook's footsteps is to make the formative leap from Staithes to Whitby, from where Cook was to launch his seafaring career. The house in Grape Lane, where Cook came as a 17-year-old to serve his seaman's apprenticeship, still stands and now houses the **Captain Cook Memorial Museum**. This is the only house in Whitby in which Cook is known to have lived. Here, Cook

The *Endeavour*

In 1768, the Admiralty decided to dispatch a ship to observe, from Tahiti, the transit of Venus as it passed across the face of the sun, as part of ongoing research into methods of fixing longitude at sea. Cook, who had been in the Navy for thirteen years and had good command of navigation, astronomy, seamanship and captaincy, was offered the post of commander. The *Endeavour* was a Whitby-built collier: strong, roomy, and could be sailed with a minimal crew. Cook knew them well. The detail of the voyages of the *Endeavour*, and Cook's subsequent ships, are beyond the scope of this book but without doubt, no detail of them is left unexplained in all the museums in and around Whitby which celebrate the life of this supreme seaman.

From Captain Cook's journal, August 1770: *'From what I have said of the natives of New Holland they may appear to some to be the most wretched people upon earth; but in reality they are far happier than we Europeans, being wholly unacquainted not only with the superfluous, but with the necessary conveniences so much sought after in Europe; they are happy in not knowing the use of them.'*

The replica of the Endeavour *in Whitby harbour.* PHOTO © LYNN KIPPS.

came into the service of John Walker and his brother Henry – local Quaker ship-owners whose fleet were engaged in the coal-carrying business.

YOUNG JAMES COOK GOES TO SEA

The first ship on which Cook was to set sail was the *Freelove*, in February 1747, bound for London with a cargo of coal. She was of a type known as a 'cat' – a broad beamed, strong, two-masted sailing ship designed for the rough and tumble of the coastal trade. Whitby, of course, was then a major port, being the only all weather harbour between the Humber and the Tyne, and shipbuilding was carried out on a large scale. The Admiralty knew the stout reputation of the Whitby ships when it came to preparing for Cook's later voyages.

Beneath the roof timbers of this classic Quaker house (after a recent £500,000 refit), you will learn how Cook eventually shunned commercial trade and opted instead for a naval career.

Cook made three voyages in the *Freelove*, then aboard the *Three Brothers*, which he rigged and fitted out. He sailed with the *Mary* to St Petersburg, and on qualifying as a mate, joined the *Friendship* and sailed with her for three years. But when the Walkers offered Cook a command of his own he shunned it, and instead signed on as an ordinary seaman with the Royal Navy. He remarked '*I had a mind to try my fortune that way*'.

Whitby and the Abbey, with the Captain Cook Memorial Museum, (white building, centre) from across the harbour. PHOTO COURTESY OF THE CAPTAIN COOK MEMORIAL MUSEUM.

Captain Cook's achievements

- The first circumnavigation of the world in both directions.
- The mapping of the Pacific Islands, and discovery of the Sandwich Islands.
- A circumnavigation of Antarctica.
- The charting of the St Lawrence River.
- The charting of the south island of New Zealand.
- The discovery of Australia.
- The discovery of Tahiti and the New Hebrides.
- He drew navigational charts which remain in use today.
- The first man to test Harrison's chronometer at sea, and thereby contributing to one of the major advances in astronomical navigation.
- The first man to appreciate that a properly-fed crew need have no fear of the dreaded scurvy.

The statue of Captain Cook at Whitby.
PHOTO © FREEFOTO.COM

■ The Whaling Trade at Whitby

Even without its Captain Cook associations, Whitby has a remarkable maritime history and the **Whitby Museum** (founded, and still run by the Whitby Literary and Philosophical Society) shows how distinguished a town it is.

In its heyday as a whaling port, the street lights of this town were lit by the burning of whale oil made from the blubber which boiled in great cauldrons on the quayside. From here sailed the Scoresbys – father and son – two of the best known whaling skippers.

William Scoresby senior sailed closer to the North pole in pursuit of whales than any sailor at the time. He can also claim to have been the inventor of the 'crow's nest' which gave the hapless crewmember, consigned to the rigging to look for whales, some protection. Until then it had been a case of climbing the rigging and hanging on, but the Scoresby crow's nest was entered by a hatch and contained a seat, a telescope and a voice-trumpet for communicating with the deck below. Luxury!

The statue of William Scoresby at Whitby.
PHOTO © WWW.BEAUTIFULBRITAIN.PLUS.COM

His son, William junior, was of a more scientific mind and although every bit as brave as his father in pursuit of whales, carried out experiments in magnetism using the ship's compass, explored the undiscovered coast of Greenland, and became famous for his intricate drawings of snowflakes. He was elected a Fellow of the Royal Society and after retiring from the whaling trade was ordained and served as the vicar of Bradford. The **Scoresby Collection** at the Whitby Museum pays tribute to both father and son with a replica of the Scoresby crow's nest, depictions of life in whaling days, and the 'Greenland Magnet' which Scoresby constructed while his ship was beset in ice and used for his magnetism experiments.

Frank Meadow Sutcliffe FRPS

In the later years of his life, Frank Sutcliffe was curator of the **Whitby Museum**, but is best known as the late 19th century photographer who captured a rapidly vanishing maritime scene in Whitby. No photographs better capture the atmosphere of the town or the way its harbour worked. His photographs are still regarded as true masterpieces, technically brilliant and evocative.

FILEY

John Wesley, the founder of Methodism, came to this small town and declared Filey to be a '*godless place*'. The criticism may have been a bit harsh but the fishermen of Filey seemed to take it to heart and formed what was to become a celebrated Fishermen's Choir which inspired some fishermen to become preachers themselves. Their inspiration was the hymns of Ira D Sankey with such maritime themes as '*Will your Anchor Hold?*' and '*Let the Lower Light be Burning*'. The Filey Fishermen's Choir travelled far and wide, singing not only at Bethels in nearby seaside towns such as Scarborough and Bridlington, but travelling inland to the West Yorkshire industrial towns. The choir still thrives.

Like many of these small coastal communities, the story is one of decline of the inshore fishing, although the town itself maintained an image of being a 'select' resort. 190 cobles were stationed on the Filey beach in the 1880s, by 2001 there were only seven.

The rocks at Filey Brigg. PHOTO COURTESY THE YORKSHIRE TOURIST BOARD.

The Yorkshire coble

The coble (pronounced with a short 'o' is Yorkshire, but with a long 'o' in Northumberland) evolved purely out of the need for a fishing vessel which could be beach-launched against heavy seas if necessary, and easily recovered. Cobles all carry high-shouldered bows, which gives the craft a deep grip on the water and help to keep her head to the seas when launching if the wind should be pressing more on one bow than the other. She has a low stern mounted on a flat floor, and two 'skorvels', or bilge keels, which help keep her upright when ashore. The fishermen of the east coast could work these craft in all weathers, using the long, narrow rudder blade to place their cobles precisely where needed; when in harbour they removed the blade to use as a plank to get ashore. Under sail, their beauty was their simplicity with a simple brown-tan dipping

lugsail set on a raked mast – a small jib being carried in fair weather. No plans exist for cobles; they were built from memory by men who understood how to shape wood to meet the demands of the sea. Cobles were always painted in bright reds, white, and sometimes yellow. Flamborough cobles were deep red, Filey cobles were blue.

The modern coble Charisma, *built in 1989, still fishes out of Whitby.* PHOTO © GLORIA WILSON.

The *Three Brothers*

The Three Brothers.

The sturdy little cobles can be found the length of the east coast, but the *Three Brothers*, which sails from Bridlington in the care of Bridlington Sailing Coble Preservation Society, is the only surviving example capable of going to sea under sail alone.

The *Three Brothers* was built in Bridlington in 1912, with somewhat less sheer than usual to allow for beam trawling. She cost £75 to build and six months to complete. Bought by the Harbour Commissioners in 1982, she is now kept alive by the enthusiasm of her supporters and can be seen, in the summer months, making limited trips between Bridlington Harbour and Flamborough Head to the north.

The *Three Brothers* holds a hugely important place in our maritime history. The word 'coble' found in Celtic (ceubal) and Breton (caubal), has been in use for over a thousand years and is recorded in the Lindisfarne Gospels.

Housed in a pair of cottages (once declared unfit for human habitation) the **Filey Museum**, with active local volunteer support, reflects the dominance of fishing in Filey's history. You will find a re-creation of a 'bait house' where mussels were attached to endless long lines to lure fish. Models of previous Filey lifeboats are on display, and the cause of many of their launchings, the notorious Filey Brigg, is remembered. This outcrop of rock is accessible by foot at low water, but a rising tide will strand unsuspecting holidaymakers. Many lives have been lost. The Paget Stone was erected as a warning, but when it became detached by erosion it was rescued and placed in this museum.

More about the coble

Conversation with a Coble Builder (1953) recorded by George Bayes: *'How is a coble built? Well, now, I should be able to tell you, if any man can. There's only three of us left between Whitby and Flamborough, so there's not many that can contradict me, eh?' Absently, he picks up an adze. 'That's what I call the shipwright's right hand, you use it see, like a croquet mallet,' he swings the heavy-headed steel thing illustratively. 'A slip, and that will give you a nasty gash. It shapes the timbers of the post and ribs. A coble may be either clincker-built – the planks overlapping each other – or caulker-built, that is with the planks flush and the seams caulked with a mixture of tar, oil and pitch.'*

The Coble Fishermen's Rule for Counting Fish: *'You pick up two herrings in each hand and that is called a warp. You give thirty two warp to the hundred making it one hundred and twenty eight herrings. The herrings were carried away by the merchants in quarter cran baskets, four baskets to the cran, which is a measure for a thousand herrings.'*

BRIDLINGTON

Bridlington Bay had always been a secure anchorage for the vast fleet once engaged in coastal trade. In February 1871, trade in coal was

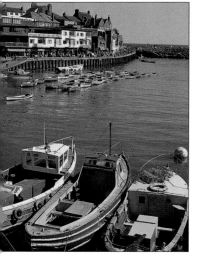

healthy between Tyneside and Paris, then under siege from Germany. Anchored in light westerly winds (a safe, offshore direction) were hundreds of sailing vessels waiting for the breeze to return to enable them to continue southwards. Just after midnight on 10 February, a sudden gale blew up from the south-east, trapping all the ships who could not recover their anchors and escape; many were driven ashore. The tales of lifeboat rescues are truly heroic. Nevertheless, by the following morning after the storm had subsided, the wreckage on the beach was nine feet deep in places, 30 ships had been lost and 70 men died.

Bridlington harbour. PHOTO COURTESY OF YORKSHIRE TOURIST BOARD.

The MP for Derby, Samuel Plimsoll, used this catastrophe as an argument for protecting seamen from careless owners and eventually the requirement for all ships to carry a Plimsoll Line, to prevent over-loading, became written into the Merchant Shipping Act. The story of the Great Gale of 1871 is brought to life at the **Bridlington Harbour Heritage Museum** by recordings of tales of local heroism enhanced by a rich collection of photographs.

Also while in Bridlington take a trip on the pleasure boat, the *Yorkshire Belle.* Once, she shared the harbour with the *Flamborian* and the *Bridlington Queen*, but now this little ship, built in 1947, is the only maritime reminder of the heyday of the English seaside resort.

SPURN POINT

It is a long a tortuous road which leads to the ever wandering Spurn Point, the crooked finger of shifting sand which beckons ships into Humber history. Its future is uncertain, for one more severe storm may turn the point into an island. It is, after all, not much more than sand and shingle held together by marram grass. Under the care of the Yorkshire Wildlife Trust it remains a remarkable environment to visit.

But for the maritime enthusiast, the black and white lighthouse is worth more than a passing glance. It has been closed since 1986 although there have been lights here since 1427. Conditions are now too unstable and buoys and lightfloats anchored in deep water are a safer bet. But nothing will remove the famous Humber lifeboat from her station within the arm of Spurn Point. This is the only lifeboat station in Britain which is manned full-time by a permanent, rather than a volunteer crew. It is such a remote spot (although a busy one, given the proximity of North Sea shipping) that there is little option other than to crew the lifeboat this way. Some remarkable rescues have been conducted by the Humber lifeboat and over the years her crew have been awarded 3 gold medals, 13 silver, 17 bronze, one MBE (Brian Bevan 1999) and one George Medal (Robert Cross).

Spurn lighthouse. PHOTO COURTESY OF YORKSHIRE TOURIST BOARD.

LEFT: The Spurn lightship; BELOW: the Maritime Museum. PHOTOS COURTESY OF HULL MARITIME MUSEUM.

The former **Spurn lightship (LV12)** (now replaced with a light float) is in retirement in Hull Marina after 48 years of service and is open to visitors who seek a flavour of life on these engineless craft which had to be anchored in turbulent waters. They were manned by men for whom the lonely life held no fears; their dedication was worth it, for within a five-mile radius of the Spurn light float, the chart shows no less than 30 wrecks, proving how dangerous this stretch of water can be.

The Spurn lightship was built in Goole in 1927 at a cost of £17,000. Unusually for a lightship, she was painted black instead of the standard red, to make her more visible in the particularly sandy waters of the Humber which, in certain light conditions, might make a red vessel hard to see at a distance.

KINGSTON-UPON-HULL

The seamen of Kingston-upon-Hull have always travelled far in pursuit of fish and whales. This was once a major port that was the base for the largest deep water fishing fleet in Britain. The long-distance fishing has

all but faded, of course, as the fish themselves became scarce due to over-fishing, and politics prevented access to the fish that the Hull trawlermen thought was rightly theirs. This led to the Icelandic Cod Wars of the 1960s and 1970s.

But maritime fortunes in this city have ebbed and flowed as fast as the notoriously unpredictable tides of the Humber, and a visit to **Hull Maritime Museum**, housed in the former Dock offices, will remind you that at one time, Hull's prosperity depended upon the whale. A vast skeleton makes visitors to the Whaling Gallery realise what an imposing and threatening creature this must have been to hunt.

Scrimshaw – the whaler's art

As holders of the Tizard Collection, the **Hull Maritime Museum** has the finest collection of scrimshaw in Britain. Scrimshaw is the etching of bone or ivory, usually in intricate and traditional designs, thought to have been first practised by the Inuit and other native groups on the north-western coast of America, and strictly speaking not originally a maritime craft. It was from the Inuit that the whaler men learnt the craft which started to appear in Britain in the mid 1800s. Whale teeth and jaw bones were the most common raw material, but walrus tusks were used too.

It was not uncommon for the whaling crews to be given part of their pay in the form of teeth, or whalebone, which commanded a good price ashore. With some of the whale-hunting trips lasting over three years or more, scrimshaw etching helped to relieve the monotony. The scenes depicted were often of ships, whales or women and could be used, for example, in pistol grips or as the heads of walking canes. Frank T Bullen, the author of *The Cruise of the Cachalot* wrote, '*The tools used are of the roughest. Some old files, softened in the fire, and filed into grooves something like saw-teeth, are most used; but old knives, sail-needles, and chisels are pressed into service. The work turned out would, in many cases, take a very high place in an exhibition of turnery, though never a lathe was near it*'.

The origin of the word 'scrimshaw' is unknown, but thought to have Dutch origins and originally meant to 'waste one's time'.

■ Fish and conflict

Through the generations many men have had to fight for their livings in the testing waters of the North Sea and beyond, and two heroic episodes are remembered in Hull. The first, the Dogger Bank Incident of 1904, is commemorated by a statue to George Smith, the skipper of the trawler *Crane* which was sunk by the Russians in what became an explosive international incident.

The Dogger Bank, only 60 miles from the Humber, was one of the richest fishing grounds in Europe. In October 1904, 40 fishing boats from Hull were working there when, unannounced, they were fired on by the

The Cod Wars

For over a century, the fishermen of Hull have had to protect their living in the rich coastal waters of Iceland where some of the best deep-water fishing was to be found. So-called 'Cod Wars' between Iceland and Britain are nothing new. There was one in 1893 when the Danish government, which then had control of Icelandic waters, resented the increased use by British fishermen of the modern, efficient steam trawlers. Gun boats were employed to arrest offending skippers and in a foretaste of the Cod Wars of the 1960s and 70s, ships were impounded and the fishing gear confiscated, if not cut adrift at sea.

The Cod War of 1958 was brought about when the Icelanders extended their fishing limit from 4 miles to 12, the second war in 1972 when they extended it to 50 miles, and the third in 1975 when the limit was extended

to 200 miles. Final agreement was not reached till 1976 when the amount of cod which could be caught by 24 named trawlers fishing within 200 miles of the coast, was limited to 50,000 tons annually. In other words, we lost. As a result 1500 fishermen became unemployed and a further 7500 lost their jobs ashore. After that, the fishing industry in Hull dwindled.

Fisheries patrol vessel Criscilla, *Hull.*
PHOTO © FREEFOTO.COM

Russian fleet bound for the Far East to fight the Japanese. The Russians thought the fishing fleet were hostile torpedo boats. The *Crane* sank instantly, with the loss of two lives. Uproar followed, with the Royal Navy preparing to confront the Russians in what could easily have escalated into a full-blown war. In the end, the matter was settled by an International Commission and compensation paid to the families of those who were lost. The statue to George Smith stands in the road known as the Boulevard.

Also to be found on the corner of the Boulevard, where it joins Hessle Road – a main thoroughfare which ran parallel to the fish docks, and where many fishing families lived – is the **Fishermen's Memorial** behind which stands a plaque in memory of the redoubtable Lil Bilocca who was born in nearby Wassand Road in 1929. After the loss of three Hull trawlers in quick succession in 1968, with the deaths of 53 men, she waged a relentless one-woman war against the trawler owners who, she believed, were putting

men's lives at risk in pursuit of profit. For her efforts she was subjected to threats, and lost her job at the fish factory. Even so, she achieved a meeting with Prime Minister Harold Wilson and brought national attention to the dangerous conditions in which trawlermen worked.

■ The *Arctic Corsair*

Although she is no battleship, the restored motor trawler **Arctic Corsair** (to be seen in the Old Harbour in Hull) has seen her fair share of conflict in the Cod Wars of the 1970s. She has probably never looked in better condition since the day she was launched, for trawlers like her were true workhorses of the Hull fishing fleet, whose business was conducted in the deep, icy Arctic waters of the distant fishing grounds. At work, a little rust or flaking paint was to be expected, but now you will find her in pristine condition.

It is difficult to sense what it was like to live and work on board one of these vessels which spent weeks on end in some of the roughest waters in which the British trawler fleet worked. The pictures on display will give you some idea, and so will the recorded voices of the men who served on her. But it is worth standing for a moment, grabbing a rail, and imagining yourself bracing against a breaking wave after a long night hauling fish. The cod on your plate will never look the same again.

J B Priestley, said that trawling ports were the homes of '.... *a race apart, perhaps the last of the wild men in this tamed island of ours; fellows capable of working day and night without food or sleep... and then also capable of going on the booze with equal energy and enthusiasm.*'

The *Arctic Corsair*. PHOTO COURTESY OF HULL COUNTY COUNCIL.

The re-generation of Hull's harbour area, following the demise of the fishing industry, includes the Marina (ABOVE); the 'Fish Trail' (RIGHT); and 'The Deep' the world's only submarium (OPPOSITE). OPPOSITE INSET: Sculpture outside 'The Deep'. PHOTOS COURTESY OF HULL COUNTY COUNCIL.

GOOLE ————————————————————————

Sitting at the head of tidal navigation on the Humber, Goole is approached by a tortuous and shifting channel that meanders between the broad banks of the river. It takes the most skilled and knowledgeable pilots to bring ships safely up to Goole.

Marking the transition from sea to inland waterway, the Goole–Knottingley canal giving access to the heart of Yorkshire's manufacturing regions. Coal came through Goole, carried in waterborne 'Tom Pudding' trains which were developed in the 1860s consisting of a series of floating boxes each carrying 40 tons of coal from the Yorkshire coalfields. On arrival at Goole, they were disconnected from each other and lifted, the contents being tipped into a waiting coaster.

The story of the transport of coal is told at the **Goole Museum**. The museum is also home to the *Audrey*, built in 1915 as a small lightship which marked the winding navigation channel of the Humber, and is now converted to a gaff-rigged sailing barge based on a design known as a Goole Billboy. She now carries twelve people on educational tours of the east coast.

You will also find *Sobriety* in the museum, a Humber Keel built in Beverley in east Yorkshire in 1910. These were versatile, tubby craft which could be pulled by horse when working the inland waterways,

The Humber Sloop Ethel *(c.1905) by Reuben Chappell of Goole.* PHOTO COURTESY OF GOOLE MUSEUM.

Sailing craft of the Humber

You might be lucky enough in the summer to see the Humber Keel, *Comrade*, and the Humber Sloop *Amy Howson* working their way along the navigable rivers between the Trent and the Ouse. They are in the care of the energetic Humber Keel and Sloop Preservation Society. The Humber Keels, like their cousins on the Tyne, are based on Viking long-ships, built with a bluff bow, but shallow draft to cope with the tidal rivers and canals. They were built for strength, too, having to cope with the vicious chop which the Humber can throw up. A Keel carried a single mast from which was flown a square white mainsail; oak leeboards replaced the keel to give the ship a grip on the water.

The Humber Sloop – a larger craft which was not constrained by the need to work canals – carried a mainsail and foresail fore-and-aft, unlike the Humber Keel which was propelled by her square sail. This enabled them to be more efficient sailing to windward and the strength with which they were built enabled them to make coastal passages from Bridlington in the north, as far south as the London River Thames.

Mention should also be given to the plucky little 'cog boats' which acted as tenders to these two crafts and without which they would have been unable to work. The cog boats were merely 12 feet long and were propelled by sculling a single oar over the stern, and were used for laying out a kedge anchor, taking warps ashore, moving crew from ship to ship. It is doubtful if any original cog boats survive, but a new one was built in 2003 to serve the two Keels.

and could raise a mast and big square sail for working the open waters of the Humber.

SOUTHWARDS TO GRIMSBY ⸻

Between Goole and the Wash, only Grimsby has any significant maritime interest. True, ship building has been going on for centuries at Barton on Humber which Daniel Defoe described in 1725 as '*a struggling, mean town noted for nothing but an ill-favoured ferry*.' The ferry has now been replaced by the stunning Humber Bridge, although the remains of the wooden ferry terminal can be seen at New Holland. Mablethorpe was the place to which Tennyson went on the publication day of his first book of poems in 1827, declaiming his work to the empty sand dunes. Further south, Ingoldmells can claim to be the site of the first Butlins Holiday Camp in 1936.

The Humber Bridge. PHOTO © FREEFOTO.COM.

Nevertheless, within this stretch of unpromising coastline are reminders of two important periods in maritime history. The first is the story of our once great fishing industry, portrayed at the **National Fishing Heritage Centre** in Grimsby, and the other is the monumental voyage by the Pilgrim Fathers to America (recalled at **Immingham Museum**), in which Immingham, now famous as a deep water oil terminal, played its part.

■ The National Fishing Heritage Centre, Grimsby

Blame the name of this town on a Danish fisherman called Grim who is said to have landed here 1000 years ago and started selling fish to the local settlers. It was the foundation of a fishing port which, only a few decades ago, was the largest in the world. What remains of the docks, which once covered 140 acres, are marked by a 309-foot dock tower modelled on the Palazzo Publico in Sienna, built to provide hydraulic power to operate lock gates.

Grimsby owes its prosperity as much to the railway as it does to the sea, for when the Manchester, Sheffield and Lincolnshire railway opened a line to the docks in 1849, it gave financial incentives to attract trawlers to land their catches and despatch them by rail. The coming of the steam trawler also meant the railways provided a direct link to the Yorkshire coal fields and so railways and fishing fleet became mutually supporting.

Like its neighbour, Hull, the Grimsby fishing fleet fished the Arctic waters largely for cod, and fought the 'Cod Wars' to protect their livelihoods. Like Hull too, the fishing industry in Grimsby has been in grievous decline from the post-war days when as many as 500 trawlers left the mouth of the Humber on a single tide. 30,000 people in Grimsby were at one time dependant on the fishing trade for their living and, until the 1970s, great fortunes were made.

The **National Fishing Heritage Centre** offers you an authentic taste of the unromantic face of the seafaring life. Staffed by retired fisherman, you will get the plain, unvarnished truth about life aboard the deep sea trawlers, the dangers and the rewards. In fact, they will ask you to sign on as crew for a journey to the Arctic, although you will not share the same fate as the apprentices who, in the 19th century, were taken on as little more than deck labourers. These youths were often gathered from orphanages as young as

Trawler wheelhouse. PHOTO COURTESY OF THE YORKSHIRE TOURIST BOARD.

12, and those who refused were brought before magistrates. It was said that the courts in Hull took a more lenient view than those of Grimsby which was only too keen on sending children to sea, sometimes in handcuffs. The loss of life was huge, estimated at one death per 1000 men employed.

BOSTON

Whilst Plymouth's famous Mayflower Steps marks for many the start of the voyage of the Pilgrim Fathers to the New World, in fact the town of Boston in Lincolnshire and the remote port of Immingham, on the southern side of the Humber estuary, truly mark the commencement of one of the most determined escapes from religious punishment and persecution ever recorded.

■ The Pilgrim Fathers of the Lincolnshire coast

The story is told both in the **Boston Guildhall Museum**, and the **Immingham Museum**. In September 1607, a group of determined pilgrims had chartered a ship to take them to exile in Amsterdam. Their meeting point was to be not far from the tower of St Botolph's Church (known as Boston 'Stump') which was visible for miles across the flat Lincolnshire landscape. Their ship approached Scotia Creek, a mile

The cells where the pilgrims were held.
PHOTO COURTESY OF THE BOSTON GUILDHALL MUSEUM.

south of Boston, in the dead of night. However, the captain had betrayed them and they were arrested, searched and imprisoned. Luckily, the strong Puritan lobby in Boston was able to pressure for their release.

Their next attempt at escape was in the spring of 1608, this time travelling in secret to the remote shores of Immingham where a Dutch ship awaited them. The men were the first to board, but just as wives and families were about to join them, armed soldiers appeared and the captain decided to raise his anchor and flee, separating husbands, wives and children. After a stormy crossing lasting no less than 14 days, those who successfully escaped made new lives in Leyden, remaining there for 10 years before commencing on the better known voyage of the Pilgrim Fathers to the New World.

THE WASH

Other than being the place where King John famously lost his jewels (now said to lie close to the 9th hole on Sutton Bridge's golf course), it is difficult to name one other thing for which the Wash is famous. It has no reputation which can match that of the other great estuaries of England; it was never the scene of famous battles, nor a place of legendary storms or tempests. It is a quiet, humble expanse of water – the drainage outlet of the fens and the rivers that cross it. The Wash is getting smaller as the years go by. Gradually, the line of the seawall which divides sea from shore has shifted seawards as the fertile hinterland has been reclaimed to provide rich soil for vegetable growing. The military love the Wash, though, which is why the peace is often disturbed by low-flying fighter planes from East Anglian bases bound for the bombing range not far offshore from Holbeach.

It is a restless stretch of water which shifts as the sand and mud swill in and out with the tide. It has few landmarks to help seafarers unfortunate enough to find themselves lost. It must, at times, feel part of a different planet.

The sea wall on the Wash. PHOTO COURTESY OF PETER WAKELY/ENGLISH NATURE.

KING'S LYNN

One of the great mediaeval ports of England, King's Lynn once traded widely with Europe. Such was its importance that it was part of the Hanseatic league, a 13th century trading partnership of largely north German merchants, but including traders in England and the low countries. Over the last 700 years, ships have left from here bound for ports from the Black Sea to Scandinavia. Its usefulness as a harbour depended much on the state of fast-flowing tides of the Wash, and so St Margaret's Church has a 17th century moon clock which tells the time of high water.

■ The King's Lynn Whalers

The **Lynn Museum** gives a good account of the importance of whaling which started in the 15th century when whales were hunted off the coast of Spain. By 1820 whaling had died out, as the demand for whale oil diminished, but it left behind some gruesome relics which can be seen in this museum. Imagine the broad strainer being stirred through the vats of fatty, bubbling blubber. Or see the surgeon's tools from a whaling ship to remind you what a dangerous game it was, and how the surgeon's cure might have been far worse than the injury. You can still go and stand by Blubberhouses Creek; now a muddy, stagnant backwater, this was where the whalers unloaded their cargo of blubber and whale bones, to be

The quay and custom house, King's Lynn. PHOTO COURTESY OF EAST OF ENGLAND TOURIST BOARD.

boiled. The foul stench was said to hang over the town, but the locals, loyal to their prosperous whale fishery, claimed it was good for them.

But much of King's Lynn's prosperity depended on its local, inshore fishery. The Wash was rich with oysters, mussels and the highly-prized pink and brown shrimps. From the quayside, a brisk trade was run in shellfish to Billingsgate, and whelks to Hull where they were used as bait on cod-catching lines.

The fishermen of Lynn, and their families, were a race apart, and their lives are celebrated in **Trues Yard**, the last remaining fishermen's yard in the town, and opened as a museum to save a pair of traditional waterside cottages from destruction. This is where you get a true picture of this crabby race of fishermen, the Northenders who lived in the part of the town they called 'Fishers End.' This was once a maze of cobbled streets and two-up two-down cottages, a typical pair of which form the heart of this beguiling museum. It is easy, while wandering through the tiny rooms, to imagine the shouts of the children who slept nine to a bed, or hear the acrimonious disputes between rival families in this little world set apart from the rest of the town.

The Northenders had their own rules, customs and traditions. They inter-married and formed their own football teams, unions, and went on outings only with each other. Some were belligerent, some were

A typical North End fisherman.
PHOTO COURTESY OF TRUES YARD MUSEUM.

frequently drunk – no sane being would dare argue with them. To meet a Northender on a dark night might also cause your heart to miss a beat, for they would be dressed in a sealskin cap, moleskin trousers, and dark guernseys (see **Cromer Museum**). For food, the women cooked Norfolk dumplings, supposedly as '*large, white and shiny as snowballs*' which were made with bread dough and should be '*as light as love*'. Enjoy the models of the working craft of the Wash in True's Yard, and imagine this tribe apart who manned them.

BURNHAM THORPE – Nelson's birthplace ──────

'*I am myself a Norfolk man and glory in being so*' – Horatio Nelson.

Wherever you travel through maritime East Anglia, you will stumble across repeated homage to Admiral Lord Nelson. His name is proudly inscribed everywhere from the **Great Yarmouth Museum**, to the smallest maritime museum in Britain, at Mundesley to the east of Cromer. But if Nelson belongs anywhere hereabouts, it is in Burnham Thorpe, his birthplace in 1758.

The precise spot on which he was born, seven weeks prematurely, can be debated. It is widely believed he was born in the rectory, since demolished, although the present rectory is pretty much on the same spot. But before you pay your respects there, consider the theory that he was born at the Shooting Box on Creake Road, because the rectory was being redecorated at the time.

The maritime atmosphere of North Norfolk, which young Nelson found so inspiring, is still there to be enjoyed, if in diluted form. It might have been at Burnham Overy Staithe where he first saw boats at work, and possibly learnt to sail them. Or perhaps it was in Wells-next-the-Sea that the sight of ships stirred his heart, for in his day this was a major port. Whatever the roots of his love of the sea, it was his native north Norfolk for which he had a deep affection and on becoming a peer, in 1798, took the title, Baron Nelson of the Nile and of Burnham Thorpe.

Captain Horatio Nelson.
COURTESY OF NATIONAL MARITIME MUSEUM.

During his youth spent at Burnham he showed all the signs of being a young man of considerable pluck. Once, failing to arrive home on time, Horatio eventually appeared at the rectory door and was asked by his mother if he had been afraid. He replied, '*I never saw fear; what is it?*'

By the age of 12, he had set his heart on the sea. He read in the Norwich Mercury that his uncle had been appointed to the *Raisonnable*, a 60-gun ship captured from the French. On Horatio's behalf, his brother wrote to seek permission for the lad to join the ship. The reply came: '*What has poor Horatio done, who is so weak, that he above all the rest should be sent to rough it at sea? But let him come and the first time we go into action a cannon-ball may knock off his head.*'

There were less exciting times spent back in Burnham. After 17 years at sea, he returned in 1787, living in the rectory where he took to gardening and dug the pond which can still be seen in the rectory grounds. Farm workers captured his interest, and he spent time studying their lives, especially the way they ploughed.

The sea was never far from his mind, though, even in this period of what must have felt like exile on the north Norfolk coast. He rode to Burnham Market to seek out newspapers through which he could follow events at the Admiralty, and learn of the revolution in France. He came to believe that somehow a black mark had been put against his name by the Admiralty: a prejudice '*which I can neither guess at or nor in the least account for*'. He wrote to the Admiralty making it clear that if he were to be offered command of a cockleboat, he would be satisfied. For more about Lord Nelson, see page 85.

WELLS-NEXT-THE-SEA ⎯⎯⎯⎯⎯⎯

This was the only commercial harbour on this coast which bravely managed to hang on to its trade until the early 1990s when the coasters finally became too big to turn in the shallow waters by the quay. From seaward, Wells is marked by a clump of trees atop an odd hill by the beach, and by the lifeboat house perched on the dunes halfway between the town and the sea. It was here that the lifeboat disaster of October 1880 took place when an onshore gale

The town sign with a Maritime theme. PHOTO © BOB BROWNJOHN.

Seals at Blakeney Point. PHOTO COURTESY OF PETER WAKELY/ENGLISH NATURE.

forced ships onto the dangerous lee shore. The lifeboat put to sea but found that for safety the sailors had climbed the rigging. The lifeboat was about to make its turn for home when a sea caught it, capsized it, and caused the mast to lodge in the sands preventing it from righting. Eleven lifeboatmen drowned. Ironically, those sailors clinging to the rigging waited till the storm had passed and then walked ashore unharmed when the tide left their ships high and dry.

THE EVER-CHANGING COASTLINE

When you have walked to Scolt Head or Blakeney Point and felt the shifting shingle under your feet, you will understand why there is little about the north Norfolk coast that is permanent. The sands shift, the tides swirl, the mud creeps in and out of gulleys while the beaches come and go. The **Cromer Museum** reminds you that in the ice age, this coast was formed by chalk and clay pushed southwards by advancing ice, which is why the glistening pebbles on display have an ancient polish to them. Its shifting nature makes this stretch of coast a geologist's dream, for here are to be found fossils of tree stumps and animal remains amongst the soft, crumbling cliffs; these are often revealed for the first time when an onshore storm shifts the sands and reveals treasures beneath. Holme-next-the-Sea is where the mystical **Sea-Henge** revealed itself. An ancient circle of 55 wooden posts with an upturned tree root in the middle is believed to be a 4000 year old ancient religious centre.

SHERINGHAM

Every town with a lifeboat is proud of it, but Sheringham is proud four times over. It is the only town in Britain which has four lifeboats in its possession. The venerable *Henry Ramey Upchurch* of 1894 (built from '*an exceptionally perfect beam of American oak*' bought in Yarmouth) can be seen in her original shed at the top of west slipway, but the other three are in the possession of the **Sheringham Museum**. For such a small museum this is a huge undertaking, in addition to which they also own a genuine 'hoveller' built by the Emery family (whose unique collection of boatbuilding tools are to be seen here) for no less than Henry Blogg of Cromer (see page 80).

It is worth remembering that there was a time when these north Norfolk beaches were far from deserted. 200 boats once fished off Sheringham beach alone, until overcrowding made it dangerous and the fishermen moved themselves to Grimsby.

CROMER

There are two kinds of crabs in Cromer: there are the ones with the claws which are a local delicacy with a national reputation, and the fishermen of Cromer who are nicknamed 'crabs' The edible crabs, the **Cromer Museum** explains, are a selfless race, especially the females who migrate northwards towards the Humber, swimming against the current, when it is time to lay their eggs. This battle against the prevailing tidal stream means that the young crabs heading for the warmer home waters have a downhill ride while their mothers have done all the hard slog in getting north. The males, incidentally, don't bother to move much at all and hang around Cromer, but pay the price for their idleness in being caught sooner.

The lifeboat JC Madge, now fully restored, served in Sheringham 1904–1936.
BACKGROUND IMAGE: *Historic photograph of Sheringham lifeboat and crew.*
PHOTOS COURTESY OF THE SHERINGHAM MUSEUM TRUST.

Cromer evolved from fishing village to resort in the early 19th century and distinguished houses still look out over the sandy shore which is pitted with saltwater pools at low tide. Although it clings on to its pier despite attempts by the weather to demolish it, Cromer has no harbour and is fully open to everything the North sea can throw at it.

Perhaps the zenith of Cromer's days as a resort were the 1950s, before cheap continental holidays drew the crowds away, and the plaster relief mural by J Mordy Smith, modelled in 1951, shows what a happy, vibrant and bustling resort this once was.

Cromer, from an old engraving. PHOTO COURTESY OF THE RNLI HENRY BLOGG MUSEUM.

■ Lifesaving on the north Norfolk coast

Being a coastline of few harbours, most of which are unsafe to approach in heavy weather, and with long banks of shifting sand lying offshore ready to entrap a seafarer who puts a foot wrong, the rescue of stranded ships and the saving of life has long formed an important part of the maritime tradition of this entire coast. To emphasise the dangers, a local saying has it that *'there are few harbours but plenty o' lifeboats.'*

One of the legendary lifeboat men of East Anglia, amongst the finest in the entire history of the lifeboat service, was Henry Blogg of Cromer whose brave life is celebrated in a museum dedicated to him. The **Cromer RNLI Henry Blogg Museum** is housed appropriately in the old Cromer lifeboat at the bottom of the 'gangway', a deep, steep ravine which links town to shore.

By the age of 12, Henry was already a crab fisherman, and at 18, a full member of the lifeboat crew. He was to witness what must be a unique occasion in Britain's maritime history when the steamer *Victoria of Yarmouth* punctured her hull on the remains of Shipden Church – a relic of a coastal village which preceded Cromer in importance and has long since been lost to the sea.

Henry Blogg '...one of the bravest men who ever lived...'
PHOTO COURTESY OF THE RNLI HENRY BLOGG MUSEUM.

The lifeboat Henry Blogg *and crew.*   PHOTO COURTESY OF THE RNLI HENRY BLOGG MUSEUM.

Henry Blogg's service to lifesaving until his death in 1954 has been unequalled. He won the RNLI Gold medal (the lifeboatman's VC) three times, the silver four times, the Empire Gallantry Medal (which was replaced by the George Cross), the British Empire Medal and the Queen's Coronation Medal. And remember, as you take in the atmosphere of this museum, or catch the steely gaze of his bust which still gazes out to sea, that Henry Blogg never learned to swim.

Fishermen's ganseys

The navy blue jumper, called a 'gansey' was found on every part of the British coast, knitted in traditional patterns and with great love, and they were a fisherman's first line of defence against the elements. The ones from Cromer, and particularly Sheringham, were considered the finest on the East Anglian coast, if not in the whole country, and the **Cromer Museum** shows five examples of fine knitting in worsted wool.

The knitting was complex, involving five or more needles of size 16 or sometimes 17, resulting in a detailed and outstanding pattern and a very tight knit which closed even tighter when the wool was wet. It has often been said the each fishing community had its own patterns and that bodies hauled from the sea could be returned to their correct villages, identified by the pattern they were wearing. But in Sheringham alone, no less than several dozen different patterns have been found which suggests this may be a myth.

The Happisburgh lighthouse

PHOTO COURTESY OF
FRIENDS OF HAPPISBURGH
LIGHTHOUSE.

The number of tragedies which have taken place off the Haisboro's Sands of the north Norfolk coast make it clear why a lighthouse was built at Happisburgh (pronounced Hazeborough) in 1791. But shipwrecks still occurred: in St Mary's churchyard is the mass grave of 119 sailors lost from HMS Invincable in 1801 on passage to join Nelson's fleet at Copenhagen.

However, after a review of navigational aid, Trinity House decided to put Happisburgh light on the closure list. The locals thought otherwise and raised money to create a trust to lease the building and maintain it. Open to the public, it is now Britain's only privately operated working lighthouse funded entirely by voluntary contributions. For more information contact happislight@keme.co.uk.

MUNDESLEY

The coastguard spirit is alive in the **Mundesley Maritime Museum** which boasts, '*probably the smallest museum in Britain*'. Nevertheless, within this small brick tower on the cliff edge, not only has a small museum been created but an active lookout station too.

It ceased to be an official coastguard station in 1990, but in recent years, Coastwatch volunteers have taken it over and now keep a watchful eye across the beach and out to the dangerous Haisboro' Sands. While the official coastguard rely on radio and radar to keep their look-

out, here volunteers employ a heavy pair of binoculars which saw service in a tank at Alamein.

One incident observed from this World War II lookout station is worth recording. The coastguard saw a foreign lifeboat creeping towards the shore, intent on landing men. As they approached, it became clear they were German officers. An invasion?

The old coastguard station. PHOTO COURTESY OF MUNDESLEY MARITIME MUSEUM.

Yarmouth beach (1847), by Alfred Stannard. COURTESY OF GREAT YARMOUTH MUSEUM, NORFOLK MUSEUMS AND ARCHAEOLOGY SERVICE.

No, it was the lifeboat from Texel, in Holland, and the men clad in German uniforms were escaping Russian prisoners of war. Nevertheless, the home guard gathered on the beach ready to repel the foe.

GREAT YARMOUTH ───────────

The newly opened **Time and Tide Museum** is housed in a converted Victorian herring curing works, and the aroma still lingers. The herring trade was once the commercial mainstay of this town, but the only remnants of it are the scents that cling to the boards and rafters of the museum.

Here you will find a full depiction of the days of herring glory, complete with herring-catching exhibits which allow children to fish for themselves. You will learn that it was once said that herring was 'eaten for breakfast, lunch and tea by the poor, and as an occasional treat for the rich'. The woven swill baskets, narrow-mouthed to prevent the herring from spilling, are emblematic of

Herrings – the 'Silver Darlin's'

For such a small fish, the herring exerted a mighty pull. It dictated the migration of the fishing fleets down the North Sea as skipper, crew and shore worker followed in the shimmering wake of the *'silver darlin's'*. In the autumn, the shoals ended their southward journey off the East Anglia coast to satisfy the huge fishing appetites of Gt Yarmouth and Lowestoft. The leading port in the herring trade can be argued, but the vastness of the industry cannot. The best fishing grounds were off the Smiths Knoll, 30 miles offshore where nets 2 miles long were set overnight. And although the herring trade can be said to have peaked in the 1920s, as far back as 1344, no less that 60 foreign boats loaded herring at Yarmouth.

Each herring drifter (see *Lydia Eva* page 93) provided work for 100 people ashore: gutting, filleting, salting and smoking. Trains arrived from Scotland as the 'herring girls' followed the fish southward, arriving usually in time for the September Yarmouth Races and returning home in the first week of December.

It was a short season but a frantic one. Sixty herrings a minute were gutted by one person working 14-hour days, and packed into 300 barrels over the course of a week. The season over, the exhausted women returned to Scotland and the Lowestoft drifters went down-Channel to fish Cornish waters, or north to the Scottish west coast, while the North Sea became quiet as the fish were left to spawn.

Scots fisher girls packing herrings.
PHOTO COURTESY OF MISS L. FLOWERDEW.

The Tower Curing Works, Great Yarmouth as it would have looked whilst in operation mid 20th century. By Gareth Sleightholme. COURTESY OF TIME AND TIDE MUSEUM.

Yarmouth, and you must remind yourself that such was the size of this industry that in 1913, two and a half million hundredweight of herring were landed, all transported in baskets such as these.

Like all contemporary museums, the emphasis here is on authentic recreations and hands-on exhibits. There is a row of Victorian shops and houses inviting you to peer through their windows; you can take the wheel of a coastal drifter and visit a barrel-maker's shop. There are tales to be heard of storms and rescues, both in sound and on video.

Many of the exhibits from the town's Maritime Museum on Marine Parade (closed in 2002) are to be found here, together with bones excavated from the North Sea and a clump of mammoth hair. A small collection of craft, which up until now has been stored in sheds around Norfolk, are at last on display. Perhaps the least significant, but most beguiling item in Yarmouth' collection is a plucky speckled hen, now stuffed and mounted in a glass case. This chicken was rescued in Victorian times from the offshore Scroby Sands when the incoming tide threatened to drown it. No one knows how it got there in the first place.

Pierhead Painters

Although this style of painting is not exclusive to East Anglia, the depiction of the sailing drifter, *Speranza* by T Swan, is a prime Yarmouth example of this style of art.

It is primitive, almost folk art, which emerged in the 18th century and became common during the 1900s. Pierhead painting doesn't get involved with the drama and tumult that seascape artists depict; instead, the artist paints a true likeness of the craft and leaves it there. However, these pictures have a quality and immediacy which can twang heart-strings in a way that more romantic painters might envy.

The paintings were often commissioned by shipowners to give an accurate record of their craft in the days before photography. The artists, mostly self-taught, had to work with speed, often capturing the image of an entire vessel in the short time between leaving the harbour and drifting out of sight. Every detail was expected to be correct – from rigging to sails and flags. No doubt with half an eye on his wage, the artist might have added a flattering touch here and there. The paintings invariably show the ship broadside-on to display her lines at their best; all sails are set to perfection, making these pictures a realisation of the shipbuilder's dream. The paintings were often sold as souvenirs of great voyages, or given to skippers and crew by grateful owners.

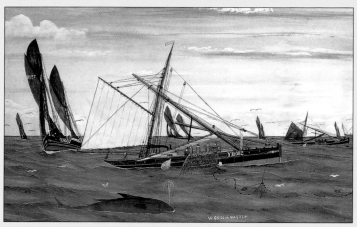

The sailing drifter Speranza *hauling her nets, by T. Swan.*
COURTESY OF GREAT YARMOUTH MUSEUM, NORFOLK MUSEUMS AND ARCHAEOLOGY SERVICE.

■ Nelson was here too!

Few places visited by Admiral Lord Nelson allow the event to go unrecorded, and Great Yarmouth is no exception – hence Yarmouth's version of Nelson's column called the Norfolk Monument.

He first came to Yarmouth two years after the Battle of the Nile where he landed and announced '*I am myself a Norfolk man and glory in being so.*' This went down well. Salutes were fired, crowds cheered, and he was hauled through the town on a carriage drawn by men instead of horses. He arrived at the Wrestler's Inn (now Hardy's) and was given the freedom of the borough. But when swearing the oath, an official noticed that Nelson had used his left hand. The unwitting official suggested the right hand more appropriate. '*That,*' replied the one-armed Nelson, '*is at Tenerife*'.

On the same visit, with Nelson's wit clearly at its keenest, a landlady asked if she might change the name of her inn to the 'Nelson's Arms.' He didn't think much of the idea and suggested not, '*Being that I have but one.*'

His next visit followed the 1801 Battle of Copenhagen at which he remarked, '*Victory is not a name strong enough for such a scene,*' It was also the occasion on which he wilfully ignored an order to cease fighting when he famously raised his telescope to his blind eye and said '*I really do not see the signal*'.

Home from the battle, he walked across the sand spit on which Yarmouth is built, to the naval hospital on a site now occupied by Sainbury's. There he found a wounded seaman who, like him, had lost an arm. Nelson said, '*There Jack, you and I are spoilt for fishermen!*'

The Norfolk Monument, 144 feet high and with 212 internal steps, is in a sorry state surrounded by remnants of Yarmouth's depressed maritime industries. It is no longer open to the public, being unsafe, and the stone head of Britannia has been removed from the top, again for safety reasons. It has been replaced by a replica made in glassfibre; the original resting in the maritime museum.

The Norfolk Monument. PHOTO © JOHN ASHLEY.
www.johnashleyphotography.co.uk

Tyne, Humber Gazetteer

Grace Darling Museum
Radcliffe Road, Bamburgh,
Northumberland NE69 7AE
☎ +44 (0)1668 214465
www.artguide.org/uk/
museumG.html
OPEN Daily, 10:00–17:00,
Easter–end Oct or BA

Marine Life and Fishing Heritage Centre
8–10 Main Street, Seahouses,
Northumberland NE68 7RG
☎ +44 (0)1665 721257
www.marinelifecentre.co.uk
OPEN Daily, Easter–Oct

Billy Shiel, Farne Islands
4 Southfield Avenue,
Seahouses, Northumberland
☎ 01665 720308
E-MAIL skipper@farne–
islands.com
www.farne–islands.com
Glad Tidings vessels have
taken passengers from
Seahouses to the Farne
Islands since the 1920s and
Glad Tidings V is the largest
of a current fleet offering
day, morning and afternoon
crossings to Inner Farne,
Staple or Longstone Islands,
with occasional trips further
north to Holy Island.

South Shields Museum and Art Gallery
Ocean Road, South Shields,
Tyne & Wear NE33 2JA
☎ +44 (0)191 456 8740
www.twmuseums.org.uk/
southshields/index.html
OPEN Daily, Mon–Sat
10:00–17:00. Closed Sun,
Good Friday. Admission free

Discovery Museum
Blandford Square,
Newcastle upon Tyne,
Tyne & Wear NE1 4JA
☎ +44 (0)191 232 6789
www.twmuseums.org.uk
OPEN Daily

Museum of Hartlepool
Jackson Dock, Hartlepool
TS24 0XZ (Adjacent to
Hartlepool Historic Quay &
HMS Trincomalee)
☎ +44 (0)1429 860077
www.thisishartlepool.co.uk/
museum.shtml
OPEN Daily

'HMS' Trincomalee
Hartlepool Historic Quay,
Jackson Dock, Hartlepool
TS24 0SQ
☎ +44 (0)1429 223193
www.hms–trincomalee.co.uk
OPEN Daily except Christmas
& New Year holidays

Hartlepool Historic Quay
Maritime Ave, Hartlepool
Marina, Hartlepool TS24 0XZ
☎ +44 (0)1429 860077,
860006 (answer machine)
www.thisishartlepool.co.uk/
historicquay.shtml
OPEN Daily

Zetland Lifeboat Museum
5 King Street, The
Esplanade, Redcar, Redcar-
and-Cleveland TS10 3PF
☎ +44 (0)1642 494311
www.redcarlifeboat.org.uk/
zetland/info.htm
OPEN Daily, May–end Sept
DON'T MISS The Zetland herself and the Call Out Drum

Kirkleatham Museum
Kirkleatham, Redcar, Redcar-
and-Cleveland TS10 5NW
☎ +44 (0)1642 479500
www.westair-reproductions.
com/mappage/clevelan.htm
OPEN Tues–Sun & BH Mon

Saltburn Smugglers Heritage Centre
adjacent to The Ship Inn,
Saltburn–by–the–Sea, Redcar
& Cleveland TS12 1HF
☎ +44 (0)1287 625252
www.redcar-cleveland.
gov.uk/museums
OPEN Daily, Easter–Sept

Whitby Museum
Pannett Park, Whitby,
North Yorkshire TO21 1RE
☎ +44 (0)1947 602908
www.spri.cam.ac.uk/
resources/museums
OPEN Daily, May–Sept;
Tue–Sun in winter

Captain Cook Birthplace Museum
Stewart Park, Marton,
Middlesbrough TS7 8AT
☎ +44 (0)1642 311211
www.aboutbritain.com/
CaptainCookBirthplace
Museum.htm
OPEN Tue–Sun, also Mon on
BH & school holidays

Captain Cook Schoolroom Museum
101 High Street, Great Ayton,
North Yorkshire TS9 6NB
☎ +44 (0)1642 724296.
www.captaincookschool
roommuseum.co.uk
OPEN Daily, 13:00–16:00,
Apr–Oct

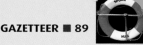

Captain Cook Memorial Museum
John Walker's House, Grape Lane, Whitby, North Yorkshire YO22 4BA
☎ +44 (0)1947 601900
www.cookmuseumwhitby.co.uk
OPEN Daily, Apr–Oct
Weekends only during Mar

Captain Cook and Staithes Heritage Centre
High Street, Staithes, (near Whitby, North Yorkshire)
☎ +44 (0)1947 841454
www.touruk.co.uk/nyorks/nyorks_staithes.htm

Filey Museum
8–10 Queen Street, Filey, North Yorkshire YO14 9HB
☎ +44 (0)1723 515013;
AH 515945.
www.fileybay.com
OPEN Daily, Easter–31 Oct, 11:00–17:00 (Sat 14:00–17:00)

Bridlington Harbour Museum and Aquarium
Harbour Road, Bridlington, East Riding of Yorkshire
☎ +44 (0)1262 670148
OPEN Daily, Easter–Sept
Weekends in winter. Edu BA

Hull Maritime Museum
Queen Victoria Square, Hull, HU1 3DX
☎ (Hull CC) +44 (0)1482 300300
OPEN Daily, Mon–Sat 10:00–17:00; Sun 13:30–16:30. Admission free

Arctic Corsair (H320)
Moored on river Hull, behind Streetlife Museum of Transport, High Street, Hull
☎ +44 (0)1482 613902;
Edu & GV bookings: 658838;
STAND: 324223
www.arctic-corsair.co.uk
OPEN Guided tours Wed, Sat & Sun; Mar–Oct. Admission free

Goole Museum
Above Goole Public Library, Carlisle Street, Goole,

East Riding of Yorkshire, DN14 5AA
☎ +44 (0)1482 392777
www.artguide.org/uk/museumG.html
OPEN Mon 14:00–17:00; Tue–Fri 10:00–17:00; Sat 09:00–13:00

Immingham Museum
Margaret Street, Immingham, North-East Lincolnshire DN40 1LE
☎ +44 (0)1469 577066
www.nelincs.gov.uk/ic/noframes/tourism-leisure/museum/immingham_museum.htm
OPEN Mon–Fri, 13:00–16:00

National Fishing Heritage Centre
Alexandra Dock, [Great] Grimsby, North-East Lincolnshire DN31 1UZ
☎ +44 (0)1472 323345
www.welcome.to/NFHCentre
OPEN Daily, Mar–Oct

True's Yard Fishing Heritage Centre
North Street, King's Lynn, Norfolk PE30 1QW
☎ +44 (0)1553 770479
E-MAIL trues.yard@virgin.net
OPEN Daily (except Christmas to New Year period)

Lynn Museum
Market Street, King's Lynn, Norfolk PE30 1NL
☎ +44 (0)1553 775001
www.norfolk.gov.uk/leisure/museums/museums.htm
OPEN Tues–Sat 10:00–17:00 (except Christmas & BH)

Boston Guildhall Museum
South Street, Boston, Lincolnshire PE21 6HT
☎ +44 (0)1205 365954
www.emms.org.uk/lincoln.htm
OPEN Apr–Sept: Mon–Sat 10:00–17:00; Sun 13:30–17:00. Closed Christmas

The Henry Ramey Upcher Private Lifeboat Museum
West End Fishermens Slipway, West Cliff, Sheringham, Norfolk

☎ +44 (0)1263 824343
www.poppyland.co.uk/norfolk/sheringham.htm
OPEN Daily (usually 12:30–16:30) Apr–Sept. GV & Edu BA

Sheringham Museum
Station Road, Sheringham, Norfolk NR26 8RE
☎ +44 (0)1263 821871, Curator: 822895.
www.sheringhamtown.co.uk/sheringhammuseum.htm
OPEN Tues–Sun, Easter–late Oct; also BH Mon

Cromer Museum
East Cottages: next to Cromer Parish Church, Norfolk NR27 9HB
☎ +44 (0)1263 513543
www.norfolk.gov.uk/leisure/museums/charges.htm
OPEN Usually daily

Cromer RNLI Henry Blogg Museum
Old Lifeboat House, The Gangway, Cromer, Norfolk
☎ +44 (0)1263 511294
www.safehavenservices.co.uk/cromer.htm
OPEN Daily, Easter–Oct or BA in winter

Time and Tide
Blackfriars Rd, off St Peter's Rd, Great Yarmouth, Norfolk, NR30 3BX
☎ +44 (0)1493 743930
FAX +44 (0)1493 743940
www.museums.norfolk.gov.uk
OPEN Daily, Mar–Oct: 10:00–17:00; Nov–Mar: Mon & Fri 10:00–16:00 (closed Tue & Thur); Sat & Sun 12:00–16:00 (check for Christmas school holiday opening times

The Norfolk Nelson Museum
26 South Quay, Great Yarmouth, Norfolk NR30 2RG
☎ +44 (0)1493 850698.
www.nelson-museum.co.uk
OPEN Daily, Apr–Oct; 10:00–17:00 weekdays, 14:00–17:00 Sat & Sun

BA: By arrangement   BH: Bank holiday   GV: Group visits

Deck and masts of the Cutty Sark.
PHOTO COURTESY OF THE CUTTY SARK TRUST.

THAMES

From Lowestoft to North Foreland

Lowestoft ■ Southwold ■ Ipswich ■ Harwich
Walton-on-the-Naze ■ Brightlingsea ■ Wivenhoe
The Thames Estuary ■ Maldon ■ Burnham-on-Crouch
The Port of London ■ Greenwich ■ The River Medway
Chatham ■ Whitstable

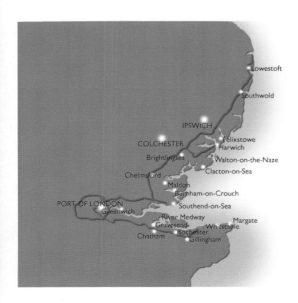

LOWESTOFT

Formerly a flourishing fishing port where at one time 700 drifters could be seen squeezed into its harbour, Lowestoft depended on the herring trade for its prosperity. The harbour itself was built by Sir Samuel Morton Peto, whose company built Nelson's Column and the Houses of Parliament.

Sadly little remains of Lowestoft's thriving fishing industry; a small fleet of inshore fishing boats helps to keep the market alive, but the majority of the fish comes in by road. Occasional visits by gas-rig supply vessels now provide most of the harbour's traffic, together with cruising yachts.

Red Herrings

Thomas Nashe, an Elizabethan writer, reported in 1599 that these highly-cured fish were used as a remedy for rheumatism, gall-stones, and if rubbed round the rim of a container holding ale, it would go flat. More importantly, they would put hounds off the scent, hence the familiar expression. Red herrings were cured in Lowestoft well within living memory. Reggie Reynolds, an old smokehouse worker, remembered: 'One old boy used to put dried horse muck on the fires and the reds he did were bloody beautiful! I put some red herring away in my mother's washhouse when I was called up in 1939 and they were still there when I was de-mobbed in 1945! Yeah, and I ate 'em as well.'

To get a flavour of this town's past glories, you must go and stand on the most eastern point in England where you find the **Lowestoft and East Suffolk Maritime Society's Museum**, and where they have created the friendliest of collections. It is stuffed with ship models – one of which will ride the waves if the clockwork key is turned. There is a reconstruction of the inside of a herring drifter's cabin, and homage is paid to the inventor of the diving helmet. Drift nets hang from the ceiling whilst, the work of pierhead painters cover the walls. There are also examples of a local style of art which used embroidery instead of paint to portray ships. This work was done by servants in the shipowners' houses using loose threads from their dresses.

■ *Lydia Eva* – the last of the steam drifters

Lydia Eva may look an antique compared with modern industrial fishing vessels, but the 138 tonne drifter was very sophisticated in her day. She had electricity and wireless, both unimagined luxuries to most

The Lydia Eva *sailing from Great Yarmouth.* PHOTO © KEN KENT.

herring fisherman then. Unfortunately she was destined to have a short career: she landed her last catch in 1938, only five years after her launch. She was built just before the final decline of the herring trade, and it is doubtful that she ever reached her full potential as a drifter.

She went on to carry out buoy work off the Welsh coast, salvage and naval duties. Incidentally, she was named after Lydia Eva Cox who, at the time of writing, is 90 and still lives in Yarmouth '*I was never allowed to go on deck. It was very unlucky for a woman to go on a boat.*' The vessel *Lydia Eva* requires constant care and restoration but remains a fitting reminder of Lowestoft's fishing heritage.

■ *Excelsior* – a grand old Lady of Lowestoft

Workmanlike, robust, yet graceful is the Lowestoft fishing smack, *Excelsior* – the last survivor of what was once a thriving fleet. To see her under full sail is an overwhelming sight. With her 100 tons of oak fully restored, and in sailing trim, she takes youngsters to sea on training cruises and takes part in Tall Ships races. She remains authentically rigged and can still trawl if required.

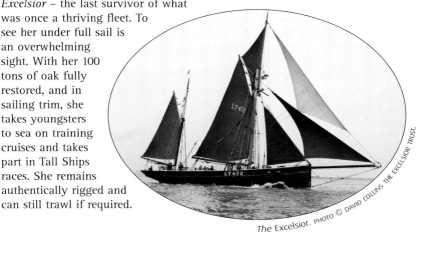

The Excelsior. PHOTO © DAVID COLLINS THE EXCELSIOR TRUST.

Built in Lowestoft in 1921, she fished the North Sea and trawled for plaice until 1935. She was then sold to Norway and brought back to England for rebuilding in 1982. Her restoration has been faithful; she has massive, fearsome tiller steering, a windlass and a steam capstan, although this is now hydraulically powered. She sets 3,400 square feet of sail and has 1.5 miles of confusing rigging for trainees to unscramble.

Opportunities to see such vessels in sailing trim are rare. It is even rarer to be able to sail them, but on *Excelsior* you still can.

■ The Royal Naval Patrol Service – Harry Tate's Navy!

This was a Navy within the Navy. A proud force, the RNPS had its own rules and regulations, and despite consisting of no more than a collection of requisitioned trawlers, yachts, paddle steamers and tugs, they made an undeniable contribution to the winning of WWII in theatres of war around the world from the Atlantic to Russia and the Far East.

Sparrow's Nest, at Lowestoft (where their museum is housed) became the centre of the RNPS operations, chosen because of Lowestoft's strategic position: facing continental Europe. It was officially known as HMS *Europa* although doubtless the members of Harry Tate's Navy had their own name for it. Together they were also known as 'Churchill's pirates'.

Much of their equipment was out of date and many of their craft were unsuitable for combat. Nevertheless, in providing escorts for vital convoys, and minesweeping, their contribution is undeniable. Their heroism was also remarkable: the RNPS lost more vessels in the course of the war than any other branch of the Royal Navy.

'*Attention is not unnaturally focused more upon famous destroyer captains and the dashing individuals who later commanded the fast, well-equipped ships of the specially formed submarine-hunting groups, such as Walker of Western Approaches. Little of the limelight falls upon the anti-submarine trawlers of the RN Patrol Service. Yet these humble, unglamorous little ships with their slow speed, limited armament and comparatively untrained crews were to prove just as much of a headache to the Nazi U-boat fleet as their bigger sisters in the Navy's general service.*' (A Cecil Hampshire *The Lilliput Fleet* 1957).

The shifting coastline

South of Lowestoft, you must make the best you can of the coastline for some of it will not be there much longer. It is constantly nibbled at by the sea. The most spectacular erosion is to be seen at Covehithe where the road ends abruptly before tumbling into the sea, making all the more dramatic the ruin of St. Andrew's church built in 1672. It was off Covehithe that the hard- fought Battle of Sole Bay took place in 1672 when the Dutch fleet, led by de Ruyter, confronted the English and French fleets, which were victorious. This coast's enemy is now the North Sea.

St Andrews church, Covehithe.
PHOTO © IAN DAVEY.

SOUTHWOLD

This has always been a nervous stretch of coast, worried about erosion, and in Southwold fearful of armed invasion too. Twenty years before the Battle of Sole Bay, Charles I gave guns to the town to protect it against privateers sailing out of Dunkirk. The existing guns, now to be found on Gun Hill overlooking the sea, were given by George II in 1745 after the town had complained *'this place is in a very dangerous position for want of guns and ammunition being naked and exposed to the insults of the Common Enemys'.*

The Museum building dates from the 18th Century. PHOTO COURTESY OF SOUTHWOLD MUSEUM.

The **Southwold Museum** celebrates the Battle of Sole Bay, and admits it is the only thing of maritime historical importance to have taken place off its shores. The museum, however, reflects a much wider maritime tradition.

For example, you will learn that you '*can never drown if you go to sea in a bowler hat*'. This was a beach fisherman's custom, and they can be seen in old photographs appearing to be dressed both for the sea and the City. There is a bowler hat for examination which will reveal that it was sturdy headgear, made from a single moulded piece of leather, resulting in a cross between a bowler and a tin helmet.

The charming figure-head 'Lucilla' was found washed up on the beach. PHOTO COURTESY OF SOUTHWOLD MUSEUM.

Southwold is almost an island, surrounded by what is now no more than a drainage ditch, called Buss Creek. Here shipbuilding took place on a grand scale: the 'busses' were stout wooden fishing vessels trading as far as Iceland and Shetland, an industry which was already thriving in 1540 and was going strong two centuries later.

As in most East coast towns, pictures in the museum of beach boats hauled above the tide line, nets drying, fish being carted, clay pipes being smoked, remind you what a thriving industry beach fishing once was.

■ The Southwold Sailor's Reading Room

A gem of a retreat, it has a panelled roof, like a small chapel, and on the matchboarded walls are pictures of old Southwold fishermen, lifeboat rescues, and four richly painted ships' figureheads which were once scattered about the town. The armchairs are soft and inviting, the newspapers are spread on the table for you to enjoy. All are welcome; there is no charge, but a donation is always welcome.

This was once a social centre for beach fishermen, where they could wait for the weather to go fishing. A stunning model of the *Bittern*, a typical Southwold beach yawl, can be found here; also a beach punt, the *Rapid*. It is a perfect place to spend a contemplative hour – accompanied only by the ticking of the clock.

Cromer lifeboat house in the 1800s; now moved to Southwold.
PHOTO COURTESY THE HENRY BLOGG MUSEUM.

■ The Cromer Lifeboat House, Southwold

Originally standing on the end of Cromer pier, this lifeboat house was declared redundant and brought to Southwold by barge where it now houses the *Alfred Corry*, the lifeboat which saw service at Southwold from 1893 onwards. She has been restored to her original seagoing state – described by a contemporary local paper, at the time of her launch, as '*a full bow to provide lift when launched over the open beach*'. As you admire *Alfred Corry*, it is worth remembering that the insignificant looking River Blyth which joins the sea between Southwold and Walberswick (crossed

The city lost to the sea

In Saxon times, Dunwich was one of the most prosperous towns in England, having three churches, a grammar school, its own bishop (which it still has) and 5,000 inhabitants. It was an important harbour and the home of merchants and traders. It was a naval centre, too, capable of sending 80 ships to war in mediaeval times and had more galleys than London.

In January 1326, its fortunes were to change forever. A ferocious storm carried over a million tons of sand and shingle across the harbour mouth, cutting off Dunwich from the sea. Dunwich's days were done, the merchants left, the naval fleets moved away and the North Sea took charge. In modern times, an army of dredgers and diggers would have restored the river mouth, but without such technology, Dunwich was left to die.

The **Dunwich Museum**'s model of disappearing Dunwich explains all. Inch by inch this huge town fell into the sea, and continues to do so. All Saints Church fell off the cliff in 1920, and the remaining archways of the mediaeval friary are dangerously close to the water's edge. On stormy nights, the legend says that the bells of sunken Dunwich churches chime out.

by a remarkable steam ferry seen in photographs in the Southwold Museum) was once a major trading river with barges and Norfolk wherrys working as far inland as Blythburgh and Halesworth.

■ The River Alde

The most northerly Suffolk river, and certainly the most unusual, is the River Alde which meets the sea at Shingle Street, where it is properly called the River Ore. It runs behind the town of Aldeburgh and eventually inland to Snape. Aldeburgh provides another stark example of the way this coast is shifting, for the timbered Moot Hall, where town council meetings are still held, now sits next to the beach – there once would have been three streets between it and the North Sea.

■ Orford Ness

The largest vegetated shingle spit in Europe, this is a wild and lonely place with an 'edge of the world' feel. Because of its remoteness, it has been the home of military experimenters for much of the twentieth century, and although rumours are thick on the ground facts are scarce. It is known that experiments were carried out here which led to the development of radar, and possibly nuclear detonators. Laboratories and experimental rigs which litter Orford Ness add to its mysterious and often sinister air.

Apart from shingle, there is grazing marshland here, salt marsh, mudflats and brackish lagoons which provide unique feeding grounds for migrating birds. It is a truly exceptional place and, thanks to the National Trust, can now be visited.

Fishing boats at Orford. PHOTOGRAPH © IAN DAVEY.

Sutton Hoo

You could argue that all of Britain's maritime history began here on the site which has been called 'page one of English history', ranking in archeological importance with Stonehenge.

In 1939, excavations revealed the richest burial ever discovered in Britain an Anglo-Saxon ship containing the treasure of one of the earliest English Kings, Rædwald of East Anglia. Nothing remained of the ship itself, although the run of the planks and the rivet marks left their impression in the soil. She was 27m long, 4.5m wide, and 1.5m high amidships, made of nine oak planks on each side. No evidence was found of a sail and it was assumed she was propelled by oars: 20 rowers per side.

The hoards of treasure, jewellery and coins discovered within the ship are priceless and can be seen in the British Museum along with more mundane items such as buckets, tubs and cauldrons, a collection of silver bowls from the eastern

The Sae Wylfing *a half-size replica of the burial ship found in mound one.* PHOTO COURTESY OF THE HERITAGE TRAIL.

Mediterranean, wooden cups and bottles, and a pair of large drinking horns. Taken together, this is one of the richest archeological sites ever discovered.

IPSWICH

The private **Museum of Knots and Sailor's Ropework** in Ipswich, reminds us of one of the most fundamental maritime skills. In the days of sail, when a ship might carry as much as twenty miles of rope and rigging, the ability of the crews to knot, splice and work rope was an essential skill. The tools of the trade are few and a rigger might work with only a knife, a fid and a serving mallet. His memory was the main tool of his craft and he would be required to hold in his head a knot for every occasion. Not every piece of ropework was used as part of a ship's rigging – the knotmaker might braid handles for seamen's chests, make covers for ships' wheels or create mats from knotted rope. In the museum you will find the largest collection of knots and ropework in Britain, collected, and sometimes constructed, by Des and Liz Pawson.

Maritime knots

All sailors need to *'know the ropes'* – that meant an understanding that a knot should be strong, secure and useful – and easily undone when needed. Although the definitive work, *The Ashley Book of Knots* lists nearly 4000 of them, arguably a sailor could get by with just three:

- *Reef knot* – known to the Romans as the Hercules knot, is the most elemental of all knots used for tying bandages and slings.
- *Clove hitch* – this was used for mooring and had the advantage of tightening under load, but easily cast off when slack.
- *Bowline* – when forming a loop in rope, this knot was supreme for it was not only secure but could be made with one hand if necessary. One of its early uses was in attaching a warp to the head of an anchor. Ashley notes 'it is so good a knot that the sailor seldom uses any other loop knot aboard a boat.'

Other knots which might justifiably join the hall of knotting fame are the Carrick bend, a round turn and two half hitches, and the sheepshank.

HARWICH HARBOUR

This is the only safe haven, in all weathers, for ships between the Humber and the Thames. Harwich itself has been eclipsed in the last 30 years by Felixstowe which now takes all the glory as the biggest container port in Britain and the busiest in Europe. (The **Felixstowe Museum** at Landguard Point traces the development of the port and its pioneering work in roll-on, roll-off technology). The fact that Drake, Frobisher, Hawkins and Nelson all set sail from Harwich does little for its status these days.

The *Mayflower*, in which the Pilgrim Fathers crossed the Atlantic, started her journey from here under the command of a Harwich man, Christopher Jones, who stopped in Plymouth to take on board the pilgrims. (*See Boston and Immingham museums for the early history of the Pilgrim Fathers.*) The story is told in an exhibition mounted by the enthusiastic Harwich Society on the **Halfpenny Pier**, which was built in 1854 as a ticket office for the first Continental ferries.

Harwich has always been the port of choice for adventurers seeking crews and captains, especially in pioneering Tudor times. Both the north-east and north-west passages were searched for (with mixed success) by ships sailing from Harwich.

MARITIME SIGHTS OF HARWICH

The Low Lighthouse, now the town's Maritime Museum.

The Treadwheel Crane, used at the Naval Yard from 1667 to 1927 and worked by men walking in the interior of the two wheels.

The Lifeboat Museum housed in the first Harwich lifeboat station (built 1876), known as the 'Number One Station'.

The Ha'Penny Pier, built in 1854, as the ticket office for the first continental ferries.

The Lifeboat Museum.

Christopher Jones' House – Master of the *Mayflower*.

The Old Custom House which was in use from about 1795 to 1935.

The High Lighthouse, built in 1818 to replace a light over the Town Gate. This and the Lower Light were used in conjunction to facilitate navigation of sandbanks until 1862, and now houses a wireless museum.

Ha'penny Pier Visitor Centre, Harwich.

The *Redoubt* built in 1808 as a large circular fort to protect the harbour from Napoleonic invasion. It was originally armed with ten guns and surrounded by a deep moat.

The Redoubt.
ALL PHOTOS COURTESY OF THE HARWICH SOCIETY.

Harwich Maritime Museum. PHOTO COURTESY OF THE HARWICH SOCIETY.

The **Maritime Museum** sits on the Harwich waterfront and could easily be confused for a low lighthouse. It is, in fact, the forward of a pair of leading lights, built in 1818, and now redundant. By lining up the forward and rear lights, ships could be safely steered between the sandbanks and into safe water, and it was the shifting sands themselves which made them redundant. Before becoming a museum, the lights were used as a station for pilots who left from here to guide ships into harbour.

The museum is as varied as Harwich's maritime history. Exhibits range from HMS *Ganges*, the naval training base across the water at Shotley, to the work of Trinity House, the lighthouse authority who have a major base here where their flagship tender, *Patricia*, is often to be seen.

But for the real maritime experience in Harwich, you must wander down the Georgian back streets between the pier and the museum to visit the old **lifeboat house** restored to its original Victorian condition, which now houses the former Clacton lifeboat. Also look out for the famous 'leg-powered treadmill' built in 1667 and restored to working order.

WALTON-ON-THE-NAZE

In a seaside town where time seems to have stood still, you will find the second longest pier in the UK (800 metres) which carries the world's oldest operating amusement park. Also, undergoing restoration, is the *James Stevens No 14* which was Walton's second lifeboat, one of the earliest to be converted to engine propulsion in 1900 at the Thames Ironworks and was intended to be launched off the beach. Proving too heavy, she was given a mooring off the pier where all Walton's lifeboats have since been moored. *James Stevens No 14* was replaced in 1928, but not before she had undertaken a monumental rescue of 92 passengers and crew from the SS *Peregrine* which had run aground on the Longsand Head in a strong gale. It was said of this rescue: '...*it would not have been possible without the engine which ran faultlessly, even when the side of the boat was stove in'.* For this rescue, the coxswain, Henry Britton, was awarded the RNLI's silver medal.

James Stevens No 14 would have long since disappeared had she not be discovered by lifeboat enthusiasts who spotted her distinctive lines clearly visible despite the unsightly houseboat superstructure which had been added to her. Now in the care of the Walton and Frinton Heritage Trust, who are restoring her, she returned to Walton in May 1998 to be met off the pier by Walton's current lifeboat. She is now on the National Register of Historic Vessels and is said to be the oldest surviving motor boat in the world.

The **Walton Maritime Museum**, housed in the RIBA award winning Old Lifeboat House, tells the story of the *James Stevens No 14,* as well as describing the peculiar geology of the fast-eroding Naze and the fossils that are often found on the beach hereabouts.

Coxwain Henry Britton.
PHOTO COURTESY OF FWHT AND KEITH RICHARDSON.

THE ESSEX COAST

South of Harwich, beyond the crumbling red crag of the Naze, the coast falls away and tucks itself into the northern fringes of the Thames estuary where the rivers Colne (which serves Colchester, Britain's oldest recorded town) and Blackwater meet. The fishermen's flint cottages of north Norfolk are replaced by Essex weather-boarded houses, painted black and white. The traditional boats are different too. The Norfolk beach fishermen give way to the Essex smacksmen who have fished for oysters in these rivers for centuries. It is also the home of the Thames barge, an unlikely looking craft: flat and stumpy, yet an efficient cargo carrier in sheltered coastal waters, having the advantage of needing only a man and boy to work her.

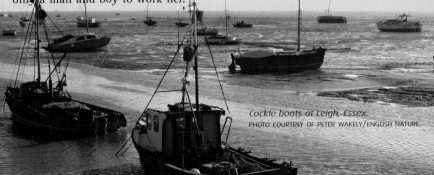

Cockle boats at Leigh, Essex.
PHOTO COURTESY OF PETER WAKELY/ENGLISH NATURE.

The *Mignonette* and the poor cabin boy

Every museum has one story to tell which is not told elsewhere. At Brightlingsea, it is the tale of the *Mignonette*, a 19 ton yawl bound for Australia in 1884. The ship foundered, the crew took to the lifeboats, and in their long days of desperation before rescue, survived by eating the cabin boy, Richard Parker. The museum, however, records that at the eventual trial, the Brightlingsea man on board was found not guilty of participating in the cannibalism. Poems were written about this terrible event, the closing verse of one of them being:

> *'We hope they will show mercy on the men at trial,*
> *They have seen such misery, there is no denial;*
> *Dick is with the angels where none can annoy,*
> *Mothers give your blessing on that sailor boy.'*

BRIGHTLINGSEA

This small Essex town on the east bank of the Colne is an unlikely member of the exclusive medieval gang of Cinque Ports, founded in the time of Edward the Confessor to provide men and ships for the King's service. In return, the ports were granted privileges and their influence was at its peak in the 13th and 14th centuries when the Navy became an organised

fighting force. Brightlingsea is the only Cinque Port outside Kent and Sussex, although technically she is a 'branch' of Sandwich. None of this stops Brightlingsea people being proud of their status and enjoying municipal exchanges with their fellows further south.

This town had a reputation for producing sailors of strength and skill, not only for the commercial trade but for yachting too. In richer days when 'gentlemen' kept yachts, it was often to Brightlingsea that they turned for their crews. This fitted nicely into the working year, for the men could yacht in the summer and fish for their livings in the winter. There were Brightlingsea men on all seven of Britain's early challenges for

Brightlingsea. PHOTO COURTESY EAST OF ENGLAND TOURIST BOARD.

the highly-prized America's Cup, although they never won it back from the Americans.

Ploughing matches were held near Brightling-sea, farmers versus sailors, to see who could cut the straightest furrow. The farmers used to steer their plough by eye, but the sailors stuck to what they knew best and lashed a compass to the plough. It is said the sailors always won.

The **Brightlingsea Museum** brings together all of this town's varied maritime heritage. It shows the method of 'stowboat fishing' which was done by the power of the sails and the strength of the men alone. Large nets were slung beneath boats which then drifted slowly with wind and tide, capable of catching ten tons of fish in ten minutes. Sprats were caught here is vast quantities, and oysters till an outbreak of typhoid in the 1930s brought the trade to a close.

WIVENHOE

In the days when it was the custom for the rich yachtsman to hand over the sailing of his craft to paid hands, the men of the Colne, Blackwater and Crouch were in huge demand, often travelling to the south coast, and Cowes in particular, at the height of the racing season. Not only were they practiced seamen, but the narrow channels in which they sailed, and the precision with which they had to steer their craft, made them ideal racing crews.

The quay at Wivenhoe. PHOTO © BONNIE HILL.

One wealthy owner, Captain Charles G Nottage, showed his gratitude to the men of Wivenhoe by leaving in his will of 1894, £3,000 for the education of seamen. **The Nottage Institute** was duly founded. It has been at its present premises on Wivenhoe Quay since 1947.

These days the emphasis is on the education of those who wish to go to sea, rather than those who were born to it. Yachtsmen come here to learn navigation, meteorology and traditional boatbuilding. A Sunday museum is open in the summer.

■ Wildfowling

Arguably a maritime sport: certainly both the **Nottage Institute**, and its neighbour across the Colne, the **Mersea Island Museum**, proudly display both a punt gun and a locally-built wildfowling punt. Hereabouts, this was not merely recreation, but a living for some. The wildfowlers required as detailed a knowledge of the tides and local waters as the fishermen because part of their skill was concealment from the wildfowl which came to the creeks and mudflats to feed. Generally, wildfowling commenced on an ebb tide before dawn, the guns returning with the flood tide many hours later. Concealment was vital, and punts were painted accordingly so as not to stand out against the glassy mud, or in the glare of the sun reflected on shallow water.

The punt guns were fearsome devices, essentially big-bore shotguns, sometimes 8 to 10 feet long, weighing many hundredweights and too large to put to the shoulder. One discharge could kill up to fifty Brent geese, mallard or widgeon, which were destined for the London market. If visiting the Mersea Island Museum, remember that although connected to the rest of Essex by a raised roadway called 'The Strood', some high tides will cover it and you might have to wait an hour till the ebb. Check the tides before you go, or ask the locals.

THE THAMES ESTUARY

At sea in the Thames Estuary, amidst the sandbanks created by the sluicing tides where North Sea meets the River Thames, who would ever guess that ahead lay, arguably, the most important maritime centre in the world? It is hardly a couple of centuries since the British Empire was ruled from London, when imperial authority was exercised by the dispatching of ships, when half the world's trade was conducted by the craft that worked these unpredictable waters.

TRADITIONAL CRAFT OF THE THAMES ESTUARY

■ The oyster smack

These traditional sailing craft are native to these waters and huge fleets were once moored at Brightlingsea, West Mersea, and at the head of the Blackwater at Maldon. It was unlikely that many of the smaller smacks would venture further than ten miles from their home ports, but, nevertheless, these were built as strongly and as powerfully as any seagoing fishing boat. These boats required versatility, for not only did they have to be nippy when it came to getting the catch home through the often choppy waters of the Thames estuary, but slowness was a requirement when hove-to, as they dredged for oysters. Constructed with vertical stems and fine bows, they are unmistakeable for their low freeboard aft to make things easier for lifting the dredge, and their flush deck to make on-board handling of the laden dredge easier.

'Nor shall I ever forget how that fleet of smacks got under way. Boat alongside, anchor windlass clicking, patent blocks clickety-clicking, peak up, jib set, anchor away, foresail set; it was all going on around me as quickly as I can write of it. So in the grey, early dawn that humble exquisite little armada, perhaps fifteen of these lovely eight to fifteen ton carvel-built cutter smacks, some of them seventy years old, streamed off out of Thornfleet and Besom Creeks.' – Edgar March remembering sailing as a novice on board the Essex smacks.

Oyster smacks racing on the Thames. PHOTO © DEN PHILLIPS.

You will hardly spot a smack working at sea today, although several are in the care of enthusiasts, kept in pristine condition and keenly raced in the summer. At one time, it would not have been unusual to have seen 100 of them at work in the mouth of the Colne and another 100 in the Blackwater. Far in the distance, on the horizon, a few might be working the shallow waters between the sandbanks, salvaging from wrecks – another of the smacksmen's legendary skills.

The **Brightlingsea Smack Dock** is in the old Aldous shipyard where many of the 100+ year old fishing smacks and bawleys that now lie in the dock were built and launched. It is open to the public at all times.

■ The Thames barge

This is the only British sailing trading vessel to have survived in any numbers to the present day.

Of the two types of craft found in these waters, the Thames barge is less sleek that the oyster smack. She is a bulky, carthorse of a craft with two masts – the mizzen being generally small – and a considerable mainsail cut square and high to catch the breeze when these shallow craft were working their way inland to quays where cargo might be unloaded. To get as far inland as possible, the barges were flat-bottomed, needing little water in which to float – as little as two feet. Instead of keels, they carried large boards which hung from each side and were lowered in deeper water to prevent sideways drift.

The rig was designed for working not only in the open estuary waters, but also in the rivers where the sails had to be set higher to catch the breeze. This meant a spritsail rather than a gaff rig, having the advantage that the sprit could also be used as a crane for cargo handling. The rig was simple, well within the capabilities of 'one man and a boy' who were the usual crew. Having no boom, a cargo such as hay could be stacked ten feet high on the deck without in any way hindering the working of the ship.

These were the days when transport in London was horse-drawn and much trade was done by these barges in bringing hay from East Anglia to feed London stabled horses. Rather than return with an empty barge, manure was brought back to be spread as fertiliser.

Thames barge Edme. PHOTO COURTESY OF THE THAMES SAILING BARGE ASSOCIATION.

These days, you can see Thames barges at Maldon, at the head of the Blackwater, where a dozen or more might be alongside, or at Pin Mill on the River Orwell, halfway to Ipswich, where barges come to dry out on the hard for repair. Annual smack and barge races are held on both sides of the Thames estuary, usually on the Blackwater, the Orwell and Medway. They offer a sight you will never forget. (See also Dolphin Yard Sailing Barge Museum, Sittingbourne, Kent.)

'The Thames barge is no modern contrivance, but she is still pre-eminent. Dependent on sail only, she is the largest sailing-vessel in the world which is regularly handled in all weathers by two men only. In and out of these channels she threads her expert course, laden with grain perhaps, or cement, and then again up some creek or inlet miles landward she searches her way to a farm wharf among the fields... All along the modern refinement of turbine and wireless of other vessels, the whole affair seems grotesquely primitive – occurring as it so often does upon London River itself; but it maintains a justification strictly up-to-date, for, in competition, it pays.' H Alker Tripp writing in the early 20th century (Conway Maritime Press).

For all its ungainly appearance, the Thames Barge could be swift, and handy provided that the right pair of hands was on the wheel. Hervey Benham, an old barge skipper describes the steering of one:

'Because she answers slowly, the amateur gives her too much helm, and leaves a wake like a serpent in pain; the experienced skipper feels and anticipates the swinging of the ship's head, checking the movement to come before the last is finished. He does not use much helm, but he is always using some.'

THE BARGEMAN'S RHYME

We've wallowed in the Wallet,
Awash with sodden deals
And slipped from Southend jetty
The sou'easter at our heels.
Stern winter had the will of us
On black December days,
Our kedge is on the Buxey
And our jib is off the Naze.

Thames barge Reminder. PHOTO COURTESY OF THE THAMES SAILING BARGE ASSOCIATION.

The Thames Barge *Glenway* at Maldon

This barge, first launched in Rochester in 1913, is a true survivor. A D-Day veteran – abandoned at Dunkirk only to be sailed home by 200 desperate soldiers. She was beached off Yarmouth in the infamous 1951 storm, refloated and left to rot at the end of Maldon promenade for much of the 1980s. Now, however, she is the centrepiece of the Thames Sailing Barge Heritage Centre at **Cook's Barge Yard** in Maldon where you can board her. This centre gives a true flavour of the life of the working bargemen, and celebrates the heyday of one of the best-loved of traditional working craft.

Sailing barges at Cooks Barge Yard, Maldon.
PHOTO © CHARLES SMITH, TRADBOAT.

Up the Thames estuary, there is no hint of London until you are almost upon it. True, the river narrows as you approach from seaward, but there is no guessing that anywhere special lies ahead. In fact, a 19th century sailor navigating the lower reaches of the Thames estuary seeing the Thames barges laden with spectacular cargoes of hay might have suspected that only an agricultural hinterland lay across the horizon. Only the fleets of colliers bound from the Tyne and Yorkshire coalfields, or the constant stream of merchantmen may have given a hint that some centre of population lay ahead. Nevertheless, London lies well hidden behind knolls, gats and swatchways which make the maritime approach to this capital city as intricate as negotiating any maze.

It is hard to imagine the port of London in its heyday, as a major employer, home to Royal dockyards at Woolwich and Deptford, a Palace at Greenwich, and an Observatory from where the world measured its time. And on the river itself, it is equally difficult to believe that this was a waterway which suffered congestion on a scale which makes London's streets these days seem free-flowing.

MALDON ─────────────────────────────────

Maldon means many things to different people. Schoolchildren may think of the Battle of Maldon fought in 991AD between the English and a ship-borne army of Danes, resulting in the first major defeat for the

English in generations. Lovers of barges will tell you that barging is what Maldon is really all about.

Cooks will have a different idea, for not only have these Essex waters been traditionally rich in oysters (blame the Romans who introduced them), but equally famous is the sea salt, purified in Maldon, which is said to be bettered by no other. Salt has been produced here since Saxon times, and although the modern Maldon Salt Works was opened as recently as 1882, it is thought they were built on the site of a similar operation. It is still a simple and natural process and would be recognized by the Romans who purified salt here to use as currency. Sea water is

Maldon. PHOTO COURTESY OF THE EAST OF ENGLAND TOURIST BOARD.

purified and then evaporated in large stainless steel pans and the resulting crystals are harvested daily using traditional long-handled rakes.

BURNHAM-ON-CROUCH

Nowadays, yachting is the principal maritime activity over much of the east coast of England, but Burnham-on-Crouch has earned itself a reputation above others. Before yachting became fashionable in the 1880s, this town with its 15 miles of navigable river depended a little on fishing, more on oysters, and certainly thrived on smuggling (all these facts are reflected in the **Burnham-on-Crouch Museum**).

The arrival of the yachtsmen was prompted by increasing traffic on the Thames which made racing at places like Erith, more difficult. The coming of the railway to Burnham meant that suddenly the unspoilt rivers Crouch and Roach were available for uninterrupted racing. Soon, major yacht clubs such as the Royal Corinthian, were to build clubhouses here. Burnham Week has always been held in high esteem by racing yachtsman and was rated second only to Cowes Week in national importance. It was, and still is, held after Cowes Week. Tradition had it that gentlemen raced at Cowes, sailed their boat to Burnham and raced there, finishing in time for the glorious twelfth of August when the yachting season was deemed to be finished and the grouse shooting season began.

The Motor Boat Museum

Well removed from the sea, at Pitsea near Basildon, the **Motor Boat Museum** has established itself as a leading authority on sporting leisure motorboats.

Motorboating began earlier than you might think – the earliest craft on display is the steam launch *Cygnet* built in 1873; the earliest racing boat is *Defender II* of 1909. Sip your shaken martini, adjust your black tie and perfect your steely gaze as you stand next to the *Fairy Huntress*, used in the James Bond film *From Russia with Love*.

The more practical minded will gasp at the world's first six-cylinder outboard, the *Soriano*, said by enthusiasts to be the most glamorous outboard engine ever built.

THE PORT OF LONDON ⸻

Strictly speaking, the Port of London begins at Clacton in the north and runs inland along the River Thames as far as Teddington, then along the north Kent coast as far as Margate. That part of the river from Docklands to Tower Bridge is properly known as the lower Pool of London, and from Tower Bridge to London Bridge: the Upper Pool. It has been the hub of the economy of London since Saxon times.

The modern history of the London docks can be traced from 1614 when the East India company first started to use Blackwall anchorage. Through the 19th century, docks were opened, including the East India docks in 1806, the St Katherine's dock in 1828 and the Royal Albert docks in 1880. In their heyday, London's docks commanded eleven miles of wharves and quays, employing 1500 cranes to handle 60,000

The Thames Barrage. PHOTO © DAVID WILLIAMS.

The London dock strike of 1889

This was a significant milestone in trade union and maritime history, and the dispute centred on the way in which labour was employed and the wages paid. Few dockers were employed full time and work was handed out on a casual, heartless basis.

'All are shouting. Some cry aloud his surname, some his Christian name, others call out their own names, to remind him that they are there. Indeed, it is a sight to sadden the most callous, to see thousands of men struggling for only one day's hire, the scuffle being made the fiercer by the knowledge that hundreds out of the number there assembled must be left to idle the day out in want. To look in the faces of that hungry crowd is to see a sight that must be ever remembered.' (Henry Mayhew, London Labour and the London Poor, 1861)

The strike began in mid-August, under the famous leadership of Ben Tillett and gained much public and press support for its lack of violence and intimidation. Large sums of money were raised to support the strikers, but a large donation of £30,000 from the Australian labour movement enabled the strikers to survive long enough to ensure a settlement.

In the fourth week of the strke, the Lord Mayor of London brought the two sides together, helped by Cardinal Manning, Catholic Archbishop of Westminster – the East End being a strong catholic community. His mediation brought the strike to a successful conclusion (from the workers' point of view) in mid September when the workers were awarded the 'dockers' tanner', or a guaranteed rate of pay of sixpence per hour.

'All along the Commercial Road, the women turned out in thousands to see their husbands and their sons pass in triumph. The sun seemed brighter, the music more inspiring, the banners more in number than ever before.' (Smith and Nash)

ships a year. It was then the largest port in the world and destined to become a major target of the Luftwaffe in the second World War.

The invention of containerisation, which required less individual handling of cargoes, did London no favours: the ships needed to be larger and the confines of the Thames was no place for the huge container carriers which were about to rule the merchant waves. The reluctance of the dockers to accept new working practices played no small part in the decline of London's docks. Many fell into disuse throughout the second half of the 20th century, only to have a rebirth as a chic and expensive place to live and do business after the docklands redevelopment.

LEFT: Docklands today, Museum in Docklands on left, Canary Wharf on right.
PHOTOS COURTESY OF MUSEUM OF LONDON.

RIGHT: Fun for children in the Mudlarks Gallery at Museum in Docklands.

■ The Museum in Docklands

In a converted warehouse, that once housed exotic spices from distant shores, this museum tells the story of London's river and its people from Roman times to the present day. For children, the Mudlarks interactive gallery gives them a working view of a nineteenth century clipper, and a diver's eye view of the docks. The modern history of docklands, too, has an importance which is expressed in a 'build it yourself' Canary Wharf.

Activities seem as important as exhibits here, and surely no better impression can be gained of Docklands than through the story-telling sessions which include the tale of the great Docklands strike of 1889, the adventures of Joseph Johnson, a black merchant sailor in the early 19th century who became a well known street entertainer, or salty tales of Caribbean adventure.

■ HMS *Belfast*

Without doubt, this is the most prominent maritime display to be seen in the Pool of London. After steaming no less than half a million miles in the course of her distinguished career, both in war and peacetime, she looked destined for the breaker's yard after paying off in 1963. But she was saved by her former captain, and others, and now provides a unique glimpse of the working life of a WWII cruiser. She is the last surviving example of the big gun cruisers.

CRUISER AT WAR

A cruiser is designed to detach itself from a fleet and operate independently as a powerful warship capable of patrolling supply routes, protecting merchant shipping, as well as engaging effectively in combat. A cruiser's size is defined by the size of its gun, and HMS *Belfast* was a 6 inch cruiser.

She scored a swift victory in WWII but soon paid a heavy price. On patrol in northern waters from her base with the 18th cruiser squadron in Scapa Flow (*see* **Scapa Flow Visitor Centre**, Orkney), she intercepted the German liner SS *Cap*

Part of the HMS Belfast *exhibition.*
PHOTO COURTESY HMS BELFAST.

Norte which was attempting to return to Germany disguised as a neutral vessel. After boarding, she was taken to a British port and reckoned worthy of 'prize money' which, under Admiralty law, the crew were entitled to for such a major capture.

Just over a month later, revenge struck when HMS *Belfast* detonated a magnetic mine while leaving the Firth of Forth causing severe structural damage (although light casualties) which took three years to repair. Later, she was to play a major part in the sinking of the *Scharnhorst* in the Battle of the North Cape, and fired the early shots in support of the British and Canadian D-Day landings on the Normandy beaches.

HMS *Belfast*'s company boasted three cats when she was first commissioned, although the most unlikely member of the ship's company was Olga, the reindeer, who was a present from the Russians. Sadly, the lengthy fighting at the time of the Battle of the North Cape caused her such distress that Olga had to be put down, although she is fondly remembered in the faithful depictions of life aboard this giant of a warship.

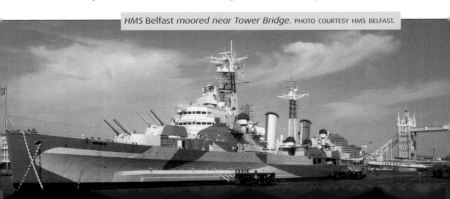

HMS Belfast *moored near Tower Bridge.* PHOTO COURTESY HMS BELFAST.

MARITIME GREENWICH – A WORLD HERITAGE SITE

Nowhere in maritime Britain is there a greater concentration of seafaring history, artefacts, art or architecture than at Greenwich. The **National Maritime Museum** cannot be bettered, not only as a resource but as an inspiration to those seeking the significance of seafaring in the make-up of Britain. Add to that the importance of the **Royal Observatory** in the history of navigation, the **Royal Naval College**, and the celebrated **Cutty Sark**, and the Greenwich experience is one which will take more than a casual visit to fully absorb.

The sense of history is almost overwhelming. Henry VIII was born here together with his daughters Queen Mary and Elizabeth I; their Tudor palace stood on the site on which now stands Sir Christopher Wren's Royal Naval College. Greenwich Park was the first royal park to be enclosed in 1443.

■ The Queen's House

It is said that the design of the USA's White House is based on the Queen's House which now forms the heart of the National Maritime Museum. The house, built between 1616 and 1635 as a hunting lodge for Anne of Denmark, the wife of James I, is the work of Inigo Jones, the first man to introduce the classical Roman and Italian ideas into English architecture, which until then had been largely gothic. For all its royal connections, usage has been limited. Anne died before its completion; work stopped for ten years, then Charles I gave the house to his new Queen Henrietta, and Jones was called back to resume the construction. Later, Charles II had more work done, but again hardly

lived there. It became the park ranger's residence in 1690.

The National Maritime Museum took up residence in 1937 and the House is now the venue for the Museum's significant collection of maritime paintings, including permanent displays and temporary special exhibitions (such as

The Queen's House. PHOTO © THE NATIONAL MARITIME MUSEUM.

The Royal Observatory. PHOTO © THE NATIONAL MARITIME MUSEUM.

Magnum photography and the the paintings of William Hodges). Architectural highlights include the delicate Tulip Staircase and the Great Hall – a perfect 40 foot cube with an original black and white stone floor.

■ The Royal Observatory

This is really a collection of buildings of various ages but all serving the common purpose of advancing astronomy, while contributing to the understanding of navigational astronomy – in particular the fixing of longitude. The oldest of the buildings, Flamsteed House, was built by Wren in 1675 as a home for the first Astronomer Royal, John Flamsteed, who did much of his work from the Octagon Room. A new planetarium, new galleries and education spaces are under construction, and many rare and beautiful artefacts pertaining to astronomy (including original Harrison chronometers) are on permanent display.

■ The Royal Naval College

This building was said to be '*one of the most sublime sights English architecture affords*'.

The site on which the Wren building now stands has a rich history, being once the site of the Palace of Placentia which was built in the early 15th century, and becoming the home of Margaret of Anjou, the wife of Henry VI. It was a royal palace for two centuries, much modified, notably by Henry VII. It was the birthplace of Henry VIII, and while living here he founded the great naval dockyards at Woolwich and Deptford. Placentia eventually fell into disrepair.

Queen Mary, wife of William III, is responsible for the building seen today. She decided to build a naval hospital on the site; Wren, assisted by Hawksmoor, was her chosen architect. Sensing that he might not live to see the building completed, Wren ordered all the foundations to be dug before any building could commence, ensuring that after his death any modification to his plans would be minimal. The building was finished in 1752

The **Painted Hall**, intended as a dining room for residents of the naval hospital, is a masterpiece of decorative art. It took the artist, Sir James Thornhill, 19 years to complete the work at a wage of three pounds a square yard for the ceiling, but only a pound for the more easily painted walls. In his lavish work (which the residents were hardly able to enjoy because there were too many of them, even for this great hall, and so they dined elsewhere) he depicts Peace and Liberty triumphing over Tyranny. William and Mary are seen ascending to heaven, keeping company with the Virtues while below them is Louis XIV clutching his broken sword. Not all the work was Thornhill's: in a series depicting the four seasons, Winter was drawn by a hospital patient, John Worley, who is recorded as having been punished for drunkenness at the age of 96. Lord Nelson lay in state here before his funeral – the precise spot on which his body lay is marked by a plaque.

Despite its distinguished surroundings, the hospital had a poor reputation for patient care and attention. It closed in 1869 to become the Royal Naval College, and after they departed in 1988 it was partly taken over by the University of Greenwich and the Trinity College of Music.

THE NATIONAL MARITIME MUSEUM ⎯⎯⎯

Without doubt this is the richest jewel in the maritime crown. It is not only Britain's premier collection, inventively shown in historic and excitingly contemporary buildings, it has grown into a major tourist attraction while maintaining its academic reputation.

It came into being in 1937, and was joined by the Royal Observatory in the 1950s. The collection consists of two and half million items, some of which are on loan to other museums. The majority of the small craft collection, for example, has moved to the National Maritime Museum, Cornwall at Falmouth although there are always some exciting smaller boats on display at Greenwich.

The Royal Naval College. PHOTO © DAVID WILLIAMS.

The Museum has a strong reputation for the quality and diversity of its exhibitions (recent shows include the widely acclaimed *Elizabeth*, the *Skin Deep* exhibition on tattooing, the cartoon reporter Tintin and the Beagle II mission to Mars).

Amongst the artefacts are collections of manuscripts, ship plans and cartography. The collection of both British and Dutch marine art is considerable, and the portrait collection is eclipsed only by that held in the National Portrait Gallery. The collections relating to Nelson and Captain Cook are unrivalled. The world's largest marine library is housed here, containing 100,000 volumes, some of which date from the fifteenth century.

Visits can also be enhanced by the actor-interpreters and a range of education workshops which complement the permanent galleries and exhibitions. The problem is – where to start?

The creative use of themed exhibitions has made it easier for you to get the best out of this museum, although you must accept that one visit will hardly give you a mouthful of a considerable feast. It is arranged on three floors, entry to which is gained through the recently built Neptune Court which boasts (at the time of building) the largest unsuspended glass roof in the world, and a high terrace surrounded by a dazzling collection of marine instruments and overlooked by the original stern-gallery of a ship which fought at Trafalgar (although it must be admitted, it fought on the French side!). The Neptune Court often becomes the venue for a range of temporary displays, including contemporary art installations as part of the Museum's New Visions programme.

■ Galleries: Level 1

EXPLORERS

This gallery tells the story of how exploration shaped the world, from the early voyages of the Vikings and Polynesians, through Columbus, Cook and Vancouver to more recent polar adventures.

PASSENGERS

Sea travel has not always been a recreational activity for the affluent classes. Sea journeys were once the only means by which the world's populations could migrate in search of a better life, or flee from a restrictive one. This exhibition is not only a celebration of the glory days of the luxury liners; it also seeks to examine the motives and experiences of the 19th and 20th century travellers who suffered conditions which were far from luxurious.

RANK AND STYLE

Naval uniform first appeared in 1748 and here you can see it in all its glories: from the dress uniforms complete with sword and epaulettes, down to the ratings' outfits which they made themselves from Admiralty cloth. Modern naval uniform now includes flash suits and other protective gear. Fishermen, too, had their uniform – intricately knitted guernseys made to traditional patterns.

MARITIME LONDON

For a young generation who might think that Docklands was always a grand housing estate – here is the true story of Britain's once premier maritime port. Shipping apart, London was once a centre of excellence in building navigation equipment and chronometers. It remains a commercial centre of the shipping world, even if the transactions these days are done in City offices, and not on the quayside.

There is also a leisure and education area here, and a lecture theatre.

■ Galleries: Level 2

HIDDEN TREASURES

This contains ship models, mainly from the 20th century. Those shown are only a small part of the museum's collection of over 2,500, most of which cannot be displayed due to lack of space. The first national ship model collection was made by Sir Robert Seppings, starting in the late 18th century, and is incorporated here.

Launch of HMS Agamemnon *at Woolwich Dockyard, 1852.* © NATIONAL MARITIME MUSEUM.

TRADE AND EMPIRE

The British Empire, which lasted for four hundred years, was the largest the world has ever known. What is often less understood is that its prosperity was based on maritime supremacy. This is the story of how the empire grew alongside maritime developments in ships and navigation. Also, how the idea of 'empire' grew to represent not only a trading convenience, but a 'civilising mission' too.

ART AND THE SEA

Artist have always turned to the sea for inspiration. For some it was the romance, but others have sought to establish national identity and pride through heroic portraits of naval commanders, or jubilant pictures of great victories at sea. The collection here is the largest in the world: from 16th century engravings to late 20th century abstract art.

Also on this level is the Caird Library, the rooms for use of the Friends of the NMM, and other exhibitions in development.

■ Galleries: Level 3
THE BRIDGE

It is one thing to create a structure which will float: it is another to get it to move successfully through the water. This interactive gallery takes you through the use of oars and rudders, to engines, paddles and propellers. By taking virtual command, here you can steer a primitive Viking ship, or become crew on a Victorian paddle steamer.

OCEANS OF DISCOVERY

This exhibitions asks the apparently simple question – how did we find our way across the oceans in the first place? The answer is broader than you might think. Here is the story of mapping and navigation, which takes us back to the early Polynesians (2000BC) who undertook wide-ranging Pacific voyages guided largely by subtle understandings of ocean currents and the positions of the stars in the skies. The mapping of the oceans became of fundamental importance, and the story is told here of how the early successes were achieved, and the developments which were to follow.

NELSON

This is a major celebration of the Britain's most famous maritime hero. Such was his status that artists did not hesitate to portray his courage either on canvas, cups or in song or verse. But what was the truth of the man? Was there another side waiting to be discovered? Might the women in his life tell a different tale? And was the veneration of his legend, in after years, a help to maritime development or a hindrance to it?

The Nelson collections are among the Museum's strongest, the uniform worn by Nelson at Trafalgar (and showing the fatal bullet hole) probably the most revered of all the objects in the collection. The Maritime Museum will always display its Nelson collection prominently, sometimes alongside superb international loan items in special exhibitions such as the *Nelson & Napoléon* feature which marks the bicentenary of Trafalgar.

SHIP OF WAR

Drawing on the museum's collection of naval models, here is the development of the sailing warship from the seventeenth century till the time of Nelson.

ALL HANDS

Aimed at a younger audience, this gallery is complete with a model of the 74-gun HMS *Cornwallis*. You can try your hand at cargo-handling, diving and gunnery with the interactive exhibits.

The people and events which come under the broad umbrella of 'maritime', from Vikings, through Tudors to a 20th century yachtswoman, are here to inspire children to delve further into this treasure house of a museum.

The Greenwich Meridian

Greenwich's fame as being the place 'from which the world's time is measured' (before the atomic clocks took over, of course) dates from October 1884. This was after an international conference (called by the President of the United States) voted 22–1 in favour of the honour going to Greenwich. The French abstained. It was agreed 'the meridian passing through the Transit Instrument at Greenwich was the 'initial' meridian and that longitude both east and west up to 180 degrees would be measured from here'. All countries would now adopt a Mean Solar Day beginning at Mean Midnight at Greenwich and measured by a 24 hour clock; the nautical and astronomical days would begin everywhere at mean midnight. Greenwich Mean Time became the world standard and the term still used these days, although for precise accuracy (which GMT does not provide because of variations in the rotation of the earth) UT, Universal Time, is used. To most of us, they are the same.

The Meridian Line at dusk.
PHOTO © THE NATIONAL MARITIME MUSEUM.

This resolution of 1884 brought about redundancy for other meridian lines, at least nine of which have passed through Greenwich. Successive astronomer Royals believed that 'their meridian' was more accurate than previous ones.

For those satisfied with a less precise measure of time, the time ball on the roof of the Greenwich Observatory is useful. At five minutes to one GMT, the ball is raised halfway up its post, fully hoisted at two minutes to one, and then drops to its starting position at precisely one o'clock GMT. Although long obsolete, this was widely used by ships anchored off Greenwich to check their chronometers.

The Altazimuth Pavilion.
PHOTO © THE NATIONAL MARITIME MUSEUM.

The Cutty Sark *at Greenwich.* PHOTO COURTESY OF THE CUTTY SARK TRUST.

THE CUTTY SARK

'*I never sailed a finer ship. At 10 or 12 knots she did not disturb the water at all. She was the fastest ship of her day, a grand ship, and a ship that will last forever.*' Captain George Moodie, first master of the *Cutty Sark*.

The *Cutty Sark* is the world's only surviving tea clipper, and she will only remain so if money can be found to make fundamental repairs to her hull which was never designed to spend time out of water. Of all the sights to be seen at Greenwich, she is the most memorable: three masted (the mainmast standing 152 feet), she is 280 feet overall, carries an incredible 32,000 square feet of canvas when under full sail, and weighs almost 1000 tons. Nevertheless, in her heyday from her launching in the 1880s, she was a true ocean greyhound.

THE GREAT TEA RACES

Held every winter for over 20 years, ships like the *Cutty Sark* raced from the Orient, fighting to be first home with a cargo of new season's tea. The route took them south from China, past Indonesia and south-westwards across the Indian Ocean to the Cape of Good Hope. From here they

Detail of wheel. PHOTO COURTESY OF THE CUTTY SARK TRUST.

raced northwards through the Atlantic, helped by the trade winds then hindered by the doldrums, but expecting to make the passage in about 100 days. The crew took huge pride in their vessel, displayed in the cleanliness of the decks, the shine on the brass and the perfection of the coils of rope.

Holder of the world record was the remarkable *Thermopylae* (Aberdeen-built like all the best tea clippers) which had sailed to Melbourne in 60 days – a record unbeaten to this day. It was the ambition of *Cutty Sark*'s owners and builders that she would outsail *Thermopylae*.

Cutty Sark was launched on 22nd November, 1869 at Dumbarton and drew her name from a Robert Burns poem *Tam O' Shanter* which featured the beautiful witch Nannie (immortalised in the ship's figurehead) seen by Tam as he rode home on his grey mare. She gave chase, but Tam headed for the river, which witches could not cross. Nannie was wearing a short Paisley shirt, known as a 'Cutty Sark'. Doubtless it was the intention of the owner that his new ship should sail like a witch too. The poem tells how Nannie pursued Tam to the river and

attempted to stop him by grabbing the tail of the mare, which came off in her hand. To keep the witch-like spirit of the *Cutty Sark* alive, after a fast passage in her racing days, the crew would make a horse's tail out of old rope and place it in the clenched hand of the figurehead.

Display of ship's figureheads on Cutty Sark. PHOTO COURTESY OF THE CUTTY SARK TRUST.

Cutty Sark *by night.* PHOTO COURTESY OF THE CUTTY SARK TRUST.

Cutty Sark's career in the tea trade was a short one: only seven years after her launch she carried her last cargo of tea. The opening of the Suez canal, and the increased power and reliability of the steam ships, relegated the great tea races to history. Having never beaten her old rival, *Thermopylae*, it seemed that she might go down in history as an 'also-ran'. But once she engaged in the wool trade, which took her from Australia via the testing southern Ocean and round the notorious Cape Horn, she proved what a remarkably strong ship she was. Under her fearless master, Richard Woodget (1885–1895) she made some remarkable passage times beating *Thermopylae* on the first five of the wool passages.

THE RIVER MEDWAY

On the banks of the River Medway, not far from where it meets the M20 motorway, what is described by historians as '*the second most decisive event in British history*' took place. The Battle of the Medway, fought in AD43 between English tribes under King Caractacus, attempted to halt the Roman advance. They failed and, as they say, the rest is history. (The *most* decisive, incidentally, is said to be the Battle of Hastings, 1066). For the Kentish people, the river marks a significant boundary – for those to the west of it are known as *Kentishmen*, and those to the east are the *Men of Kent*.

Flowing for some 70 miles from Sussex through deepest Kent, the Medway meets the Thames at Sheerness. Although it has doubtless been a commercial waterway since man learnt to carry cargo by boats, it is the lower reaches, as far as Rochester and Chatham, where the rich maritime history is anchored.

Sir Francis Drake, at the age of eight, lived on a ship moored off Chatham, his father being the vicar of Upchurch. It is thought that the sight of the Naval fleets at Chatham stirred the young seafaring soul. It was from the Medway that Drake took his early commands, trading from the Thames estuary to the Channel ports and becoming a full skipper while still a teenager.

Two centuries later, Horatio Nelson arrived on the Medway shores to join his uncle's ship, the *Raisonable* as a midshipman, spending a year learning basic seamanship. Nelson took his first command here at the age of 13, which required him to take charge of the tender to *Triumph* on which he had just returned from the West Indies. *HMS Victory*, aboard which he was to seal his reputation, was built at Chatham, commencing in 1759 and launched in 1765. She spent many years in Medway waters before sailing to Trafalgar and immortality.

Henry VIII is largely responsible for the naval significance of the Medway, and in 1550 it was decided that all the ships which had made their base in Portsmouth should be moved to Chatham,

Sir Francis Drake (detail). © THE NATIONAL MARITIME MUSEUM.

Sheerness marine parade. PHOTO © HAROLD WYLD.

which was strategically more useful when facing the enemy of the day: the Dutch. By 1688, when peace was finally made, the French were now proving troublesome. Portsmouth once again became more convenient, and the fleets returned there.

■ The Troubled Medway

The waters where the Medway meet the Thames seem to have had more than their fair share of troubles. 1797 saw the famous Nore Mutiny, off Sheerness – where the first dockyard of 1665 was built under the direction of Sir Samuel Pepys, Charles II's Secretary to the Admiralty.

In April of 1797, a mutiny had already taken place at Spithead (Solent) when 16 ships of the line refused to set sail until demands for better pay and generally better treatment were met. It was an orderly kind of mutiny, and within a few weeks the seamen had won. A month later, the mutiny at the Nore was more demanding, involving issues of shore leave and changes to the Articles of War. The mutineers attempted to blockade the Thames in pursuit of their demands. Having conceded at Spithead, the Admiralty was going to give no ground at Nore. In the end, the mutiny crumbled and the leader was hanged from the yardarm of HMS *Sandwich*.

The Medway was also the scene of one of worst recorded tragedies in naval history. HMS *Bulwark*, a 15,000 ton battleship, was loading coal in Saltpan Reach when a huge explosion ripped her apart, enveloping the entire ship in flame and smoke. 700 men were lost which was more than in any naval incident in peacetime or war.

Even today, approach to the Medway must be made with care, for at her mouth lies the wreck of the potentially lethal USS *Richard Montgomery* which sailed from America to London in 1944 with a cargo of munitions. Having escaped the attention of the Germans throughout the entire passage, she may have felt safe at anchor off Sheerness. However, as the tide fell she ran aground and all attempts to refloat her failed. Realising the danger that her 1400 tons of explosives presented in the middle of one of Britain's most strategic waterways, immediate attempts were made to remove them. It was judged too dangerous. It was calculated that should she explode, every building in Sheerness would be destroyed and a tidal wave was likely to affect nearby shores. The *Richard Montgomery* remains on the bed of the Thames estuary, still laden with her increasingly volatile cargo, countless prayers having been said that no ship will collide with her wreck.

■ The *Medway Queen*

This grand old lady, built for pleasure-cruising on the sheltered waters of the Medway, eventually found glory on the beaches of Dunkirk and is one of the last estuary paddle steamers left in Britain.

The paddle steamer was a hugely popular part of seaside tourism from Victorian times through to WWII, as these ships could land close to beaches and utilise shallow harbours. The *Medway Queen* was designed for those pre-package overseas tour days when a trip to our own seaside was a treat and getting afloat was a bonus. She boasted four public saloons serving teas and refreshments, but the sight of her labouring compound diagonal engines was the major attraction.

Built in 1924 on the Clyde, she provided boating pleasure between Strood and Southend and was considered to be of sufficient importance to attend the Spithead review of 1937. Her war record is hugely distinguished: as part of the evacuation of families from town and cities to the country, she ferried young evacuees across the Thames from urban Kent to rural East Anglia, and no sooner had the war started than she was requisitioned and fitted out as a minesweeper.

PS Medway Queen. PHOTO COURTESY OF THE MEDWAY QUEEN PRESERVATION SOCIETY.

At the time of Dunkirk evacuation, she saved the lives of no less than 7000 soldiers, shuttling between England and France pausing only to refuel. Many of her crew were given awards for bravery and she earned the title 'Heroine of Dunkirk'. However, on her last trip she was badly damaged and assumed lost. On her eventual arrival at Dover, limping home on one paddle, all saluted her.

The rest of her story is a familiar one of gradual decline, dereliction, attempted rescue and failure. But she refused to lie down. Now in the care of her Preservation Society, funds are urgently being raised for her complete restoration. She now lies in Damhead Creek on the Medway near Rochester.

The Golden Dustman

This was the title bestowed on Henry Dodd by no less than Charles Dickens. Dodd (born 1801) had made a fortune in refuse disposal having started his working life as a ploughboy on fields near St Paul's Cathedral. His talent was in spotting the increasingly urgent need for an expanding London to get rid of its refuse. His business eventually employed five barges of which he was extremely fond,. He was also a caring employer of the crews. On overhearing a conversation between two skippers as to whose barge could sail the faster, Dodd organised the first ever barge match, which one of his own barges won.

By bringing a racing element to the barges, he can be credited with doing much to accelerate the development of these craft, making them speedier on the water and easier to handle. His grave, in Slough, is decorated with barges and plough teams – the two great loves of his life.

Sailing barges racing on the Thames. PHOTO COURTESY OF THE SAILING BARGE ASSOCIATION.

PS Kingswear Castle. PHOTO COURTESY OF PADDLE STEAMER KINGSWEAR CASTLE TRUST.

■ The Paddle Steamer *Kingswear Castle*

The *Kingswear Castle* is in fine shape, and sails regularly from Rochester Pier or the Historic Dockyard at Chatham. Unlike her less fortunate relations, this coal-powered paddle steamer has benefited from a full restoration, having been saved from the breaker's yard on at least two occasions. She is a first-class example of an excursion paddle steamer, has huge charm and is much loved. She faces one problem – good quality steam coal is becoming increasingly difficult to obtain because of little demand, and there are fears her engines may have to be converted to oil. In the meantime, enjoy the sound, sight and smell of her engines on one of the many cruises she undertakes on the waters of the Medway.

■ Dolphin Yard Sailing Barge Museum

The traditional industries of north Kent, such as cement, bricks and paper, were well served by the ever versatile Thames barge, and no less than 500 of them were built in Milton Creek, a tidal inlet running from Sittingbourne to the Swale. Of those yards, Burley's, renamed Dolphin Yard, remains as a museum in praise of this work-horse of the Thames estuary. Barges come and go, but it is the ambition here that there should always be at least one visiting barge. All the barge builders' crafts are displayed, from carpentry and ironwork to sail making and you can hear the swish of the adze through timber, smell the hot tar that caulked the seams. Work continues on the SB *Cambria* – the last UK vessel to carry a commercial cargo under sail. Launched in 1906, once complete she will be open to the public – the museum already has a reconstruction of her skipper's cabin.

The brick trade was of huge importance here, especially at the time of the rapid expansion of London, and the main work of the barges was bringing in raw materials and removing finished bricks. Each brickyard would boast of their own fleet of barges which fuelled the pride of the skippers and kept their competitive edge.

■ The Guildhall Museum, Rochester

Described as the gateway to the Medway's history, this museum takes a broader view than just the maritime history of the river. However, the story of the Convict Hulks should not be missed for they were a grim part of the Medway landscape for many years. In Charles Dickens' *Great Expectations,* it was from a prison hulk which '...*lay out a little way from the mud of the shore, like a wicked Noah's Ark.*' that Magwitch escaped.

When it became impossible to deport prisoners to the colonies after the American War of Independence, the only option for confining felons was to employ prison ships, many of which were moored in the Medway with the intention of using prisoners for hard labour ashore, and returning them to prison at night. At one stage, 60 of these hulks were in use, but the most notorious was the *Brunswick* where almost 500 prisoners were kept in an inhumanely small space.

To pass the time, prisoners worked with bone and straw to produce items for sale, and also built more complex ship models, some of which are on display here. No prison hulks survive.

The museum weathervane, and one of the elaborate ship models on display. PHOTOS COURTESY OF THE GUILDHALL MUSEUM, ROCHESTER.

CHATHAM: THE HISTORIC DOCKYARD

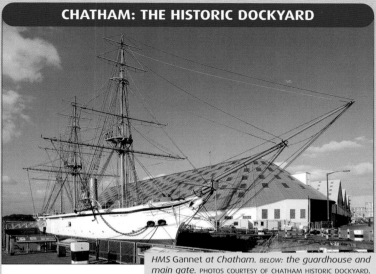

HMS Gannet *at Chatham.* BELOW: *the guardhouse and main gate.* PHOTOS COURTESY OF CHATHAM HISTORIC DOCKYARD.

When the end of the Cold War signalled a major slimming down of Britain's Royal Navy, it became clear that many of the infrastructures were no longer needed. High on the redundancy list was Chatham Dockyard. Its future could easily have gone in several directions: flattening for redevelopment, dereliction, or resurrection. Because the latter was wisely chosen we now have, within a hour's journey from London, a truly World Historic Site and the European Museum of the Year 2003. So extensive and thorough are the collections here, from warships to lifeboats, shipbuilding to sail-making, that few visitors intent on seeing everything manage to consume the feast in less than five hours.

You are effectively visiting a small, self-supporting city built for the construction and maintenance of ships and support systems for the Navy. And when you consider that they have been doing that at Chatham from Elizabeth I through to the Falklands War, you realise the huge importance of this site in our maritime history.

There are 80 acres here, and if you do nothing else but marvel at the architecture then that might be sufficient for some. There are no less than 47 scheduled ancient monuments and Georgian buildings of mouth-watering aspect. The Royal Dockyard Church of 1806 has a gallery supported by cast-iron pillars which was the first use of this ground-breaking material in the dockyard.

To make Chatham Dockyard easier to comprehend, think of it as five museums in one:

■ Wooden walls

This exhibition depicts the way ships were built in the days of sail. The building of masts, the shaping of the hull, the carving of the timbers are all shown here in a recreation of the building of the *Valiant* of 1758, a 74 gun ship-of-the-line. The gallery consists of seven timber-framed masthouses, constructed largely from ships' timbers. Above the gallery is the 'mould loft' where it is thought the

Scene from the 'Wooden Walls' exhibit. BELOW: Large scale model of HMS Victory. PHOTOS COURTESY OF CHATHAM HISTORIC DOCKYARD.

original lines for HMS *Victory* may have been drawn. The dockyard employed wheelwrights, not only in the maintenance of carts and wagons, but in building ships' steering wheels. During the renovation of the workshop, a collection of ships' timbers were discovered and identified as being parts of a ship which was built at Chatham during the 1770s and broken up after the Napoleonic wars. It is said that this is the most impor-

tant maritime archeological discovery in northern Europe since the finding of the *Mary Rose.*

■ Lifeboat!

This is the RNLI's National Collection of Lifeboats. Sixteen full-sized lifeboats are on display from early pulling (oars) and sailing craft to powerful examples of 20th century lifeboat development.

HMS Cavalier. PHOTO COURTESY OF CHATHAM HISTORIC DOCKYARD.

▪ Historic warships

The warship HMS *Cavalier*, which saw active service in WWII is here, and the submarine *Ocelot*, a warrior from the Cold War.

Cavalier was one of hundreds of destroyers built to maintain the shipping lanes around Britain and escort merchant convoys, also keeping lines of supply open. *Cavalier* – not launched till 1944 – started her career in Arctic convoy work, later escorting the *Queen Elizabeth* and the *Queen Mary* ferrying troops across the Atlantic. Her place in the record books is owed to her winning a race with the frigate HMS *Rapid*, held in the Firth of Forth in 1971. Over a 64-mile course she averaged 31.8 knots and was declared '*the fastest ship of the fleet*'. A year later she was returned to Chatham to await the breakers, a fate which she avoided by becoming a museum ship.

Ocelot is known as the first of the 'plastic' submarines. Strictly speaking, her casing was built of glass fibre and alloy and in the early 60s, when she was built at Chatham, this was the first use of plastics in submarine construction. The Cold War was at its most intense when she was built as an Oberon class attack submarine, employing silent electric engines which made her almost undetectable. Her work remains a secret, although she is now on full display here. Nevertheless, it is known that during her career, which ended in 1992,

RIGHT: Ocelot *in dry dock; ABOVE:* exploring the submarine. PHOTOS COURTESY OF CHATHAM HISTORIC DOCKYARD.

Exploring the Ocelot – *up periscope!*
PHOTO COURTESY OF CHATHAM HISTORIC DOCKYARD.

she sailed over 90,000 miles. This is not a visit for the claustrophobic – 68 men served in these cramped quarters.

HMS *Gannet*, undergoing restoration, is a survivor of a time of huge transformation in the navy. At the start of Victoria's reign, many of the methods used for ship-building had changed little since Nelson's time, but by the time of her death, at the beginning of the 20th century, steel and steam had taken over and the most fundamental changes were taking place. *Gannet* had a foot in both camps, being rigged both as a sailing barque but also carrying a two-cylinder horizontal compound engine. The propellor could be lifted to reduce drag when under sail, and the funnel could be collapsed to prevent interference with sails and rigging. The order was often heard 'up funnel and down screw' as she switched from sail to steam. After paying off at Sheerness, having done patrol duties in the Far East, she became a training ship. *Gannet* was then much modified and her engines removed. After this she served as RNVR headquarters before being renamed *Mercury* and then towed to the River Hamble where she lay until 1968 as a training school. Her full restoration is nearing completion.

RIGHT: HMS Gannet *is a sailing barque with an engine; BELOW: her elegant figurehead.*
PHOTOS COURTESY OF CHATHAM HISTORIC DOCKYARD.

■ The Ropery

Although traditional rope-making has been undertaken at Chatham since at least 1618, the rope-making that takes place today is no reconstruction but a commercial operation by Master Ropemakers Ltd. The process of making natural fibre rope hasn't changed in a fundamental way for almost 400 years. There are three stages: raw fibres are spun into yarn, the yarns are twisted to form a strand and usually three strands are laid together to form the rope. The strength of the rope and its ability to hold together and not unravel, comes from the fact that the strands are twisted against the direction of the yarns, and the finished ropes against the strands.

The hunger for rope in the days of sail was almost insatiable, with a ship requiring about 20 miles of it. So it was to Chatham that huge cargoes of Russian hemp were brought to be stored in the Hemp Houses, three of which survive. After the combing of the raw hemp fibres, they were taken to the Double Ropehouse to be spun into yarn. At the time of construction, this remarkable building, was the longest brick building in Europe measuring 1,135 feet.

Preparing hemp bundles for use in 'The Ropery'. PHOTO COURTESY OF CHATHAM HISTORIC DOCKYARD.

■ Museum of the Royal Dockyard

The history of Chatham is as distinguished as any naval history could be. From the small dockyard of Elizabeth I through to the Falklands War of the 20th century, Chatham has played its part, including the Dutch wars and the 18th century disputes with France – building huge numbers of ships in the years of the Napoleonic wars. New methods of wooden construction were developed here in less troubled times and the coming of steam meant huge changes and adaptations. Early experiments in propeller power were carried out here, amidst huge suspicion.

The first major iron ship that the navy built in any of its dockyards, the *Achilles*, was constructed here. Submarines were built throughout the 20th century and the traditional work of a naval dockyard in supporting a massive navy continued. Simply to stand in Chatham Dockyard, you will feel part of a mighty chunk of Britain's maritime history.

Whitstable harbour. PHOTO © HAROLD WYLD.

WHITSTABLE

Whitstable has long been a base for oyster, whelk and cockle fishing, and although the shrimping, the sailing barges and the shipbuilding have gone, the oysters remain, and so do the black, tarred fishermen's huts which line the beach. Although oysters have been farmed in the Thames Estuary from Orford Ness to the North Foreland, they have always done especially well in the shallow waters off Whitstable where the sea and fresh waters mix, providing ideal conditions for the growth of algae on which oysters feed. At one time the industry, along with other fishing activities, was so important here that the row of black beach huts would have been continuous, and the shipyards teaming with folk. **The Whitstable Museum and Gallery** tells the story of the oyster fishery.

The traditional oysters boats have long gone, although the *Floreat* is in the care of the museum and forms part of their expansion plans, and the *Favourite*, an oyster yawl (although with only one mast) built in 1890, is in the care of the Favourite Trust, awaiting restoration, and is displayed on the beach. She is the last remaining craft of her kind, out of 150 which were once beached here.

Thames Gazetteer

Lydia Eva (YH 89)
www.lydiaeva.org.uk
OPEN temporarily closed for
extensive restoration work

**Lowestoft and East Suffolk
Maritime Heritage Museum**
Sparrows Nest Park, Whapload
Road, Lowestoft, Suffolk
NR32 1XG
☎ +44 (0)1502 561963
www.aboutbritain.com/
LowestoftMaritimeMuseum.htm
OPEN Daily, mid-Apr to early Oct.
Group visits (6 or more) by
arrangement out of season

Excelsior LT472
Riverside Road, Lowestoft
NR33 0TU
☎ +4401502 585302
marina.fortunecity.com/
reach/318
Call for sailing programme

**Royal Naval Patrol Service
Museum**
Sparrows Nest Lowestoft
NR32 4PR
OPEN All summer. Private tours
by arrangement

**Southwold Sailors' Reading
Room**
East Cliff and East Street,
Southwold
www.suffolkcc.gov.uk/tourism/
dayout/section_1_index.html
OPEN Usually open daily

**Southwold Alfred Corry
Museum**
Ferry Road, Southwold Harbour,
Suffolk

Southwold Museum
9–11 Victoria St, Southwold,
Suffolk IP18 6HZ (opposite
the Church of Saint Edmund,
King and Martyr)
☎ +44 (0)1502 723374
www.southwoldmuseum.org/
OPEN Daily, Easter to end Oct
(pm only; am also in August)
or by arrangement

Dunwich Museum
St. James' Street, Dunwich,
Suffolk
☎ +44 01728 648796
OPEN Mar: Sat and Sun
14:00–16.30. Apr to Sept: daily
11.30–16.30. Oct: daily
12:00–16:00. Free

Felixstowe Landguard Fort
Viewpoint Road, Felixstowe,
Suffolk
☎ +44 (0)1394 277767.
www.landguard.com/
OPEN Tue, Wed, Sat pm June to
Sept. Also Sun & BH Mon at
Easter

Felixstowe Museum
Ravelin Block, Viewpoint Road,
Felixstowe, Suffolk (adjacent to
the Landguard Fort and harbour
viewing area)
☎ +44 (0)1394 672284
(Secretary), 674355 (museum
answerphone)
OPEN Sun & BH Mon, Easter to
Oct, also Wed Jun to Sept.
13:00–17:30
DON'T MISS Decorated paddle
box from the steamer *Royal
Sovereign* 1893, 19th century
double-frame sextant, 5 foot
model of motorlaunch ML442
built by ex crew member

*Ship model from Southwold
museum.* © SOUTHWOLD MUSEUM.

Sutton Hoo Ship burial site
Woodbridge, Suffolk (2 miles
E of Woodbridge on B1083)
Sutton Hoo, Woodbridge,
Suffolk IP12 3DJ
☎ +44 (0)1394 389700
www.nationaltrust.org.uk/
places/suttonhoo/index.html
OPEN Daily, Jun to Sept
Wed–Sun, in Oct. Weekends in
winter (phone)

**Museum of Knots and
Sailor's Ropework**
501 Wherstead Road, Ipswich,
Suffolk IP2 8LL
☎ +44 (0)1473 690090
knots@footrope.fsnet.co.uk
OPEN By arrangement
DON'T MISS A painted Portuguese
bow fender, Ship's serving
mallet, from New Zealand,
handed down from rigger to
rigger since 1840, a sennit mat
from old rope yard, 1930s

Harwich Maritime Museum
The Low Lighthouse, Harbour
Crescent, Harwich, Essex
☎ +44 (0)1255 503429
www.harwich-society.com/
OPEN Daily, May to Aug. Also
Easter weekend and other
occasions (enquire)

Harwich Lifeboat Museum
Wellington Road, Harwich
☎ +44 (0) 1255 503429

Walton Maritime Museum
Old Life Boat House, East
Terrace, Walton-on-the-Naze,
Essex
☎ +44 (0)1255 678259 (AH)
www.james-stevensno14.
org.uk/ james_stevens.html
OPEN Daily, pm only, Jul to Sept,
and BH weekends, or by
arrangement
DON'T MISS the James Stevens
lifeboat display, cliff fossils, the
Naze Tower story

Brightlingsea Museum
1 Duke Street, Brightlingsea,
Essex CO7 0EA
☎ +44 (0)1206 303286
(evenings)
www.brightlingsea-town.
co.uk/history/museum.htm
OPEN Easter to end Oct,
Mon (pm), Sat and Sun

Nottage Maritime Institute
The Quay, Wivenhoe, nr
Colchester, Essex CO7 9BX
☎ +44 (0)1206 824142
homepages.rya-online.net/ not-
tage-maritime-institute/
OPEN Sundays, 14:00–17:00,
early May to mid Sept, or by
arrangement
DON'T MISS the launching
cradle from local boatyard,
James Cook; the punt gun;
tools used to build wooden
minesweepers in WWII

Mersea Island Museum
High Street, West Mersea,
Colchester, Essex CO5 8QD
☎ +44 (0)1206 385191; AH:
383050; Edu: 382533
www.mersea-island.com/
about/Museum.htm
OPEN Wed–Sun & BH, pm only,
May to Sept. Open am for
Special Events

Maldon District Museum
47 Mill Road, Maldon, Essex
CM9 5HX
☎ +44 (0)1621 842688
OPEN Wed–Sun & BH, pm only,
mid-Apr to Oct. Educational and
group visits by arrangement
DON'T MISS The painting of
Record Reign one of the largest
barges built locally; a full set of
sailmaker's tools presented by
Taylor (once sailmakers of
Maldon)

**Thames Sailing Barge
Heritage Centre** (aboard *SB
Glenway*)
Cook's Barge Yard, Maldon
☎ +44 (0)1621 857567
www.cooksbargeyard.co.uk/
OPEN Easter Fri to end Sept,
Wed, Sun 11:00–17:00
Winter weekends (Oct– Dec),
Sun 12:00–16:00

Brightlingsea Smack Dock
The Smack Dock, Waterside,
Brightlingsea, Essex CO7 0AX.
For information contact
Hon. Secretary, Colne Smack
Preservation Society, c/o James

Lawrence, The Sail Loft, 22-28
Tower Street, Brightlingsea,
Essex CO7 0AL
☎ +44 (0)1206 302863

**Burnham-on-Crouch and
District Museum**
The Quay/Coronation Road,
Burnham-on-Crouch, Essex
CM0 8AS
☎ +44 (0)1621 783444, 783901
www.burnham.org.uk/museum.
html
OPEN Mar to Nov: Wed, Sat, Sun
& BH. June and school holidays:
daily, pm

The Motor Boat Museum
Wat Tyler Country Park, Pitsea
Hall Lane, Pitsea, near Basildon,
Essex SS16 4UH
☎ +44 (0)1268 550077
www.steamboat.org.uk/
historic.htm
OPEN Thur–Mon (daily during
school holidays) 10:00–16:30
DON'T MISS The Carstairs
Collection of racing trophies;
the Soriano outboard motor;
steam boat *Cygnet*, 1873

PS Tattershall Castle
King's Reach, Victoria
Embankment, London
(between Charing Cross &
Westminster Piers)
☎ +44 (0)20 7839 6548
myweb.tiscali.co.uk/tramways/
TattershallCastle.htm

Museum in Docklands
No. 1 Warehouse, West India
Quay, Hertsmere Road, London
E14 4AL
☎ +44 (0)20 7001 9800
www.museumindocklands.org.uk
OPEN Daily 10:00–17:00
(12:00 –17:00 Sun)
DON'T MISS Sailortown –
reconstruction of the streets
of Wapping 1830s; a pirate's
gibbet; items from the *Princess
Alice* disaster

Sailing barges on the Thames.
© SAILING BARGE ASSOCIATION.

Display on HMS Belfast.
© HMS BELFAST.

HMS Belfast
Morgans Lane, Tooley Street,
London SE1 2JH
☎ +44 (0)20 7940 6300, 7940 6328
www.hmsbelfast.org.uk
OPEN Daily
DON'T MISS exploring the 6 inch gun turrets and magazine rooms; the Upper Bridge and its views of London; number 2 deck and visit the surgery, dentist, bakery and galley

Cutty Sark Clipper Ship
King William Walk, Greenwich,
London SE10
☎ +44 (0)20 8858 3445
www.cuttysark.org.uk
OPEN Daily, 10:00-17:00
DON'T MISS Long John Silver Collection of merchant figureheads

National Maritime Museum
(including the Queen's House and Royal Observatory)
Romney Road, Greenwich,
London SE10 9NF
☎ +44 (0)20 8858 4422
www.nmm.ac.uk
OPEN Daily except Christmas,
10:00–17:00 (10:00–18:00 Jul to Sept)

The Royal Naval College, Greenwich
No public access to the larger part (now a university) but the Painted Hall and Chapel are generally open to visitors daily between 10:00 and 17:00. The grounds of the Old Royal Naval College are open to the public from 8:00 until 18:00.
The College will be closed to the public on 24, 25 & 26 Dec

PS Medway Queen
Damhead Creek, River Medway, Hoo Peninsula near Rochester, Kent (contact MQPS for detailed route instructions)
☎ +44 (0)1634 252848
www.medwayqueen.org.uk

PS Kingswear Castle
Historic Dockyard, Chatham
ME4 4TQ
+44 (0)1634 827648
www.pskc.freeserve.co.uk

Rochester Guildhall Museum
High Street, Rochester, Kent
ME1 1PY
☎ +44 (0)1634 848717
www.medway.gov.uk
OPEN Daily
DON'T MISS the prison hulks experience; Medway gallery of ships models, 17th century Guildhall chamber

Dolphin Yard Sailing Barge Museum
Crown Quay Lane,
Sittingbourne, Kent ME10 3SN
☎ +44 (0)1795 424132
www.thamesbarge.org.uk/
barges/charter/dolphinyard.html
OPEN Sun & BH, Easter to Oct 31
DON'T MISS the collection of sailing barge models; captain's cabin of SB *Cambria*; barges under restoration

HMS Cavalier (D73)
Chatham Historic Dockyard,
Dock Road, Chatham, Kent
ME4 4TE
☎ +44 (0)1634 823800
www.hmscavalier.org.uk
OPEN see entry for Chatham Historic Dockyard

Chatham Historic Dockyard
Dock Road, Chatham, Kent.
☎ +44 (0)1634 823800,
823807
www.chdt.org.uk
OPEN Daily, Apr to Oct. Closed 1 Dec to 15 Feb. See website for details
DON'T MISS historic warships; Wooden walls exhibition of ship construction; and the Ropery

Whitstable Museum and Gallery
5a Oxford Street, Whitstable,
Kent CT5 1DB
☎ +44 (0)1227 276998
www.whitstable-museum.co.uk/
index.html
OPEN Mon–Sat 10:00–16:00
(+ Sun pm July & Aug). Not Good Friday

BA: By arrangement
BH: Bank holiday
GV: Group visits

DOVER, WIGHT

From North Foreland to Anvil Point

Goodwin Sands ■ Ramsgate ■ Cinque Ports ■ Deal
Dover ■ Dungeness ■ Hastings ■ Eastbourne
Beachy Head ■ Newhaven ■ Brighton ■ Shoreham-by-Sea
■ Littlehampton ■ Selsey Bill ■ Chichester ■ The Solent
Spithead ■ Portsmouth ■ Gosport ■ Southampton
Isle of Wight ■ Poole

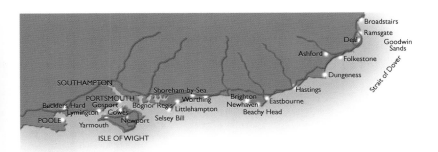

Foreness Point Coastguard station. PHOTO © HAROLD WYLD.

NORTH FORELAND

North Foreland is one of the great maritime turning points of the British Isles. It marks the end of the Thames estuary and opens up the waters of the English channel with their promise of a passage to distant shores. It marks the division between the sheltered, shoal waters of the North Sea and the deeper seas that turn into oceans. We are also very close to mainland Europe here, and the coastline speaks of battles ancient and modern between the ever-changing foes that the passing centuries have thrown at us. Along this stretch of coast, the Romans landed, the Normans invaded and the Germans were kept at a distance. From the naval dockyards at Portsmouth, the Cold War was waged, and from here ships were sent to fight in the Falklands and the Gulf.

Yet it is also one of the most recreational coastlines in Britain, with resorts which saw splendour in Victorian days. At Southampton, the greatest liners the world has ever seen set sail for the Americas, Australia and Africa. And across the Solent, at Cowes on the Isle of Wight, the sport of yacht racing has been elevated to new competitive and social heights. It is a length of coastline which presents an ever-changing maritime view.

Yachts on the Solent. PHOTO © DAVID PACKMAN.

Picnics were popular on the Goodwin Sands in the early 1900s.
PHOTO COURTESY OF DOVER MUSEUM.

THE GOODWIN SANDS

The Goodwin Sands sound harmless. It could be a name for a sunny strand on which long, hot summer days might be spent. In fact, although they are called 'sands', they are as hard as rock with the added peril that they are continually on the move – all 12 miles of them. They are named after Earl Godwin, father of King Harold, who is said to have farmed an island of 4,000 acres protected by a seawall which collapsed in 1100 turning the island into a sandbank.

Whatever the truth, this extensive, shifting sandbank consists of an ever-changing maze of shallows, gulleys, and tidal islands. They could not be in a worse place for they sit no more than a few miles offshore, stretching from just south of the North Foreland almost to Dover. This is

The Goodwin Sands disaster of 1954

On 26 November 1954, the greatest disaster in the history of the lightship service befell the South Goodwin lightship. The marking of the Goodwin Sands was done by three lightships. These floating lighthouses were moored on station and showed a brighter light than a conventional navigation buoy. They were used because the sands provided no foundation for a proper lighthouse. Lightships have no engines and rely on anchors for their security. A strong southerly gale, up to force 11, was blowing, causing huge seas in the Dover Strait. The South Goodwin maintained her station until the tide started to run to the north which brought enormous strain on her chain and anchors. Despite an estimated breaking strain of 90 tons, the mooring broke and the lightship was adrift. It was not long before she was driven onto the sands, capsizing before her crew of seven were able to escape. The only survivor was a student monitoring bird numbers. The bodies of the others were never recovered and the lightship was soon swallowed by the sands that she was intended to guard.

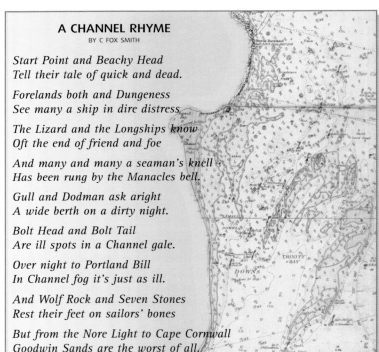

A CHANNEL RHYME
BY C FOX SMITH

Start Point and Beachy Head
Tell their tale of quick and dead.

Forelands both and Dungeness
See many a ship in dire distress.

The Lizard and the Longships know
Oft the end of friend and foe

And many and many a seaman's knell
Has been rung by the Manacles bell.

Gull and Dodman ask aright
A wide berth on a dirty night.

Bolt Head and Bolt Tail
Are ill spots in a Channel gale.

Over night to Portland Bill
In Channel fog it's just as ill.

And Wolf Rock and Seven Stones
Rest their feet on sailors' bones

But from the Nore Light to Cape Cornwall
Goodwin Sands are the worst of all.

where the North Sea narrows into the Dover Strait and the huge commercial traffic bound from the Atlantic to the European ports is squeezed together like rush hour traffic hitting a contra-flow. Using traditional methods of navigation, there were few shore marks hereabouts with which a mariner might fix his position, and the confusing meeting of the North Sea and Channel tides gives added difficulties. Consequently, the Goodwin Sands lie there, waiting to entrap those who have made the slightest mistake.

■ The last manned lighthouse in England
The North Foreland lighthouse is one of the many lights hereabouts whose function is to guide ships clear of the Goodwins (as well as marking its own headland, of course) and a light has burnt here since 1499 – then an iron basket in which wood was burnt. The present light dates from 1866,

North Foreland lighthouse. PHOTO © HAROLD WYLD.

but what sets it apart from the rest is that this was the last manned lighthouse in England to be automated. A closing ceremony took place on the 26 November 1998, in the presence of the Duke of Edinburgh, Master of Trinity House, when the last six keepers left the lighthouse, bringing to an end a long tradition of keeping the lights burning.

The **North Foreland lighthouse**, in the care of East Kent Maritime Trust, is open to the public.

RAMSGATE

The only 'Royal' harbour in England, thanks to the enthusiastic welcome given to George IV in 1821 who returned the compliment by conferring this unique title. With its proximity to the lethal Goodwin Sands, it was suggested in 1750 that Ramsgate, then a small fishing harbour, be upgraded to '*harbour of refuge status*' employing the legendary engineer John Smeaton to advise on the construction.

The **Ramsgate Maritime Museum** is housed in the 19th century clock tower by the Royal Harbour, and while telling tales of Thanet sea-faring life, inevitably the dramas played out on the Goodwin Sands feature large. In particular, the Great Storm of 1703 which was of hurricane proportions

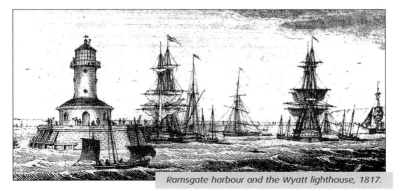

Ramsgate harbour and the Wyatt lighthouse, 1817.

Ramsgate harbour. PHOTO © HAROLD WYLD.

and more violent than any storm recorded, caused devastation throughout the English Channel and North Sea. It is claimed that as many as 10,000 lost their lives in the course of the storm, including the 3rd Rate Man of War *Stirling Castle* which was driven aground. Recovered artefacts are on display in the museum. There is also a reminder that Ramsgate once claimed its own time zone, defined by the Ramsgate Meridian Line, distinct from the one at Greenwich, as part of the protracted search for a method of measuring time, and thereby longitude, while at sea.

■ Dunkirk little ships at Ramsgate

Ramsgate has a strong association with the WWII Dunkirk evacuations, and the 1912 Admiralty Steam Launch, *Sundowner*, played her part. She was converted to a pleasure craft for Commander Charles Lightoller (senior surviving officer of the *Titanic*) and answered the call which led to that famous fleet of small ships rescuing an army of 338,000 men, stranded on the far side of the Dover Strait. The *New Britannic* also saw service at Dunkirk having been built in 1930 as a pleasure launch.

Also on display in Smeaton's restored dry dock (1791) are three interesting vessels: *Strandby*, a 1941 Danish carvel-built fishing trawler once common in Ramsgate; *Khaki*, a Deal beach boat built for inshore fishing in 1929 and the steam tug *Cervia* (1946).

THE CINQUE PORTS —————————

Five harbour towns make up the Cinque Ports – Hastings, Romney, Hythe, Dover and Sandwich. Arguably there is a sixth, Brightlingsea in Essex, although it is admitted that technically this is a 'branch' of Sandwich and not a Cinque Port in its own right.

They were formed in 1050 by Edward the Confessor who ordered that it should be the responsibility of these five towns to provide important defences along the stretch of coastline closest to Europe. In return for this, the towns were granted an unprecedented degree of self-government.

Ignoring their failure to prevent the Norman invasion and subsequent Battle of Hastings in 1066 (they were otherwise engaged defending England against Norwegian attack), the Cinque Ports were responsible for what is regarded as the first occasion on which a fleet of ships fought as a single, orchestrated unit making the battle of 1216 the first-ever proper naval battle to be fought off these shores.

Hubert de Burgh, Regent of England, saw a French fleet gathering off Sandwich which was 3 times the size of the 16 ships he had at his disposal. However, working as a unit under a single command (in contrast to the every-man-for-himself style of fighting which had been the norm until then), de Burgh moved his smaller fleet to windward, perplexing the French who had never seen this tactic. Assuming a mistake, the French sensed victory and jeered at de Burgh's fleet. This was the cue for the English to throw quicklime into the air which blew down-wind, blinding the French. The English archers swiftly got to work and victory was soon theirs.

There was no doubt about it – a new style of warfare had been invented and the post of Lord Warden of the Cinque Ports (a post held more recently by Sir Winston Churchill and the Queen Mother) was given to Hubert de Burgh

TOP: *The Hastings common seal, late 13th century.*
RIGHT: *The coat of arms of the Cinque Ports.*
PHOTOS COURTESY OF DOVER MUSEUM.

with a brief to strengthen the fleets of the Cinque Ports. This was to be their heyday, although not long-lasting. Their methods were soon copied, then their harbours (notably Sandwich) started to silt, and by 1588 they made their last modest contribution of a dozen ships to fight the Armada.

DEAL AND THE DOWNS

Deal was the landing place of Julius Caesar on 25 August, 55BC, his galleys having crossed from Europe. He chose well, for Deal sits opposite a stretch of water known as 'the Downs' which has provided a safe and secure anchorage for ships ever since.

The Downs have the advantage of sufficient depth of water to give access to all but the biggest ships, and are effectively protected on three sides by the arm on Sandwich Bay to the north, the cliffs of Dover to the southwest, and the Goodwin Sands to the east. There are few anchorages where a sailing ship may feel safe in any shift of wind, but this is one of them.

Because of its importance, Henry VIII built a castle at Deal for its protection in the 1530s, when the Catholic powers in Europe were a threat to him.

Its importance as an anchorage lasted into the twentieth century. To assist ships in their navigation, Deal's Time Ball Tower was constructed in 1855, resembling the Time Ball at Greenwich. At precisely 12.55 each day, the ball was raised to the top of its 14 foot mast, and released at precisely 1pm by an electric impulse sent directly from Greenwich. With this information, ships could check chronometers before proceeding down Channel.

■ The Deal luggers

Like many small coastal towns, Deal lived off a little fishing and smuggling, but the Downs anchorage provided much employment in provisioning and servicing waiting ships. The Deal boatmen were called 'hovellers' and would carry

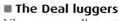
Time Ball Tower, Deal. PHOTO COURTESY OF DOVER DISTRICT COUNCIL.

The Martello Towers

These Napoleonic defences are to be found at frequent intervals all the way from Aldeburgh in Suffolk (the most northerly) to Seaford in Sussex. In the early 19th century, when a cross-channel invasion looked increasingly likely, this string of strong but simply-built fortresses was hastily erected. Of the original 103 Martellos (named after a fort of similar design at Mortella in Corsica which had withstood a heavy bombardment) 45 still stand, all of similar squat design. Although each was equipped with a roof-mounted cannon and living space for 24 men, no shot was ever fired in anger from them.

The Martello Tower at Sandgate, now converted to an unusual home. PHOTO © HAROLD WYLD.

food, water and chandlery to the anchorage. They provided a salvage service, recovering spars and anchors lost overboard; also plundering ships lost on the Goodwin Sands for their cargoes. Before the introduction of lifeboats, they also provided a rescue service.

The Deal luggers are remembered, in model form, in the **Deal Maritime and Local History Museum**. Also another of the Deal boats; the four/five-oared Deal galley *Saxon King*, was built for speed. In fact, the speed of the galleys was such that by law they were prohibited from using more than four oars as they were proving useful to the smugglers who could easily flee from the Excise men.

DOVER

> *'The sea was confined by mountains so close to it that a dart could be thrown from their summit on to the shore'* – Julius Caesar describing the approach to Dover.

Dover is Britain's front door. Certainly almost every major figure in European history has come knocking on it from Caesar, through William the Conquerer, Philip of Spain, Napoleon and Hitler, plus a few. Hence the need for its castle which is one of the strongest in the country.

Dover castle. PHOTO COURTESY OF WHITE CLIFFS COUNTRY.

■ The White Cliffs of Dover

You are looking at what was once the bottom of a deep tropical ocean – rock which was formed 200 million years ago. As recently as 26,000 years ago, Kent was joined to France, but the sea cut through the range of hills we now call the North Downs to create an initially narrow Dover Strait. The soft chalk was quickly (in geological terms) eroded to give an ever-widening waterway between Britain and Europe. They have come to be associated with patriotism and a longing for home, bolstered in no small way by Vera Lynn's wartime song.

■ The Bronze Age Dover Boat

Radiocarbon dating suggests that the Dover Boat (in the **Dover Museum**) is 3,550 years old – we are talking about something from the same era as Stonehenge. Only 10 metres of it have been recovered, and it is thought that this is only half of the original which was of sufficient size to make Channel crossings, suggesting early international trade.

It was built from six oak timbers, lashed with yew, and moss appears to have been used to 'caulk' or seal the leaks between the planking. It employed paddle power. The Bronze Age Dover Boat is of international maritime significance and experts agree that it may yet have many secrets to yield.

■ Cross-Channel ferries

Numbers of foot passengers began crossing the Channel in the early 19th century with the introduction of paddle steamers. These proved fast and

The bronze age boat on display in Dover Museum. PHOTO COURTESY OF DOVER MUSEUM.

effective passage, if uncomfortable in the choppy waters for which the Straits were famous. The main problem was one of landing, as neither Dover, Calais nor Boulogne harbours were deep enough for ships to be able to enter at every state of tide. Ships might anchor and the passengers would then be at the mercy of a rowing boat operator who would ferry them ashore, for a price. It was not until the Admiralty Pier at Dover was built in 1850 that passengers could step ashore with ease.

The carrying of cars across the Straits has been going on for scarcely a century, commencing in 1908. The first car ferry was the inspiration of Captain Townsend (of Townsend Thoresen fame) who bought a minesweeper and converted it to carry cars which were loaded by crane. By 1939, he was carrying 31,000 cars a year. The convenient 'drive on' terminals did not appear till 1953.

Drive-on, drive-off was a trick that the railways had perfected in 1936 when the Southern Railway operated a service between Dover and Dunkerque with SNCF, the French operator. The ship was moored in a special dock in which the level of water could be adjusted to align the incoming rails with those laid on the ship's deck.

Dunkirk memorial, Dover. PHOTO COURTESY OF WHITE CLIFFS COUNTRY.

Dover coastguard

High on the top of the white cliffs of Dover, overlooking the world's busiest stretch of seaway, sit the Dover coastguard. They observe and plot with sophisticated radar, sometimes pursuing ships which flout the rules of navigation. Their role here, and around the coast of Britain, is well understood. But in the history of the coastguard service, their terms of employment has not always been so clearly defined.

Smuggling, and the prevention of it, was the original focus of the coastguard who were formed as the Preventative Water Guard at a time (late 1700s) when it was estimated that half the tea drunk in England had been smuggled ashore. Their duties expanded to taking responsibility for shipwrecks in the early 1800s and they were trained in lifesaving.

Their remit grew until by 1920 the coastguard could be said to be working and aiding the Admiralty, the Hydrographer, the Customs and Excise, Lloyds, the Air Ministry, the RNLI and the Fishery Department. Now, from atop the White Cliffs, Dover coastguard observed 46,000 ships in 2000, of which 36,000 were carrying dangerous cargo.

Coastguard cottages. PHOTO COURTESY OF WHITE CLIFFS COUNTRY.

The train then simply steamed aboard the ship and was re-railed in a similar way at the destination. The most famous train to travel this way was the luxury *Golden Arrow* between London and Paris.

■ Cross-Channel swimmers

Captain Matthew Webb dived off the end of Admiralty Pier in Dover on 24 August, 1875 and swam the English Channel for the first time taking 21 hours 45 minutes from Dover to France. It wasn't the first attempt: this honour goes to J B Johnson in 1872, but he gave up after an hour.

Other than providing sport for the determined and hardy, Channel swimming helped in the development of Clark S Merriman's India-rubber survival suit, tested by a Captain Boyton in the same year that Webb made his more sparsely-clothed crossing. A report of the time says:

'On 10 April 1875 he stepped into the water at Dover with only a double-bladed paddle and headed out to sea, followed by reporters in the steam tug 'Rambler'. For the crossing a two foot square canvas was fitted as a sail into the left boot of the suit. On the way Boyton consumed a mixture of beaten eggs, a couple of cherry brandies and a cigar (but no solids). However, the crossing was eventually abandoned when the weather worsened and the pilot of the French boat became concerned for Boyton's safety, threatening to surrender all charge of his boat at darkness if Boyton failed to come aboard'.

After the success of Webb, Channel swimming became almost a national sport, and newspapers organised relay races. The slowest crossing of the Channel was by an American, Henry Sullivan, taking 26 hours 50 minutes in 1923.

DUNGENESS

It has been said that if 'Kent is the Garden of England, then Dungeness is the back gate!' Built entirely of sand and shingle, and very steep-to at its tip (it is said a yacht may pass close enough for the skipper to be able to touch the shore with his boathook – but don't be tempted to try this), it is a world apart from the rest of Kent, with a bohemian feel amongst those who live there and sufficiently remote from any centre of population for it to be made the site of a nuclear power station. For this reason, there are two lighthouses here – the new one was built when it was seen that the power station would mask the older one.

The marking of this headland has always been a crucial matter, for it is low-lying and hardly discernable from sea till a ship is almost upon it in precisely the place where the Channel narrows into the Dover Strait. It was said, as far back as 1615, that '1,000 people perish here every year from want of a light'. But the sands that form the promontory are in constant flux and lighthouse construction proved troublesome when the first light was built in the same year. A second, coal-burning tower replaced it which served till 1792. Later in the 1850s, early experiments in electric light were carried out, after Michael Faraday (no less) had achieved some success at the South Foreland. Further shifting of the land required a new light (still standing) in 1904. Its modern neighbour was erected in 1961.

Dungeness lighthouse. PHOTO © HAROLD WYLD.

HASTINGS

The Battle of Hastings, 1066, took place six miles inland, so was hardly a maritime affair. However, at the entrance to the pier stands the Conqueror's Stone where, it is said, William paused for a bite to eat before pressing on to one of the most famous battles in English history.

■ The Hastings Stade

But the longest running battle at Hastings has been the attempt, since the 1500s to build a proper harbour; all attempts having been defeated by the sea. Instead, the fishermen hauled their boats to safety above the high water mark on the shingle beach known as the 'Stade'. A harbour wall was eventually built causing an unexpected but welcome enlargement of the beach. In the 1850s, 85 boats were registered here.

Hastings fishing beach and East Hill Lift.
ABOVE: Hastings castle.
PHOTOS COURTESY OF HASTINGS BOROUGH COUNCIL.

On the Stade you will still find Europe's biggest fleet of beach-launched boats – mostly engaged in net fishing for sole, plaice and cod. There are some trawlers, but they are in the minority. Although this may seem an antiquated method of fishing nowadays, it is precisely the kind of environmentally sensitive fishing method that we need if the seas are not to be emptied of fish. Because the boats have to be hauled up after every trip, their size and fishing gear is limited, and consequently their catch. If you see what appears to be a pile of black, garden sheds sitting on top of each other, these are merely the 'net shops' built for the storage and mending of fishing nets. With beach space at a premium, the fishermen have built upwards to provide the space they need. They have been building net shops like this since the days of Elizabeth I.

Fish caught here are mostly sold in the local fish market (usually late morning) built in 1993, but Hastings has two museums – the **Shipwreck Heritage Centre**, and the **Fishermen's Museum** which together give as broad a view of the maritime traditions to be found anywhere along this stretch of coast.

■ Hastings Fishermen's Museum

Housed in a church, the star of the show in this museum is the 29 foot *Enterprise* – a Hastings sailing lugger which was built on the beach in 1912 and is typical of the boats which worked here in the days of sail. The first Hastings boat to be built with an engine, the *Edward and Mary* (1919) sits outside. The stuffed albatross may be an import.

■ Hastings Shipwreck Museum

If ever a coastline invited a shipwreck, it is this one. There are no safe harbours in the event of a storm, and the

Fishing boat and 'net shops'. PHOTO COURTESY OF HASTINGS BOROUGH COUNCIL.

shoreline is often low and featureless, particularly in Rye Bay, making position fixing uncertain. The **Shipwreck Heritage Centre** offers exhibits from a Roman ship to a Victorian river barge plus many relics from the wreck of the *Amsterdam*, a Dutch East Indiaman which was blown ashore in 1748 after rudder failure. The 28 chests of silver she carried were valued at £200,000 in the currency of the day.

EASTBOURNE

Were it not for the assassination of the actor, William Terris in 1897 – killed outside London's Adelphi Theatre – the memorial boathouse in Eastbourne might never have been built. In the event, money raised after an appeal in the *Daily Telegraph* led to its construction and it was opened in 1898 by the Duchess of Devonshire. The first occupant was a 35 foot self-righting boat which carried the not uncommon name *James Stevens* (see Walton-on-the-Naze) The Eastbourne lifeboat was *James Stevens No 6* and was one of a series built from a legacy of £50,000 he gave to the RNLI. The William Terriss Lifeboat House was declared the country's first permanent Lifeboat Museum in 1937.

Beachy Head. PHOTO COURTESY OF *ALL ABOUT SUSSEX.*

BEACHY HEAD

Beachy Head is the most impressive of the Channel headlands at 530 feet, and the highest chalk sea cliff in Britain.

It is a common source of specula- tion as to why the lighthouse should be built at the foot of it, and not on the top from where its light would carry further. It is true that the Belle Toute light (made famous both through tele- vision and for the expensive efforts taken to move it backwards 15 metres from the crumbling cliff edge a few years ago) is on top of the cliff. But this was replaced in 1904 by a stat- uesque example of the lighthouse builder's art at sea level, complete with rings of red and white paint. It was sited on a shelf of rock extending well away from the shore which uncovers at low water making for a strenuous walk (not for public access). At sea level, the light is less prone to being shrouded in the low cloud and mist that often hangs over Beachy Head – which was the main drawback with the Belle Tout light.

The light itself was provided by a paraffin vapour burner, and 'ampli- fied' by the revolving optics to create a beam, which appeared to a distant ship as a flash of light. During WWII, the lighthouses were shut off to prevent their use by the enemy, but were switched on again on the orders of the Admiralty to aid returning ships and aircraft. However,

The Dieppe Raid of 1942

Partially launched from Newhaven, there was a disastrous attempt in August 1942 to make a successful raid on German-occupied France. 5,000 Canadians joined with 1,000 British troops in a raid which, with hindsight, was premature. The RAF and RCAF conducted its most intense air battle to date in a single day, losing 106 aircraft to the Germans' 48 making it the highest daily loss in any air battle of the entire war. On land, the fighting lasted for nine hours with no real advance by the allies. One thousand died and two thousand were taken prisoner. If the loss served any purpose, it was to provide harsh lessons which led to the successful D-Day landings in 1944. The story of the Dieppe Raid, and the history of the Newhaven ferry service, is told at the **Newhaven Local and Maritime Museum**.

the paraffin light took 15 minutes to come to full brilliance, which was not fast enough. The problem was solved by making a small wooden platform next to the burner, on which was placed the keepers' two-wick kitchen lamp. Once it was placed at the focal point of the optics, it provided the light that the air crews needed for the five minutes it took for the aircraft to fly over. Many aircrews will have owed their safe homecomings to the lighthouse keepers' kitchen lamp.

NEWHAVEN

Although it is not the most popular route for making a Channel crossing, the ferry service from Newhaven was an enormous success when the railway first arrived here in 1847 and a Marine Passenger Terminal was built. It meant that the distance from London to Paris, via Newhaven, was 90 miles less than travelling through Dover. The early ferries did not benefit from the shelter of the Chain Pier, built in the 1820s, and so embarkation may have been a troublesome business by contrast with the destination, Dieppe, which had a fine, sheltered harbour.

Newhaven ferry terminal. PHOTO COURTESY OF ALL ABOUT SUSSEX.

Brighton Beach and pier. PHOTO © FREEFOTO.COM.

BRIGHTON

If Brighton has any single natural asset, it is of course its beach. And in the days when a beach was a place of work and not leisure, Brighton thrived as a fishing community, launching its craft from the sand and shingle in the manner common on this stretch of coast. But when the Prince Regent (later George IV) visited in 1783, this became the fashionable place to retreat to from the squalors of London, and from then on

the beach fishermen felt the squeeze as play took precedence over work. Now, with its marina which is the largest man-made yacht harbour in Europe, the leisure industry has taken over the sea as well, and the fishing conducted from Brighton is now minimal. The writing has literally been on the wall since the 1860s when the council built the vast sea wall, dedicating only three of the arches to the fishermen, and the rest to the growing leisure business.

However, one arch remains dedicated to the memory of the men who earned a hard living off this beach, and the **Brighton Fishing Museum** holds a 27 foot beach boat of the type

The Arches, Brighton. PHOTO © FREEFOTO.COM.

that was common here, and gives a nod in the direction of the pleasure boating industry which now rules.

'We're the men of Sussex, Sussex by the Sea,
We plough and sow and reap and mow,
And useful men are we;
And when you go to Sussex, whoever you may be,
You may tell them all that we stand or fall for Sussex by the Sea!
Oh Sussex, Sussex by the Sea! Good old Sussex by the Sea!
You may tell them all that we stand or fall, for Sussex by the Sea.'

SHOREHAM-BY-SEA

There are few museums where the building is older than its contents, but the **Marlipins Museum**, run by the Sussex Archeological Society, is housed in an early 12th century building which is said to be one of the oldest secular buildings in Europe still in use. Origins of its distinctive chequer board stone façade are from both Sussex and France. Part of this museum tells of seafaring life hereabouts. It also reminds us that Shoreham was the home (18 Church Street) of Captain Henry Roberts who circumnavigated the world twice with Captain James Cook and was in command of the boat which took Cook ashore to meet his death.

The meeting point of the River Adur and the sea make this one of the few natural harbours on this stretch of coast and in the 1300s there was

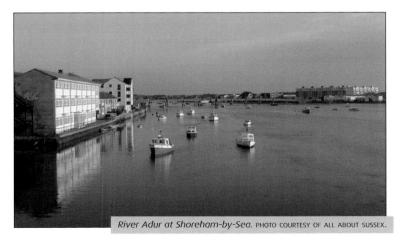

River Adur at Shoreham-by-Sea. PHOTO COURTESY OF ALL ABOUT SUSSEX.

much trade in wool and salt, alongside a shipbuilding industry which took timber from the then forested South Downs. In 1766, pressure from local business interests forced the building of a proper harbour mouth and in the early 1800s, when Brighton was prospering as a resort, the coal trade here was substantial and brought much prosperity – but not for long. Shoreham had no skills in building iron ships, which were the new requirement, and after the 800 ton *Osman Pasha*, a square-rigger, was launched in 1878, the ship building more or less folded, although wooden torpedo boats were built here during WWII.

Incidentally, much has been said of the quality of the light to be found on Shoreham beach and in the 1920s it became a home to the silent film industry, using locals as extras.

LITTLEHAMPTON

Many of the great castles and churches of Sussex were built with stone imported from France through Littlehampton, which stands at the mouth of the River Arun. It has always considered itself a smart little town, and at the height of the seaside holiday era, always attracted a 'better class of visitor'. In the 1930s, there were a quarter of a million visitors a year.

Apart from oyster fishing in the specially built Oyster Pond near the river, shipping and shipbuilding have been the maritime business here and one in five men of the town were employed in one or the other in the mid 19th century. The **Littlehampton Museum** boasts 200 ship models, tells the story of the 'Great Wanderer' or Trisantona (as the River Arun was once called) and warns of a depiction of the world's scariest landlady.

Selsey. PHOTO COURTESY OF PETER WAKELY/ENGLISH NATURE.

SELSEY BILL

> *'Saint Wilfred sailed to Sussex, an' he come to Selsey Bill,*
> *An' there he built a liddle church upon a liddle hill:*
> *He taught the starving pagans how to net fish from the sea,*
> *An' then he them converted all to Christianitee.*
> From 'Song of the Sussex Men' by Arthur Beckett.

The poem tells of the arrival of Wilfred in Sussex, and how he taught the men to fish. The first church in Sussex was built in his honour, now alas beneath the waves and known as 'the cathedral under the sea'.

There are few towns which can claim to have the sea on three sides, but Selsey is one of them. But given that it is a major headland it may come as a surprise to find that it carries no lighthouse. This is because the hazards hereabouts are not Selsey Bill itself but the myriads of shoals, in particular the Owers which has caught many a careless craft which has left the Solent bound eastwards. Even so, the Mixon, Pullar Bank, Grounds and the Head Rock can be equally lethal to any ship. Marked now with a high intensity light buoy, the Owers has long been the station for a lightship used as the navigation mark for rounding Selsey Bill.

The lifeboat, the *Friend*, did not come to Selsey till 1861 (remembered in the **Selsey Lifeboat Museum**) at which time there was not a single lifeboat between Worthing in Sussex and Lyme Regis in Devon.

Despite its remoteness, Selsey always commanded an important strategic position; at one time it had three coastguard stations and a Lloyds signal station through which ships could send messages of their intended arrivals and departures. The Spanish Armada passed close to here in 1588, and the famous Mulberry Harbours – Churchill's inventive moveable harbours – were stored here in readiness for the D-Day invasion. The most remarkable survivor of wartime at Selsey is the WWI listening post which employed a concrete dish, like a satellite dish, to listen for the early approach of Zepplins.

CHICHESTER HARBOUR

Yachts moored in Chichester harbour.
PHOTO COURTESY OF PETER WAKELY/ENGLISH NATURE.

An inland sea, almost, Chichester Harbour has only a narrow entrance between sand and shingle spits, and is of great environmental significance. The sands here shift with the action of the wind and the sea, nevertheless the rubbery-leaved sea holly thrives, and the sea bindweed. To the lee of the dunes is a saltmarsh providing winter habitat for redshank and plover. The rare glasswort plant is found here, the ashes of which were once part of the glassmaking process.

The business of Chichester harbour has always been maritime. These days it is an enormous yachting centre, but in the 13th century it was a key player in the wool export trade; by the 18th century, corn was going out while coal was coming in, and by the 19th century it was on the wane as a working harbour, except for fishing.

The **Emsworth Museum** tells the story of the town, once the major port within Chichester harbour. It contains a walking stick made from a sailor's love letters. Take note, too, of the technique of 'mud walking' perfected by the Chichester fishermen.

An appeal is currently underway to raise money for the restoration of *Terror*, the last of the open working boats of the harbour which was once engaged in the oyster trade.

The mill at Langstone, near Emsworth. PHOTO © DAVID PACKMAN.

The Nab Tower

This guardian of the eastern approach to the Solent must be one of the least attractive navigation marks to be found anywhere around the coastline of Britain – certainly it has none of the elegance of a lighthouse.

It was never intended for such service. After the damage caused by enemy submarines in WWI, a floating barrier of steel wire nets was built across the Dover Strait, forcing the submarines issuing from German harbours to take the longer route via the north of Scotland. The nets were suspended from buoys but in order to make a more permanent defence, it was decided that a chain of concrete structures would be laid across the channel.

The Nab Tower. PHOTO COURTESY OF THE CORPORATION OF TRINITY HOUSE.

Work started in Shoreham on the octagonal buildings which were to be 24 metres high and built in four tiers of hexagonal cells. This amounted to 9,000 tons of concrete. The budget was an enormous £1.25 million, which looked destined to be wasted when the war came to an end and the first structure was not even positioned.

Urgently seeking a use for them, it was decided that the Nab light vessel should be replaced with one, and the first was towed from Shoreham on the 12 September 1920. The tower was constructed in such a way that it could be floated into position, and then slowly flooded till it stood on the seabed. In the event, it filled too quickly, the tower settled and assumed an angle of 1.5 degrees to the vertical, which it still has to this day. It was also a mile from its intended position. For all its unattractiveness, the lighthouse keepers who manned it claimed it was comfortable, having been built to house 90 naval personnel, and there were never more than a handful of lighthouse keepers at any one time.

THE SOLENT

This stretch of water between the Isle of Wight and the Hampshire mainland – a drowned river valley when the island and rest of Britain were connected – has two distinct faces. Firstly, it is the major yachting centre of Britain and the starting place of some of the greatest yacht races in the world, such as the first ever America's Cup and Fastnet Races. It is home

Yachts and container ships share Southampton Water. Calshot Coastguard tower is seen in the background; detail, left.
OPPOSITE: Brent geese over the Solent. PHOTOS © DAVID PACKMAN.

to the Royal Yacht Squadron, the most distinguished of all yacht clubs. The Rivers Hamble and Beaulieu, together with the town of Lymington, afford vast yacht marinas providing berths for 30,000 yachts. This is the pleasurable face of the Solent.

But the Solent has always been home to seagoing warriors from the days of Henry VIII's navy to the present day. Portsmouth is still the premier naval base in the country and it is from here that fleets have departed in modern times to wage war in the Middle East and the Falklands. Trade has been important, too: with container ships making for Southampton, and vast tankers squeezing themselves round the tight bends of the narrow channels of deep water that lead to the largest oil refinery in Europe, on Southampton water.

Fishing has always been carried out here, especially for oysters in the rivers, but it has hardly been a prominent activity. Instead, the never-ending movement of warships, liners, cargo ships, tankers, yachts and ferries provide the abiding maritime image of the Solent.

There would be every reason to believe that the Solent has been spoiled by its proximity to industry, but this is far from the case. The waters are still abundant in molluscs and crustaceans on which large numbers of over-wintering birds feed. Although green algae appears to cover many of the mudflats at low water, this is not entirely without benefit for the Brent geese which feed on it. The Solent still supports the largest flat oyster fishery in Europe, as its waters are rich in plankton. Only vigilance will keep the Solent healthy, but for a major waterway it is not doing badly.

SPITHEAD

For all its fame, this is no more than a convenient anchorage off the mouth of Portsmouth harbour, sheltered by the Isle of Wight to the south. Its reputation comes from the grand Reviews of the Fleet which have been conducted here by monarchs at the times of Coronations or Royal anniversaries. The Royal Navy, of course, has shrunk and at one time its ships might have filled the waters between the two shores; these days it is a much thinner affair. In the 20th century there were eleven reviews, but the one planned for the Queen's Jubilee in 2002 was cancelled due to cost.

In contrast, the review of 1856 as recorded by the *News of the World*: '*26 screw line-of-battle ships; nearly 40 frigates, paddle and steam; 2 mortar frigates; 4 wrought-iron floating batteries; 50 13-inch mortar vessels; 20 sloops, corvettes, and brigs; and 164 screw gun boats; in all upwards of 300 sail of men-of-war, having an aggregate tonnage of 150,000 tons, manned by 40,000 seamen, carrying 3,800 guns, and firing at one discharge a broadside of nearly 90 tons of solid iron.*'

The Spithead Mutiny

As well as being the spot on which the Royal Navy has shown its best face, in the Mutiny of 1797 it showed a less pleasant aspect. The press gangs were still active, not only catching new recruits but forcing men back onto ships when they had hardly set foot ashore, thus committing them to years at sea. Provisions were poor, fresh vegetables unavailable, scurvy widespread. The practice of flogging remained.

When the *Queen Charlotte* refused to put to sea, with the crew demanding better terms of service, the mutiny rapidly spread, not just through Spithead but as far as the Nore in the Thames Estuary. Faced with a continuing war with the French, and the perceived reasonableness of the demands, 59 of the Navy's most brutal officers were dismissed, pay and conditions improved, and a Royal pardon granted for the mutineers.

PORTSMOUTH HARBOUR

The Sail Training Association ship the Prince William *at the entrance to Portsmouth Harbour.* PHOTO © DAVID PACKMAN.

No harbour in Britain is richer in Naval history, providing an intense concentration of maritime history from HMS *Victory*, *Warrior*, the *Mary Rose* through to the military museums which have based themselves here: the **Royal Naval Museum**, the **Royal Marines Museum** (in Southsea), the **D-Day Museum**, the **Royal Armouries**, the **Museum of Naval Firepower** and the **Royal Navy Submarine Museum**.

A military presence was established here in 1194 when the first dock was built and a wall erected round it on the orders of King John in 1212. Since then, mostly after the time of Henry VIII, it has become the Royal Navy's home, and a fertile ground for huge technological developments. The world's first dry dock was built here in 1495; the making of metal bands by rolling iron (for mast hoops) was first practiced here, and the father of Isambard Brunel invented a steam machine here which automated the making of wooden blocks (pulleys).

It is difficult to point to any particular period and say that this was Portsmouth's heyday. Perhaps it was in the time of the Napoleonic wars when the need for new ships was urgent and streams of timber were hauled, by horses, to be crafted into ships of the line by a well-paid workforce that numbered thousands.

Or perhaps it was in the days of the construction of HMS *Dreadnought* in 1906, which represented the zenith of 'Pompey's' naval contribution. A massive battleship carrying ten 12-inch guns, and propelled by Parsons' newly developed steam turbines, she was more powerful than anything afloat. Few shipyards can claim to have made all the world's other warships obsolete overnight, but in this case Portsmouth can.

Portsmouth remains an important naval base, and families still stand at the harbour mouth to wave loved ones off to war, as generations have done before. But it is her newly-developed talents as a provider of maritime heritage that sets her apart from any other harbour in Britain.

■ HMS *Victory*

Without doubt the prize of the entire harbour is HMS *Victory*, Nelson's flagship at the Battle of Trafalgar, 1805. But even without that honour she would still be remarkable for she is the oldest commissioned warship, and is still manned by naval officers and is the flagship of the Second Sea Lord. She is the only 18th century ship of the line to be found anywhere in the world.

She was ordered in the same year that Nelson was born, and built at Chatham in 1759. She was not brought into immediate service and this may have allowed her timbers to mature without the stress of active service, so helping her preservation, for she was abandoned for almost a century before being taken into care – other ships would have rotted away in that time.

The gun deck, HMS Victory. PHOTO COURTESY OF HMS VICTORY.

The Battle of Trafalgar and the 'Nelson Touch'

No dramatist could have bettered the real events that marked both the pinnacle and the finale of Nelson's naval career. Here was a sailor who had already captured the public imagination with his victories at Cape St. Vincent and at the Battle of Nile. He had lost the sight of his right eye in the Corsica campaign in 1794 and three years later lost his right arm after being hit with grapeshot at Santa Cruz, Tenerife. Already knighted, and created Baron of the Nile, he now sailed to confront Napoleon's navy off the south western coast of Spain and achieve the greatest-ever victory in naval history.

It had been Napoleon's intention to invade Britain in the summer of 1805 and to achieve this he needed naval supremacy in the Channel, which would allow his armies to cross the water unchallenged. To do this, he ordered his fleets to meet in the West Indies, where they would gather and sail in formation for England. The drama unfolded like this:

- March 1805 – The British attempted a blockade of the French ports to prevent the French leaving.
- April 10 – Nelson learned that Villeneuve had evaded the British and joined up with the Spanish and was bound for the West Indies. Nelson pursued him, Villeneuve lost his nerve and headed back to Europe and ended up effectively imprisoned in Cadiz. Napoleon, not best pleased, abandons attempts at an invasion of Britain and instead turns his attention to the troublesome Austrians and Russians.
- October 19 – A British frigate, keeping careful watch, sees the French/ Spanish fleet attempting to leave Cadiz (bound for the eastern Mediterranean to support Napoleon's armies). Nelson's fleet is 48 miles offshore, and Nelson orders the French to be chased.
- October 21 – The British fleet are a mere 9 miles from the enemy. The fight is on.

THE BATTLE PLAN

At 11.50 am Nelson gave the famous order, transmitted by flags to the fleet: 'England Expects that Every Man will do his Duty'. This was not Nelson's first choice of message: he had wanted to send 'England confides that every man will do his duty' followed by the order for 'close action'. He was advised that the word 'confides' required several flags to be hoisted, but if he wished to change it to 'expects' then one single flag would do, this being covered by the Admiralty Code of Signals. 'That will do,' said Nelson. Collingwood received the message and is said to have replied, 'What is Nelson signalling about? We all know what we have to do!'

HMS Victory. PHOTO COURTESY OF HMS VICTORY.

The 'Nelson Touch', as his tactic has been described, was to sail towards the French fleet at right angles to them and in two lines. This confounded the French for their guns were unable to direct any fire towards Nelson's fleet without turning through ninety degrees, which they chose not to do. Also, by splitting the French fleet into three, it allowed each section to be crushed by the superior fire power of the British without the remainder coming to its rescue.

Even so, it was a bloody battle with much close quarters fighting. The British, including *Victory*, suffered severe damage but 18 enemy ships were captured by the time Villeneuve surrendered at 13.45. In the entire battle, the death toll on both sides was 8,500, the British taking 20,000 prisoners.

The course of world events was changed by the Battle of Trafalgar. Napoleon never again turned towards Britain, the Germans were not unified and Russia had no proper navy. For the next century, Britannia ruled the waves.

THE DEATH OF NELSON

'Thank God I have done my duty' Nelson's final words.

A musket ball, fired from the *Redoutable* at 1.30pm, hit Nelson in the shoulder, piercing his left lung. 'They have done for me at last, my backbone is shot through' were his words. He was taken below, his face covered in case he was recognised and morale suffered. Although in pain, he continued to give orders and did not finally die until a total victory had been reported.

The song, *Death of Nelson* by S J Arnold was popular with Victorian tenors, and on hearing it caused Lady Hamilton to leave the theatre in hysterics.

RECITATIVE:

O'er Nelson's Tomb,
With silent grief oppress'd,
Britannia mourns her Hero,
Now at rest:
But those bright laurels
Ne'er shall fade with years,
Whose leaves are water'd
By a Nation's tears.

ARIA:

'Twas in Trafalgar's bay
We saw the Frenchman lay,
Each heart was bounding then.
We scorned the foreign yoke,
For our Ships were British Oak,
And hearts of oak our men!
Our Nelson mark'd them on the wave,
Three cheers our gallant Seamen gave,
Nor thought of home or beauty.
Along the line this signal ran,
England expects that ev'ry man
This day will do his duty!

And now the cannons roar
Along th'affrighted shore,
Our Nelson led the way,
His Ship the Vict'ry nam'd!
Long be that Vict'ry famed,
For Vict'ry crowned the day!
But dearly was that conquest bought,
Too well the gallant Hero fought,
For England, home and beauty.
He cried as 'midst the fire he ran,
'England shall find that ev'ry man
This day will do his duty!'

At last the fatal wound,
Which spread dismay around,
The Hero's breast received;
'Heav'n fights on our side,
The day's our own,' he cried!
'Now long enough I've lived!
In honour's cause my life was past,
In honour's cause I fell at last,
For England, home and beauty.'
Thus ending life as he began,
England confessed that ev'ry man,
That day had done his duty!

Nelson's funeral procession on the Thames.
PHOTO © NATIONAL MARITIME MUSEUM.

In service, *Victory* was hugely popular and she was well used as a flag-ship by several Admirals before coming under the command of Nelson. After the Battle of St Vincent she was thought to be past her best and taken out of service at Chatham where she underwent £70,000 worth of rebuilding before coming back into service two years before Trafalgar.

■ HMS *Warrior* – the end of the 'Wooden Walls'

The mood of the Royal Navy when Victoria came to the throne was one of complacency – they thought themselves invincible behind the 'wooden walls' of their timber ships. The threatening sight of the iron-clad French-built *La Glorie* was to change minds forever. Brunel had proved that iron ships could work, and his *Great Western* had started a transatlantic paddle steamer service. The French, not willing to remain second best to the British navy, saw virtue in iron for warship construction, although the cost prevented them from building the fleet they wished. Instead, they clad wooden hulls in five inches of iron above the waterline, as in *La Glorie*, and bolstered the British view that once again the French were a threat.

At first, Britain was going to follow the French and simply clad our existing ships in iron. But the idea was mooted that a ship might be built in which the 'vital organs' of guns, boilers and engine were shrouded within a protective iron 'box' carried on a ship which could choose between steam or sail. This was to be *Warrior*.

HMS Warrior's *wheel.* PHOTO © PETER MILFORD.

She was to have many advantages over wooden warships which had evolved as far as their designs would permit. Now, with an iron warship 100 feet longer than any previous warship, guns could be mounted on a single deck, avoiding the instability problems of multi-decked ships. Her guns were twice the size of any guns previously carried afloat (six 68 pounders and ten 110 pounders) and she displayed an almost invincible firepower which few enemies would dare to engage. She became the largest, fastest and strongest and most powerfully armed warship in the world and the Royal Navy could sigh with relief on her launching day, 29th December 1860 – once again they ruled the waves. However, it marked the end of the hopelessly vulnerable and weak wooden walls which had been the pride of the Navy since the time of Henry VIII.

THE RESCUE OF *WARRIOR*

The finely-restored ship you see in Portsmouth today would have been unrecognisable 30 years ago. Like many pioneers, her achievements were soon eclipsed as engines became more efficient and designs improved. Within ten years she became an antique and was eventually moved to Milford Haven where she was used as a scruffy refuelling barge. With much impetus from the Duke of Edinburgh, she was towed to Hartlepool for restoration, with the added bonus of providing jobs to what was then a depressed part of Britain.

The restoration of *Warrior* was to make Hartlepool a world class centre for work of this kind. The restoration was not achieved, however, until 80 tons of rubbish had been removed from her – 200 tons of concrete cladding from her deck alone. An almost forensic examination of her history has been carried out to ensure to she is restored to her original condition. Remarkably, after 120 years afloat, experts judged that her hull had not let in as much as a drop of seawater.

■ The *Mary Rose*

'The flower I trow of all ships that ever sailed'.

It is difficult to know which caused the most public attention – the sinking of the *Mary Rose* at Spithead in 1545, or her rise from the seabed in 1982. She was built soon after Henry VIII became King as part of his expansion of the Navy and named after his favourite sister Mary Tudor. She was the second most powerful ship in his fleet and in her part in the Battle of Brest may have been the first ship ever to have fired heavy guns through gun ports.

ABOVE: The Mary Rose *in the ship hall, viewed from the stern.* RIGHT: TOP; *Some of many personal items excavated from the* Mary Rose. MIDDLE; *1000's of artefacts were recovered from the wreck.* BOTTOM; *Cast bronze, muzzle loading, bastard culverin on display in the* Mary Rose *museum.* ALL PHOTOS COURTESY OF THE MARY ROSE TRUST.

Mystery surrounds her sinking which happened in the sheltered waters of the Solent. The French claimed that one of their cannons had done it, but other reports spoke of her capsizing as a result of some instability, perhaps because the gun decks were positioned one on top of the other making the centre of gravity dangerously high.

She lay on the bed of the Solent, broken-backed, till 1971 when a remarkable piece of underwater archaeology in the fast flowing, murky Solent waters proved her identity. It was decided she could be raised.

Sixty million television viewers worldwide watched as a giant floating crane raised her to the surface on 11 October 1982. The raising, in a sense, had been the least of it, for the engineering expertise to build a steel cradle beneath this fragile wreck, without causing fundamental damage, is breathtaking. Add to that the problems of achieving this in swirling waters with limited visibility, and the true scale of this recovery becomes clear. Not only were the timbers of the ship rescued, but also 19,000 artefacts which gave an unprecedented insight into the workings of the Tudor navy.

During her first 12 years ashore, she was gradually raised to an upright position, making it easier for the untrained eye to appreciate her. During this time she was sprayed with water to prevent rapid deterioration of the timbers due to contact with the air. Since 1994, a ten year programme of preservation has been carried out which will remove the need for constant 'watering'.

■ The D-Day Museum

The invasion of Normandy by the allied troops on the 6 June, 1944, was the greatest military operation ever to be conducted both by land, sea and with air support. Between dawn and nightfall, 165,000 troops had landed and although much fighting and loss of life was to follow, it turned the tide and the grip of Nazi Germany on Europe was broken.

The entire story, not only of D-Day but of the progress of WWII, is told in the remarkable Overlord Embroidery to be found in the **D-Day Museum**. It was inspired by the Bayeaux tapestry which tells of the events leading up to the Battle of Hastings in 1066, and in 34 panels it depicts events from 1940 to D-Day itself. Designed by Sandra Lawrence, it was made by the Royal School of Needlework using techniques in use at the time of Mary Rose.

Detail of a panel from the Overlord Embroidery.
COURTESY OF PORTSMOUTH MUSEUMS & RECORDS SERVICE.

■ The Royal Marines Museum

Who are the Royal Marines? In short, they are the sea-going soldiers of the Royal Navy. But the complete answer might not be quite as simple as that, for in their history there has been more than a little confusion about who the Marines belong to.

This hugely distinguished fighting force can trace its history back to 1664 when they were described as a 'Maritime Regiment of Foot'. They defended Harwich from the Dutch in 1667, fighting on foot, but suffered heavily in the battle of Sole Bay, 1672, but this time fighting at sea. So are they sailors or soldiers? The question was eventually raised by Samuel Pepys who declared in Parliament, '*this house has no regular information as to what a marine is.*'

No matter, in 1775 the order was given for the creation of 50 companies of marines to be based at the major dockyards of Portsmouth, Chatham and Plymouth and the Royal Marines have been at the heart of every conflict since, ranging from the 'Imperial policing' of far-flung parts of British Empire to the maintaining of coal supplies in the Newcastle coal dispute of 1831.

There is no greater testament to the courage of the Royal Marines than the sight of the 7,000 awards, including ten Victoria Crosses, on display in their museum.

Be warned – your children might find this museum addictive: they will be able to carry a Marine's rucksack and scramble over a Rigid Rider, fire flintlock pistols, and mingle with the snakes and scorpions which Marines regularly confront in jungle warfare. Great military careers have been founded on less inspiration that this.

The Royal Marine with the biggest question mark

James Gray, Worcester-born, joined the marines in 1747, enlisting at Portsmouth and sailed to India to fight the French. After being wounded (in the groin) and having taken part in several sieges, Gray returned to England in 1750 without any of his shipmates realising that James Gray was, in fact, the audacious Hannah Snell who had managed, remarkably given the proximity in which these marines must have lived, to conceal her true sex from her shipmates. As if to prove that little has changed, her first act on returning to England was to sell her story to a publisher and take to the stage, where her appearances became a sensation.

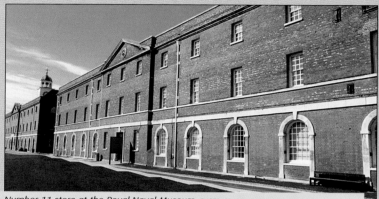

Number 11 store at the Royal Naval Museum. PHOTO COURTESY OF THE ROYAL NAVAL MUSEUM.

■ The Royal Naval Museum

This is one of the major maritime museums in Britain which has recently undergone a substantial facelift. The result is a happy blend of entertainment, education and academic precision. Set in the heart of Portsmouth's naval dockyard, and housed in three storehouses which were built to supply Nelson's fleet, it sits within sight of HMS *Victory*. As you tread the timbered floors, remember that these might have been from captured French and Spanish warships. Where better to explore the long and distinguished story of the Royal Navy.

The Sailing Navy exhibition, however, will give you pause for thought. The traditional view of wooden warships is that they were cramped and miserable to live on, particularly for their crews. The exhibition tries to correct that view. As a modern museum (although first established in 1911) it provides a computer-interactive 74-gun ship for you to steer into battle.

SCURVY AT SEA

This dreaded 'disease' caused immense suffering among sailors until it was discovered to be due to a simple vitamin deficiency, mainly vitamin C, in their diet. Without it, the basic function of body cells could not continue, leading to wasting of flesh in a hideous manner, and in some cases loss of mental function. It baffled the medical experts at the time who knew that the only certain cure was for the men to go ashore where they were said to weep with joy at the sight and smell of fresh food.

Captain James Cook became determined that his crews would not succumb during his long Pacific voyages, and took with him supplies of 'portable soup', made from dried vegetables, and sauerkraut. This appeared to solve the problem.

William Bowles wrote in his poem *The Spirit of Discovery* (1804):

Smile, glowing health!
For now no more the wasted seaman sinks,
With haggard eye and feeble frame diseased;
No more with tortured longings for the sight of fields
    and hillocks green, madly he calls.

However, modern experts believe that Cook might have just been lucky. One of his measures was to prevent fat being eaten from boiling pans. This fat had been in contact with the copper from which the pans were made, forming chemicals which prevented the gut from fully absorbing vitamins. This alone may have been as valuable as his soup, which, after repeated boiling, would have lost most of its nutritional value.

The museum tells the story of the Modern Navy with films on WWII, especially made from a naval point of view, and the tale of the often forgotten Pacific campaign. The progress made in naval warfare becomes starkly evident when the battle at Jutland (1916) is compared with the Falklands operations of 1982.

Perhaps the most profound, and unique collection is to be found in the tapes of the Oral History collection which contains the voices of naval seafarers in peace and at war describing not only the great naval battles in living memory, but also painting a vivid picture of the routine of life aboard ships, in dockyards and Admiralty offices. These recordings form part of the permanent collections (not all on display), which includes much fine art, manuscripts, photographs and artifacts.

Of course, given the proximity of HMS *Victory*, and the overwhelming presence of Nelson in Portsmouth, the story of his flagship and her battles figure large here. But just as intriguing is the question of what Nelson himself was like.

The Trafalgar Experience. PHOTO COURTESY OF THE ROYAL NAVAL MUSEUM.

The Nelson gallery. PHOTO COURTESY OF THE ROYAL NAVAL MUSEUM.

As part of a major redevelopment programme, the Royal Naval Museum decided to commission a new model of him, and this resulted in much academic searching to come up with a totally new impression of the man.

Two myths have been overturned. Firstly, he never wore an eye patch because he never lost an eye. True, he lost the sight of one but this did not result in an empty eye socket. Secondly, he wasn't particularly small: at the time, 5 feet 6 inches was average height for a man. Also, thanks to research carried out by this museum, we have an accurate impression of his face. A mask in the museum's care, thought to be a death mask, has been revealed to have been taken in Vienna in 1800 when he was still alive.

The result is that you can now stand in front of this model, within the shadow of HMS *Victory*, and be as close to Nelson as it is possible to be.

Explosion! Museum of Naval Firepower, Gosport

While much thought and analysis is given to the tactics of warfare, in the end it comes down to someone shooting at someone else – warfare is ultimately about big bangs. The delivery of the explosion has changed somewhat from the crude cannonball to the Exocet missile, but in the converted Powder Magazine of 1777 at Priddy's Hard, in Gosport, you will see the whole story from small arms bullets to the atom bomb, which 'greets' you on arrival.

But it is a human story too, of those who worked here in the days when safety regulations were unheard of, and mutilation was common. There is tribute paid, too, to weapons' designers who were required to be every bit as inventive and precise in their work as the architect of a warship.

This is an award winning museum and a highly popular family attraction.

GOSPORT

The submarine was viewed with enormous scepticism when it was first introduced into the Navy in 1910. It was said that '*submarining was no occupation for a gentleman*'. Since then, it has not only become a principal weapon of war but a keeper of the world's peace.

You can see *Holland 1*, the Navy's first sub, in the **Royal Navy Submarine Museum**, and progress through to HMS *X24* which was in service in WWII, and to HMS *Alliance*, commissioned in 1947 – for the full underwater experience.

HMS *Alliance*. PHOTO COURTESY OF ROYAL NAVY SUBMARINE MUSEUM.

■ Submarine Pioneers

The first underwater attempt (excluding Alexander the Great's descent in a glass barrel) was by William Bourne, a Navy gunner of 1578 who designed a boat with a wooden framework bound in leather. It could be rowed underwater, and by pumping air in or out of it could be made to rise and fall in the water. It never got off the drawing board, but something similar was built in 1605, but got stuck on the mud of the riverbed.

The first 'working' submarine was the invention of a Dutch doctor, living in England, Cornelius Van Drebbel, and employed snorkels which floated on the surface of the water, the craft working 12 feet below the River Thames. There was no military interest in it.

Holland 1 was the Royal Navy's first submarine, brought into service in 1901. She was the first of five built by Vickers of Barrow. At 120 tons, they were driven by a 4-cylinder petrol engine when on the surface and an electric motor when submerged. It was a craft of limited use, being able to travel no more than 60 miles before either the batteries went flat or the air ran out. The systems were crude: the measurement of toxic exhaust gases in the submarine was achieved by three white mice who, it was assumed, would die of asphyxiation before the men. The early submarines were used mostly for coastal defence and not thought highly of: '*underhand, under water and damned un-English*'.

However, their potential was soon realised and by the start of WWI, the Navy had 100 of them, now powered by diesel and with a longer range. They soon proved themselves in combat, the crews collecting five VCs in the course of the war. By the end of WWII, British submarines could claim to have sunk 2 million tons of enemy shipping and 57 warships.

The submarine service has its own flag which depicts the piratical Jolly Roger. It follows a remark of Admiral Sir Arthur Wilson (First Sea Lord 1909–1912) who said '*The crews of all submarines captured should be treated as pirates and hanged*'.

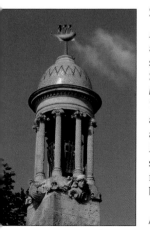

SOUTHAMPTON AND THE GREAT LINERS

Although merchant shipping and shipbuilding have all been conducted at Southampton on a substantial scale, it is as one of the great liner terminals that Southampton is famous, and the **Southampton Maritime Museum** pays full tribute. Famously, the *Titanic* departed from here on her first and last voyage, but the luckier *Queen Mary* was a regular visitor, and later the *QE2*. A substantial model of the *Queen Mary* evokes an age of transatlantic travel that was soon eclipsed by the speed of air travel. However, a new wealthy clientele have discovered that travelling by liner is every bit as good as it was – the massive

Mayflower Memorial, Southampton. PHOTO © DAPHNE GRANT.

Queen Mary 2 and QE2 pass at Southampton. PHOTO © LUKE SANDERSON.

Queen Mary 2, as high as a 21-storey building, left from Southampton on her maiden voyage in January 2004.

But there is more to Southampton's maritime story that just the liners. This former Saxon fishing village grew into a thriving mediaeval walled town, becoming a spa and resort well before the age of the liner. And here we again meet the Pilgrim Fathers who first entered the story at Boston and Immingham in Lincolnshire. This was one of the stopping places for the *Mayflower* on her way to Plymouth, and it was through Southampton's Mayflower Gate (through which you can still walk) that the Pilgrims embarked in 1620.

■ The *Titanic* – not a good start

Although *Titanic*'s problems were yet to come, her departure from Southampton on her maiden voyage went far from smoothly. Britain was in the grip of a six-week coal strike but her owners, White Star Line, were determined that she should sail on time. Consequently, 4,500 tons of coal were scavenged from six other ships, as well as officers and crew. Nothing was going to stop the *Titanic* – in Southampton anyway. On the morning of departure, she was hardly ready to sail and carpenters, painters and carpet fitters were still at work (nothing changes). At noon, her whistle finally blew and with the help of tugs she steamed into the River Test. It was lucky that the nearby *New York* was not rammed in the process, for she had broken her moorings and was drifting into danger.

Maritime Museum, Southampton. PHOTO © DAPHNE GRANT.

Titanic, however, departed unhindered bound for Cherbourg to take on passengers, then to Queenstown (Cork), after which she set off on her final voyage.

The **Southampton Maritime Museum** has the chilling voices of those who remember her loss.

■ Bucklers Hard Maritime Museum

After the frantic feel of the Solent's towns and cities, Bucklers Hard on the banks of the Beaulieu River will come as welcome relief. Even so, warfare has touched this secluded spot over the years and several ships of Nelson's fleet, *Agamemnon* (said to be Nelson's favourite), *Euryalus* and *Swiftsure* were built here and all saw action at Trafalgar. In the 18th century an attempt was made by the Duke of Montague, the local landowner, to establish Bucklers Hard as a port where he could unloaded the valuable sugar from his Caribbean estates. In WWII, Mulberry harbours were built on the old oyster beds as preparation for the D-Day landings, and special operations, clouded in secrecy, were practised here.

In this museum you can learn of the discriminating Puckle's Gun which was designed to fire round bullets at Christians and square ones at the others!

Yachts moored at Bucklers Hard. PHOTO © DAVID PACKMAN.

Passing the Needles during the Round the Island race. PHOTO COURTESY ISLE OF WIGHT TOURISM.

THE ISLE OF WIGHT

The maritime history of the Isle of Wight is either bound up with the gentlemanly sport of yachting, or the less dignified business of smuggling. Both have been practised successfully and on a grand scale from this island's shores.

■ Cowes Week – the story of yacht racing

The first official regatta took place at Cowes in 1812 and it has been known as a yachting centre ever since. The 'Week' quickly became part of the established social scene.

As a place to be seen, Cowes was helped in no small way by Queen Victoria and Prince Albert who bought the nearby Osborne Estate in 1845 and made it their home. Interestingly, the fashionable aspects of Cowes Week left the town and its own people largely untouched, and this is still the case. The unusual name of the town comes from the two forts (or Cows) built at either side of the Medina River by Henry VIII of which it was written in 1545 *'The two great Cows that in loud thunder roar, This on the eastern that on the western shore.'*

If it were not for piracy, there might never have been any yachting. It was in order to escape the clutches of these sea thieves that swift, nippy craft were built called *'jaghtschips'* or hunting ships – *'jaght'* is a Dutch word meaning to hunt. The word evolved into 'yacht' at the hands of the

Uffa Fox

Without doubt, the most famous man of Cowes – designer, racer, yachtsman and character – was born on the Isle of Wight in 1898 and grew up on the Cowes waterfront. His great achievement was the design of the planing dinghy, fuelled by a belief that given the right design of hull, a small sailing boat could be made to plane, or ride the surface of the water, rather than plough through it. The culmination of this ambition was the International 14 *Avenger* which won 52 of the first 57 races she entered. It made this a much sought-after design, and some of Fox's early experiences in a local shipyard, building high-speed power craft, must have helped to refine his thoughts.

With a reputation now behind him there was no stopping him, and designs came thick and fast. But Uffa Fox was never a man to turn his back on his eccentric streak and so there was little surprise when he took off across the Channel on a two-seat canoe of his own design. It was always his claim that his best work was the Airborne Lifeboat carried beneath planes and dropped by parachute to the survivors of ditched aircraft. After the war he created the *Flying Fifteen* class which is enthusiastically sailed to this day.

He sailed the famous Dragon, *Bluebottle* with the Duke of Edinburgh, and achieved some fame for that. His third and final marriage was to a French woman – he spoke no French and she no English.

'A man needs a foot of boat waterline for every year of his age'
– UFFA FOX

English, and the ability of these craft to move through the water at speed, outwitting opponents, caught the imagination of a few of the aristocracy.

Charles II might be called the first yachtsman, having received the gift of a yacht from the Dutch. Although credit for the world's first ever yacht club

goes to the Cork Water Club in Ireland (now the Royal Cork Yacht Club), the Royal Yacht Club, now the exclusive Royal Yacht Squadron was created at Cowes in 1815, but the Royal Thames Yacht Club predates this.

The Prospect.
PHOTO © DOUGLAS COX.

■ The Museums of Cowes

Cowes has always attracted the wealthy, but few took up any kind of residence here. Sir Max Aitken (late press baron and founding father of the London Boat Show) is the exception and his pink house, 'The Prospect', a converted sail loft in a commanding position on the Cowes waterfront, now houses the museum that carries his name. It contains the many trophies he gathered in his sailing career, as well as marine paintings.

The **Cowes Maritime Museum**, although paying due homage to the yachting for which the town is most famous, reminds us that ship building in the 19th and 20th century was no small part of the town's heritage. The Boat Trail, which includes all of Cowes' maritime sights is a four-mile stroll along a marked route and includes the famous yacht clubs as well as the Columbine Yard used since 1935 for the building of flying boats.

■ Newport Classic Boat Museum

This riverside museum houses a unique collection of historic small craft – unique in that all the exhibits have been restored and maintained in a seaworthy conditon and are used on the water as often as possible. These range from canoes and rowing boats to lifeboats,

Two classic craft. PHOTOS COURTESY OF NEWPORT CLASSIC BOAT MUSEUM.

The Maritime Museum, Bembridge.
PHOTO © DOUGLAS COX.

sailing craft and powerboats and even a 1969 hovercraft. You can also visit the restoration shed to see work being done on current projects.

■ Bembridge Maritime Museum and Shipwreck Centre

Often the most intriguing museums are a result of individual inspiration, and this museum devoted to the ship-wrecks of the island has been devised by Martin Woodward who first started diving hereabouts in 1968. His speciality is the uncharted wreck.

The waters around the Isle of Wight are fertile ground for him and displayed here are many artefacts including ships' bells, foghorns, cannonballs and portholes. Of his many discoveries, the most famous is that of the submarine *Swordfish* which left Gosport in November 1940 bound for the western approaches and was never seen again. Having assumed for many years that she had been sunk in Biscay, she was discovered south of St Catherines Point on the island in 150 foot of water. All 40 of her crew were lost, and the secret position of the wreck is now their official war grave.

■ St Catherine's Quay

The steep ravine known as Blackgang Chine, bought by a local businessman in 1842, might now be described as a theme park. It plays its part in the maritime scene, however, by offering **St Catherine's Quay** which offers a glimpse of the 'back' of the Isle of Wight with its shipwrecks and smugglers, depictions of coastal erosion, the skeleton of an 87-foot whale, a lifeboat, paddle steamer and 19th century beach scene.

■ The Museum of Smuggling History

This museum at Ventnor, tells of the tales and tricks used by smugglers on this less policed side of the island where landings were more easily made and gaps in the cliffs provided safe havens for the smugglers' boats. Writing about the village of Niton, on the south side of the island, one observer remarked:

The Wightlink ferry docking at Yarmouth. PHOTO COURTESY OF ISLE OF WIGHT TOURISM.

'The whole population here are smugglers. Everyone has an ostensible occupation, but nobody gets his money by it, or cares to work in it. Here are fishermen who never fish, but always have pockets full of money, and farmers whose farming consists in ploughing the deep by night, and whose daily time is spent standing like herons on lookout posts.'

■ Fort Victoria Museum

Yarmouth is the home to the Island's museum of marine archaeology. The raising of the *Mary Rose* at the eastern end of the Solent was one of the great such achievements of modern times, but this museum shows how marine archeologists piece together the shapes of craft from as far back as the 16th century, and how they recreate the lives of those of lived aboard. So, you will learn how a 16th century Venetian cargo ship, which sank off Yarmouth, was excavated, and see a recreation of a 'First Fleet Ship' which set off 250 years ago, loaded with convicts bound for Australia.

POOLE

Remarkably, Poole harbour has 14 hours of high water a day due to complex tidal movements created by the Solent and the Isle of Wight. It forms one of the largest natural harbours in the world with a shore line 100 miles long. In the middle of the harbour sits Brownsea Island, famous for being the place where the Boy Scouts' organisation was born.

Poole quay. PHOTO © WWW.FREEFOTO.COM.

Poole Quay is where you breathe the town's tradional maritime air these days, and where you will find the **Old Lifeboat House** and the **Waterfront Museum**. Housed in historic buildings close to the quay, the museum houses the Poole Local History Centre and features a display on the Studland Bay wreck excavations.

It seems unlikely that Poole can owe much of its prosperity to a rather chilly island on the far side of the Atlantic, but the Newfoundland fishing trade of 16th century brought the town great wealth. The discovery of Newfoundland by John Cabot in June 1497 also revealed the largest and richest fishing ground ever known. The waters were said to be so thick with cod that ships were forced to plough through the shoals of them. The enterprising seafarers of Poole thought they might engage in this rich fishing, and the records show that much salt (used for preserving) was imported at that time. The fish, though, was not for consumption here; salt cod was much prized in Europe and during the Napoleonic wars, the salt cod eating countries of Portugal, Italy and Spain had not been able to obtain supplies from the French or the Americans, who would have been the natural suppliers. Instead, Poole fishermen filled the gap.

It was Nelson's victory at Trafalgar which helped to bring about the demise of this lucrative trade, for the defeat of Napoleon allowed the French once again to enter the market and Poole's fish were no longer sought. The decline was rapid and harsh.

Poole was a centre for the import and export of wine, fruit and canvas in the 16th century.

Dover, Wight Gazetteer

Ramsgate Maritime Museum
Clock House, Pier Yard, Royal Harbour, Ramsgate, Kent CT11 8LS
☎ +44 (0)1843 587765
www.ekmt.fsnet.co.uk
OPEN Tues–Sun 10:00–17:00, Apr–Sept; Thurs–Sun 11:00–16:30, Oct–March. Groups BA

Deal Maritime and Local History Museum
22 St George's Road, Deal, Kent CT14 6BA
☎ +44 (0)1304 3811344
www.dover-web.co.uk/visitorattractions_dealmaritime.asp
OPEN Mon–Sat (pm only) Apr–Sept

Dover Museum
Market Square, Dover, Kent CT16 1PB
☎ +44 (0)1304 201066
www.dover.gov.uk/museum
OPEN Daily, 10:00–18:00 summer; 10:00–17:30 winter

Hastings Fishermen's Museum
Rock–a–Nore Road, Hastings, East Sussex TN34 3DW
☎ +44 (0)1424 461446
www.1066country.com/fishermuseum.htm
OPEN Daily (except Christmas). 10:00–17:00 summer; 11:00–16:00 winter

Shipwreck Heritage Centre
Rock–a–Nore Road, Hastings, East Sussex TN34 3DW
☎ +44 (0)1424 437452
(AH: 445642)

www.nautical-heritage.org.uk/aboutus.html
OPEN Daily, Apr–Oct, or BA for groups

Lifeboat Museum
King Edward Parade, Eastbourne, East Sussex BN21 4BY
☎ +44 (0)1323 730717
www.eastbournelifeboats.org.uk/museum.html
OPEN Daily, Apr–Dec

Newhaven Local and Maritime Museum
Paradise Family Leisure Park, Avis Road, Newhaven, East Sussex BN9 0DH
☎ +44 (0)1273 612530
www.newhavenmuseum.co.uk
OPEN Daily, 14:00–16:00 Apr–late Oct. Weekends only in winter

Brighton Fishing Museum
201 King's Road Arches, Brighton, East Sussex BN1 1NB
☎ +44 (0)1273 723064
www.sussexmuseums.co.uk/brighton_fish.htm
OPEN Daily, usually 10:00–17:00 but may vary

Marlipins Museum
High Street, Shoreham–by–Sea, West Sussex BN43 5DA
☎ +44 (0)1273 462994; (0)1323 441279
www.sussexpast.co.uk
OPEN May–Oct: Tues–Sat 10:30–16:30.
BH 10:30–16:30

Littlehampton Museum
The Manor House, Church Street, Littlehampton, West Sussex BN17 5EW
☎ +44 (0)1903 738100
www.sussexcoast.co.uk/art/littlehampton.php
OPEN Tue–Sat 10:30–16:30 (closed Gd Fri & Xmas to New Year)

Selsey Lifeboat Museum
Kingsway, Selsey, Chichester, West Sussex.
☎ +44 (0)1243 605282
www.selseylifeboat.co.uk/index.html
OPEN Daily, Easter–end Sept. Confirmation advisable.
GV: BA

HMS Victory
H.M. Naval Base, Historic Dockyard, Portsmouth
☎ +44 (0)23 9272 3111
www.historicdockyard.co.uk/welcome.html
OPEN Daily

HMS Warrior 1860
Victory Gate, H.M. Naval Base (Historic Dockyard), Portsmouth
☎ +44 (0)23 92778600
www.hmswarrior.org
OPEN Daily except Xmas Day

The Mary Rose
Mary Rose Trust, College Road, HM Naval Base, Portsmouth PO1 3LX
☎ +44 (0)23 92750521
www.maryrose.org
OPEN Daily, except Xmas, from 10:00

Royal Marines Museum
Eastney, Southsea, City of
Portsmouth PO4 9PX
☎ +44 (0)23 9281 9385
www.royalmarinesmuseum.
co.uk
OPEN Daily

Royal Naval Museum
HM Naval Base, Historic
Dockyard Portsmouth
PO1 3NH
(Part of Flagship Portsmouth
Trust historic grouping)
☎ +44 (0)23 92727562
www.royalnavalmuseum.org
OPEN Daily, from 10:00
(except Xmas Day)

The Royal Navy
Submarine Museum
Haslar Jetty Road, Gosport,
Hampshire PO12 2AS
☎ +44 (0)23 9252 9217
www.rnsubmus.co.uk
OPEN Daily, except 24 Dec–1
Jan 10:00–17:30
(10:00–16:30 in winter)

Explosion! Museum of
Naval Firepower
Priddy's Hard Heritage Area,
Gosport, Hampshire
PO12 4LE
☎ +44 (0)23 9250 5600
www.explosion.org.uk
OPEN Daily from 10:00,
Apr–Sept & school hols.
Winter: check first

D-Day Museum
Clarence Esplanade,
Southsea PO5 3NT
☎ 0239 2827261
www.ddaymuseum.co.uk
OPEN Daily except 24–26 Dec.
Apr–Oct 10:00–17:30;
Nov–Mar 10:00–17:00

Emsworth Museum
10b North Street, Emsworth
(near Havant), Hampshire
PO10 7DD
☎ +44 (0)1243 378091
(373780 for Hon. Sec.)
www.emsworthmuseum.
org.uk
OPEN Sat, Sun & BH, Easter–
end Oct and Fri in Aug

Southampton Maritime
Museum
The Wool House, Town
Quay, Southampton
SO14 2AR
☎ +44 (0)23 8063 5904
www.southampton.gov.uk/
leisure/heritage/maritime.
htm
OPEN Daily, ex Mon & BH

Buckler's Hard Maritime
Museum
Buckler's Hard Village,
Beaulieu, Brockenhurst,
Hampshire SO42 7XB
☎ +44 (0)1590 616203
www.bucklershard.co.uk
OPEN Daily (times vary with
season)

Bembridge Maritime
Museum and Shipwreck
Centre
Sherbourne Street,
Bembridge, Isle of Wight
PO35 5SB
☎ +44 (0)1983 872223,
873125 (24 hr)
www.isle-of-wight.uk.com/
shipwrecks
OPEN Daily 10:00–17:00,
Mar–Oct, or GV BA

The Classic Boat Museum
The Quay, Newport, Isle of
Wight PO30 2EF
☎ +44 (0)1983 533493
www.harbours.co.uk/
newport/newport.html
OPEN Daily, Apr–Sept

Sir Max Aitken Museum
83 High Street, West Cowes,
Isle of Wight PO31 7AJ
☎ +44 (0)1983 295144,
293800
www.cowes.co.uk/retai67.
html
OPEN Tues–Sat, May–end
Sept or BA

Cowes Maritime Museum
Library & Maritime Museum,
Beckford Road, Cowes, Isle
of Wight PO31 7SG
☎ +44 (0)1983 293394
www.cowes.co.uk
OPEN Mon–Wed, Fri & Sat

Museum of Smuggling
History
Botanic Garden, Ventnor,
Isle of Wight PO38 1UL
☎ +44 (0)1983 853677
www.plymouthdome.info/
index
OPEN Daily, Apr–Sept

Blackgang Sawmill and
St Catherine's Quay
Blackgang Chine, near
Ventnor, Isle of Wight
PO38 2HN
☎ +44 (0)1983 730330
www.blackgangchine.com
OPEN Daily, 26 Mar–29 Oct,
10:00–17:00

Fort Victoria Museum
Fort Victoria Country Park,
Westhill Lane, Yarmouth,
Isle of Wight PO41 0RW
☎ +44 (0)23 8059 3290
www.myweb.tiscali.co.uk/
fortvictoria/fortvic.html
OPEN Daily, Easter–Oct

Old Lifeboat House
Fisherman's Dock, East Quay
Road, Poole, Dorset
BH15 1HZ
☎ +44 (0)1202 663000
www.nmm.ac.uk
OPEN Daily, Easter–end Sept

Waterfront Museum
Old High Street, Poole
BH15 1BW
☎ +44 (0)1202 262600
www.swggfl.org.uk
OPEN Apr–Oct: Mon–Sat 10:00
–17:00, Sun 12:00–17:00;
Nov–Mar: Mon–Sat 10:00–
15:00, Sun 12:00–15:00

BA: By arrangement
BH: Bank holiday
GV: Group visits

PORTLAND, PLYMOUTH

From Anvil Point to Land's End including the Isles of Scilly

Weymouth ■ Portland Harbour ■ Portland Bill
Chesil Beach ■ Bridport and West Bay ■ Teignmouth and
Shaldon ■ Brixham ■ Dartmouth ■ Salcombe ■ Plymouth
Polperro ■ Fowey ■ Charlestown ■ Mevagissey ■ Falmouth
The Lizard ■ Mount's Bay ■ Land's End ■ Isles of Scilly

THE DORSET COAST

The coastline of Dorset carries the weight of more history than merely maritime. Within its 95 miles is to be found evidence of three great geological eras: east Devon reveals the rocks of the Triassic period and is reckoned as one of the major ancient reptile sites in Britain. Dinosaurs once stalked this part of the world in the Mesozoic era, and remarkable fossils, found along the entire length of the coast, are remnants of the Jurassic age. Yes, this could have been the original Jurassic Park, complete with stunning scenery where the soft, chalky cliffs of Purbeck have been eroded over centuries into spectacular sculptures, the most impressive being a natural arch of Portland limestone at Durdle Door, just to the west of Lulworth Cove.

All this makes our maritime history seem distinctly modern.

WEYMOUTH

God Save King George! Sea-bathing was invented at Weymouth, and George III (he who suffered the 'madness') is to blame. Prior to the first royal immersion, in 1763, Ralph Allen of Bath, took the radical advice of his doctor who suggested that a bathe in the English Channel might ease his health problems. But how to achieve it? There were no

Weymouth harbour. PHOTO COURTESY OF DORSET COUNTY COUNCIL.

Durdle Door. PHOTO COURTESY OF DORSET COUNTY COUNCIL.

'swimming costumes' and so rather than be seen naked he devised a hut on wheels which could be taken to the water's edge. This new therapy might have never gone any further had not Mr Allen told his friend the Duke of Gloucester, who told King George III.

The King's doctors thought it would be an ordeal beyond him, but George persisted and, to the strains of the national anthem, duly entered the water from a bathing 'machine' like the one Allen had used. Word spread, and from that moment on bathing in seawater became the height of fashion,

King George liked Weymouth, and it liked him. Although seaside amusements were yet to be invented, the royal family are said to have enjoyed a local competition which gave the prize of a pound of tobacco to the local with the broadest grin.

PORTLAND HARBOUR

The Isle of Portland always provided shelter from westerly gales, and it was a well-used anchorage for coastal traffic caught out in bad weather between Plymouth and the Solent. But the anchorage was exposed to the east and became a dangerous lee shore in such weather. This prompted the Victorians, never fearful of a major engineering project, to use six million tons of stone to create Europe's largest deepwater harbour.

Portland lighthouse. PHOTO COURTESY OF DORSET COUNTY COUNCIL.

Construction started in 1849 with a foundation stone laid by Prince Albert, and finished in 1872 with a stone laid by his son Edward.

It soon became an important coaling point on the Channel route, and an anchorage much used by the Channel Fleet, although it was never considered a naval base on the scale of Portsmouth or Plymouth. In WWII, it was, together with Weymouth, a major gathering point for the invasion fleet and the US 1st Division (known as 'The Big Red One') left from here to fight on Omaha beach.

PORTLAND BILL

There are two stretches of water around the British Isle with a ferocious reputation, both due to accidents of geography coupled with unhelpful effects of the tide. One is the Pentland Firth off north east Scotland, and the other is here off Portland Bill where the notorious Portland Race runs.

Even in reasonable weather, giant seas can build within five miles of the Bill; the waves are often of sufficient majesty to make warships think twice about taking a short cut through them. Certainly, small craft avoid the place. The Race occurs as the flood tide makes its way up channel and finds Portland Bill in its way. The landmass of the Bill deflects it southwards, which causes it to pick up speed. This fast flowing water, now heading offshore, eventually meets the main stream of the flood tide and the result is turbulence on a grand scale, compounded by a sudden shallowing of the water over the Portland Ledge. Add even a modest wind against the tide, and this becomes a fearsome place, fit only for the Weymouth lifeboat crew, who have to face it on a regular basis.

Chesil beach. INSET: *Swans at Abbotsbury.* PHOTOS COURTESY OF DORSET COUNTY COUNCIL.

CHESIL BEACH

This is one of the natural wonders of the British coastline. The beach, 10 miles long from Abbotsbury to Portland, consists of shingle piled up to 40 feet in places, sitting on top of blue clay. It encloses a lagoon, called the 'Fleet', which floods with brackish water and provides a feeding ground for the famous Abbotsbury swans. The most remarkable thing about Chesil beach is the way the combined action of the tides and the sea causes a grading of the shingle from one end to the other. You find shingle-sized stones at Abbotsbury, and cobbles as big as your fist off Portland. For a taste of the 19th century smuggling atmosphere of this stretch of coast, try J Meade Faulkner's *Moonfleet*. The beach, or 'bank' as some people call it, is a notorious graveyard for sailing ships trapped in Lyme Bay in a southwesterly storm. Hence Deadman's Bay to be found towards Portland.

West Bay. PHOTO COURTESY OF DORSET COUNTY COUNCIL.

BRIDPORT AND WEST BAY

The wide streets with long, straight alleyways are the clue to inland Bridport's maritime connection. For centuries they have made rope and twine, and in the days of sailing ships, to be hanged was known as being 'stabbed with the Bridport Dagger'. Ropemaking here can be traced back to the Middle Ages when King John gave the order to the people of Bridport to make, '*night and day as many ropes for ships both large and small and as many cables as you can*'. In those days, a square-rigged ship might require 20 miles of cordage, so it made this a prosperous town. In 1530, in order to protect Bridport's industry, all ropemaking was banned within five miles of the town. One mile away on the coast lies the village of West Bay, formerly Bridport's harbour.

THE ENGLISH RIVIERA

The protection given by the bulge of Devon creates a micro-climate from Exmouth to Start Point, and gives this stretch of coastline a reputation for more sunshine and less rain than in other parts of the southwest. Palm trees flourish in Torquay where frosts are rare.

Tor Bay is appreciated by ships as a protected anchorage in bad westerly weather, and the deep and sheltered waters, close to the shore,

The boyhood of Raleigh

Raleigh. © THE NATIONAL MARITIME MUSEUM.

To the north-east of Exmouth, in the village of Hayes Barton, Sir Walter Raleigh was born. It was at nearby Budleigh Salterton that Sir John Millais' famous oil painting of 1870, *The Boyhood of Raleigh* was painted. The seawall, clearly seen in the picture, still stands. The painting, reckoned by some not to be Millais' best work, was used to inspire schoolchildren in the late 19th and early 20th centuries; it was found in almost every schoolroom of the period to drive home the message that ambition can take a youngster as far as any horizon – if he follows the wisdom of his elders.

Raleigh (1554–1618) was a politician, soldier, adventurer and courtier to Queen Elizabeth I. He famously spread his cloak on the ground at Greenwich Palace so the Queen might not have to tread in a muddy puddle. This story may not be true.

Raleigh studied seamanship and navigation and built a warship, modestly named *Ark Raleigh*, which became *Ark Royal*, and fought against the Spanish Armada. With the death of the Queen, he found no favour with James and was eventually executed for treason after long imprisonment in the Tower of London.

mean that there is rarely a day when a vast tanker is not at anchor within sight of the coast. In fact, Tor Bay is often used as a giant ship park as carriers with no cargo wait for orders.

Exmouth is thought to be the first resort to be established in Devon where its salt waters were reputed to have curative properties, which were keenly sought by gentlemen of wealth.

Sir Walter Raleigh departed on some of his voyages from here and, given that no seaside town in Britain can shun a Nelson connection, Exmouth boasts that his wife once lived in the town.

TEIGNMOUTH AND SHALDON

These two towns stand on opposite banks of the River Teign where it meets the sea at Torbay. Small coasters still use Teignmouth, with over 1000 ship movements a year exporting granite, timber and clay. The Dartmoor granite used in the building of the first London Bridge (now in America) was carried to London on ships leaving from here. The Burton Room of the **Teignmouth and Shaldon Museum** houses what is known as the

Artefacts from the Church Rocks wreck: ABOVE LEFT AND RIGHT: Gold merchant's seal, 'Cherub' decoration on gun; BELOW: Bronze steel-yard weight. PHOTOS COURTESY OF TEIGNMOUTH AND SHALDON MUSEUM.

Burton Maritime Collection. Of all the exhibits, the most curious are the artefacts recovered from a mystery shipwreck which have aroused the interest of marine archeologists the world over. The wreck was discovered accidentally by a 13 year old boy who was spear fishing, and is now thought to be the remains of a 16th century Venetian ship. From the sea bed around her, canons, shot, pottery and bones have been recovered and, curiously, what is thought to be an Elizabethan version of a petrol bomb.

BRIXHAM

With so much of Britain's coastline reflecting a decline in the fishing trade, both inshore and offshore, it is heartening to come to Brixham and see the

fleet thriving. This is the home of the largest fleet of beam trawlers to be found in the UK, and their living is earned searching for Dover sole, turbot, brill and plaice. The larger 'beamers' will stay at sea for five days at a time; but the inshore fleet is active too, fishing for whiting, cod, scallops and crabs.

One of the fleet of Brixham trawlers.
PHOTO © MIKE MILLAR, BRIXHAM HERITAGE MUSEUM.

Two famous seafarers of Teignmouth

It is difficult to think of more contrasting maritime careers than those of the 19th century Admiral Sir Edward Pellow, a man of tactical brilliance and enormous courage, and Donald Crowhurst, the 20th century solo round-the-world yachtsman who disappeared at sea, overwhelmed by the pressure of completing his voyage.

Pellow had already achieved a remarkable naval career even before he was given command of the Mediterranean fleet after Trafalgar, succeeding Nelson. Amongst his crews he was respected as a captain and risked his own life more than once to dive overboard to save a drowning man. After the defeat of Napoleon, he led an allied army assault (on horseback) against the French revolutionaries. This might have been enough for one career. However, he then led the assault on Algiers, to crush the trade in Christian slaves which was operating from north Africa, undaunted by the 100 guns and 8,000 gunners of his enemy. Showered with honours, he died in 1833.

The world of Donald Crowhurst could not be further removed from that of Pellow. Crowhurst's ambition was to race single-handed around the world in the first event of its kind – the *Sunday Times* Golden Globe. In a poorly prepared trimaran called *Teignmouth Electron* (he ran a company making electronic navigation equipment) he set sail in October 1968. The pressure of publicity seems to have prevented him from admitting that he was unready for such a voyage. He radioed reports back to England suggesting the race was progressing well, but these are now thought to be fictional and he may never have left the Atlantic. The last entry in his log was dated 1 July 1969 after sailing 16,591 miles in 213 days. He was never seen again.

Brixham has benefited as a bay sheltered by the long arm of Berry Head to the south. Since the building of the substantial breakwater in 1843, completed in 1916, it became a secure harbour which could be entered in any weather. A ship building industry thrived alongside the fishery and in 1850 Brixham was described as the '*largest fishery in England ... more than 270 sail of vessels, comprising 20,000 tons of shipping and employing about 1600 seamen*'. In the 1840s, '*140 merchant schooners of 80–200 tons, 120 sailing trawlers of 20–40 tons and 100 smaller vessels*' were built here.

For vessels making for Brixham, the light on the top of Berry Head is the most important navigation mark. This light is unique, since it is merely a squat structure six feet high sitting on the top of a very high cliff (over 200 feet). This makes it not only the highest, but also the shortest lighthouse in Britain. The light is said to be the inspiration for John Henry Newman's famous hymn, *Lead Kindly Light*:

> *Lead, kindly Light, amid th'encircling gloom, lead Thou me on!*
> *The night is dark, and I am far from home; lead Thou me on!*
> *Keep Thou my feet; I do not ask to see*
> *The distant scene; one step enough for me.*

The Brixham trawler

A monarch amongst the sailing trawlers, this was the most powerful class of vessel of its size ever built. The first ship was constructed in Brixham in the late 18th century and then widely copied by other fleets when more distant waters started to be used as fishing grounds.

You can still see them at Brixham today, although converted for use as charter vessels. These ships carry substantial amounts of canvas and there seems to be hardly a job on board which might come under the heading of 'light work'. It is thought that the Brixham fleet might have been the first to employ the trawling method of catching fish, much of which came from a particularly rich ground to the north of the Skerries; this was a reef extending north eastwards from Start Point. Strong breezes often blew here, which the heavy trawlers needed; there was also shelter from the channel swells which hindered the recovery of the trawls. The three Brixham trawlers operating today: *Leader*, *Provident* and *Golden Vanity*, are regular visitors to their home port. Under extensive restoration is *BM45 Pilgrim*, built in Brixham in 1895. Also at Brixham is *Regard*, built in 1933 to the design of a Brixham trawler, but as a yacht; apparently she was used for trawling diamonds off the South African coast.

Brixham sailing trawlers. PHOTO © MIKE MILLAR, BRIXHAM HERITAGE MUSEUM.

The **Brixham Heritage Museum** reflects Brixham's long standing maritime traditions, both in peace and at war. The British Seaman's Orphans Home was here, and nearby Berry Head served as an important fortification in the Napoleonic wars. Also, the famous hymn *Abide with Me* was written in Brixham by the Reverend Henry Francis Lyte as he approached death. The tune is played on the bells of his church, All Saints, Brixham.

The Berry Head lighthouse. PHOTO COURTESY OF BRIXHAM MUSEUM & HISTORY SOCIETY.

Brixham was also the scene, in 1688, of what has become known as the 'bloodless revolution'. On the spot now marked by a statue, Prince William of Orange landed. He went on to claim the throne as King William III. His promise to the people was, '*The liberties of England and the Protestant religion I will maintain*'.

The Great Gale of 1866 is well remembered, since this prompted the establishment of the first Torbay lifeboat to be stationed at Brixham. In one disastrous night, an unexpected wind of hurricane strength blew ashore 40 ships sheltering in Torbay with a loss of nearly 100 lives. There has been a lifeboat at Brixham ever since.

■ The *Golden Hind* at Brixham

No, not the real one which Sir Francis Drake sailed aboard on his 16th century circumnavigation, but a replica. Never mind, there is much aboard to thrill and inspire a younger generation about our seafaring history with much talk of pirates and treasure. The *Golden Hind* replica has been a feature of Brixham harbour since 1963.

The replica of the Golden Hind. PHOTO COURTESY OF THE *GOLDEN HIND*.

ABOVE AND RIGHT: Dartmouth Museum and some of the exhibits; TOP: Dartmouth and the Mouth of the Dart by Thomas Luny (about 1815); BELOW: An early steam engine of the Newcomen type (Newcomen lived in Dartmouth). PHOTOS COURTESY OF DARTMOUTH MUSEUM.

DARTMOUTH

For sheer splendour, the rooms which house the **Dartmouth Museum** take some beating. This is where Charles II held court while stormbound here in 1671. The entire Dart valley is breathtaking. From seaward, there is hardly a hint that, behind the cliffs, sits one of the safest and most attractive of English harbours, where tiers of cottages cling to the steep hillsides. Once past the impressive 15th century Dartmouth castle, which guards the river mouth, you find the harbour bursting with moored yachts, tripper boats, and the ferry that runs between Dartmouth and Kingswear. Overlooking all this is the distinguished presence of the Britannia Royal Naval College, the Navy's principal seat of learning.

Dartmouth Castle, which started construction in 1481, may have been the first fortification to use canon to defend a stout chain stretched across the harbour mouth. The chain's mooring ring on the opposite shore can still be seen.

No period in maritime history has left Dartmouth untouched. In the 12th century it was the embarkation point for Crusaders; in Elizabethan times, Sir Walter Raleigh opposed the Armada with ships from here. The *Mayflower*, with the Pilgrim Fathers aboard, put in here for repairs, *en*

The Royal Naval College and one of the museum displays. PHOTOS COURTESY OF THE ROYAL NAVAL COLLEGE.

route for Plymouth. In 1944, this was a major base for D-Day operations with 400 craft setting sail from both here, and Slapton Sands to the south. The Naval College acted as the centre for Combined Operations.

■ The Britannia Royal Naval College

Kings George V, VI, the Duke of Edinburgh, and the present Prince of Wales were cadets in the college, built in 1905 to replace the training ships, *Britannia* and *Hindostan* which had been moored in the river since 1863. The architect was Sir George Aston who can claim credit for Admiralty Arch and the east frontage of Buckingham Palace. The college houses its own small but rich museum, and tours of the entire college operate, depending on term times.

SALCOMBE

Like Dartmouth, from seaward you would never guess that Salcombe existed. You need to peer round the bend in the Kingswear estuary before you see the town itself and the 2000 acres of tidal creeks which make this the West Country's finest natural harbour. The protection given by the

Salcombe harbour. PHOTO COURTESY OF DEVON COUNTY COUNCIL.

hills and cliffs creates a warm micro-climate, and bananas, figs and palm trees grow without greenhouse protection.

Like Dartmouth, Salcombe has a harbour-mouth castle, Fort Charles, built by Henry VIII as protection against the French and Spanish.

Salcombe has seen ship building, smuggling and fishing in its long history, and this was a home port for the fruit schooners who raced with fresh fruit from the Bahamas, the Mediterranean and the Azores. These ships were built in local yards, and being the first home with the fruit was hotly contested.

Salcombe has two museums: the **Museum of Local and Maritime History** gives a hands-on experience for children, and tells the story of the part both Salcombe and Slapton played in the D-Day invasion.

The **Overbeck's Museum** (National Trust) is housed in an elegant Edwardian mansion and is the creation of Dr Otto Overbeck who collected model boats and local shipbuilding tools. Overbeck's garden provides stunning views across the estuary.

THE EDDYSTONE LIGHTHOUSES

No offshore reef proved more of a challenge to the pioneering lighthouse builders than the Eddystone Rocks, 14 miles south of Plymouth, in a position which made them a mortal danger to ships, both when making for the safety of the harbour after a channel crossing, or on a coastal passage. Masters had long sailed in fear of being brought up on the spiky red granite shoals around which swirled confusing tides, and over which built enormous seas in severe gales. Christopher Jones, the master of the *Mayflower* said of the rocks '*Twenty-three rust-red ragged stones around which the sea constantly eddies, a great danger for if any vessel makes too far to the south she will be caught in the prevailing strong current and swept to her doom on these evil rocks*'. It was to tame these 'evil rocks', that ship-owner Henry Winstanley built the first Eddystone light in 1698.

There was nothing Winstanley enjoyed more than a mechanical challenge. A man of means, something of a dandy, his house was littered with mechanical tricks to amuse guests. He was famous for having created

The *Herzogin Cecile*

The **Overbeck's Museum** has photographs of the wreck of the *Herzogin Cecile*, one of the last of the great clipper ships which foundered in Starhole Bay at the western entrance to Salcombe harbour. Known affectionately as the '*Duchess*', in 1936 she was engaged in one of the great Grain Races in which clippers raced each other from Australia with cargoes of cereal. It was to be her last voyage. She had made splendid time to Falmouth – only 86 days – and beating her old rival the *Pommern* by eight days. She was under orders to proceed to Ipswich to discharge her cargo but in thick fog and strong winds, she foundered on the Hamstone, a few miles from Salcombe. The sightseers, many of whom turned into looters, hampered the rescue but there was no loss of life. She remained stuck for many weeks; the invading saltwater caused her grain cargo to swell, breaking her timbers apart. However, she was refloated and beached in Starhole Bay when the authorities refused to allow her entry into Salcombe on health grounds. Here she broke her back, lost her masts and settled. Her remains may still be visible at low water, and are much visited by divers who say she is a 'pretty' wreck.

'Winstanley's Waterworks'; a tableaux employing water fountains and fire. Having invested his growing wealth in shipping, he was distressed at losing two on the Eddystone, and vowed to build an enduring light.

It was a slow process. He drilled holes one summer, then, the following year, fixed iron bars into the rock with molten lead. After a brief absence as a prisoner of the aggressive French, Winstanley continued until, on 14 November 1698, he climbed to the top of his new tower and lit the candelabra which provided the first Eddystone light. Crowds

The Eddystone lighthouse

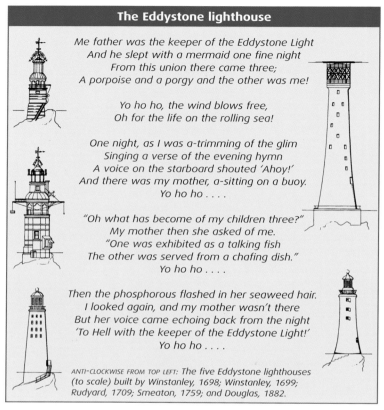

Me father was the keeper of the Eddystone Light
And he slept with a mermaid one fine night
From this union there came three;
A porpoise and a porgy and the other was me!

Yo ho ho, the wind blows free,
Oh for the life on the rolling sea!

One night, as I was a-trimming of the glim
Singing a verse of the evening hymn
A voice on the starboard shouted 'Ahoy!'
And there was my mother, a-sitting on a buoy.
Yo ho ho . . . .

"Oh what has become of my children three?"
My mother then she asked of me.
"One was exhibited as a talking fish
The other was served from a chafing dish."
Yo ho ho . . . .

Then the phosphorous flashed in her seaweed hair.
I looked again, and my mother wasn't there
But her voice came echoing back from the night
'To Hell with the keeper of the Eddystone Light!'
Yo ho ho . . . .

ANTI-CLOCKWISE FROM TOP LEFT: The five Eddystone lighthouses
(to scale) built by Winstanley, 1698; Winstanley, 1699;
Rudyard, 1709; Smeaton, 1759; and Douglas, 1882.

gathered on Plymouth Hoe to see the sight. The light was soon put to the test by a strong gale which confined Winstanley till almost Christmas, but the light stood the test. But by spring, winter had taken its toll on the masonry and he ordered a rebuild.

Although built with heavier stone, and iron bound, the new light was no match for a severe gale on 25 November 1703 in which 8,000 seamen drowned in the channel in one night. By dawn, there was hardly anything left of Winstanley's Eddystone.

John Rudyard was the next lighthouse builder, and his more 'conventional' looking light, survived for nearly 50 years before fire in the keepers' quarters spread to the light and eventually destroyed the structure.

John Smeaton, the greatest of the English civil engineers, was the next to have a go, employing some of the lessons learnt by Rudyard who had dovetailed the stone together to provide strength. He also had the use of a quick-drying cement which he had invented. It took three years to complete and the first light was shown on 16 October 1759. It was a triumph of engineering, especially when the candlelights were replaced with oil, but the rock on which it had been built proved unstable and in the late 1870s, the decision to rebuild was taken. However, Smeaton's tower was held in

Smeaton's tower still stands on Plymouth Hoe. PHOTO © TIM STANGER LRPS/COAST CARDS.

sufficient esteem by the people of Plymouth to be removed block by block and rebuilt on Plymouth Hoe. The present light, built by James Douglas replaced it – finally lit in the summer of 1882.

The current lighthouse, completed in 1882.
PHOTO COURTESY OF CORPORATION OF TRINITY HOUSE.

PLYMOUTH

For the last 500 years, the maritime history of Plymouth has been firmly tied to its military connections. Its geography provides a two-pronged harbour for shelter, and it inevitably became a convenient base for a large proportion of the Royal Navy. However, compared with others, the Navy have had only a recent presence here. In the 16th century, Sir Walter Raleigh had suggested that a base might be built here, but Queen Elizabeth thought it too expensive. Instead, Portsmouth and Chatham remained the favoured Royal Dockyards. It wasn't until 1693 that the first docks at Devonport were brought into service, and not a moment too soon, for the next 100 years were going to see the Royal Navy engaged in endless wars with the French and Spanish. Devonport grew to be the largest naval base in western Europe with 15 dry docks, 4 miles of waterfront and 25 berths covering a total of 640 acres.

Some of the greatest voyages in the world have started from Plymouth. Sir Francis Drake set out on his circumnavigation from here. The Pilgrim Fathers, aboard the *Mayflower*, set sail from Plymouth. The voyages of James Cook started here, and also Darwin's aboard the *Beagle*. In more recent times, Sir Francis Chichester made his record-making Atlantic crossing and round the world passages.

■ The Plymouth breakwater

Safe harbour though it might have appeared, it offered no real protection to a southerly gale which could throw large seas to the very feet of the town. In the early 1800s, it was proposed that a breakwater be

Plymouth, the Barbican district. PHOTO COURTESY OF DEVON COUNTY COUNCIL.

The Plymouth breakwater. PHOTO © TIM STANGER LRPS/COAST CARDS.

built at a cost of the huge sum (at that time) of £1.5 million. It was built along a line of rocks and 3 million additional tons of rock were dumped to form it; this effectively removed 27 acres of Plymouth. Measuring 40 feet across the top, it stands 200 feet above the sea bed. At the eastern end is a strange conical construction with a ball on the top. This is intended as a refuge for any seafarer who finds himself washed onto the breakwater. Here he could climb above the high water mark and 'shelter' in the cage until rescued.

■ Plymouth Naval Base Visitor Centre

Despite being one of the Navy's busiest bases with over 5,000 ship movements a year, the base provides room for a **Visitor Centre** which offers tours of the modern submarine refit complex, as well as historical exhibitions including the Field Guns and what it described as the 'only working hangman's cell in the country'. The oldest naval dock at Plymouth dates from 1689 and here you will get a flavour of Plymouth's naval history, and smell the tarred twine and rope in the Ropery and White Yarn stores. There are figureheads, dockyard fire fighting, and a large collection of documents relating to dockyard history.

Also see **Plymouth City Museum**, and in particular, its collection of maritime paintings and ship models: the work of prisoners of war.

Smeaton's Tower, standing proudly on Plymouth Hoe is open daily in the summer, and is a good place to reflect on the engineering battles that have been fought to light the Eddystone Rocks nearby. (See page 206.)

Sir Francis Drake

DRAKE'S DRUM *by Sir Henry Newbolt*

Drake, he's in his hammock and a thousand miles away
Capten art thou sleepin there below
slung atween a round shot in Nombre Dios bay
and dreaming arl the time of Plymouth Hoe
yonder looms the island, yonder lie the ships
with sailors lads a dancin heel and toe
and the shore lights flashin and the night tide dashin
he sees et arl so plainly as he saw et long ago
Drake he was a Devon man and ruled the Devon seas
Capten art thou sleeping there below
rovin thro his death fells he went with heart at ease
and dreaming arl the time of Plymouth Hoe
take my drum to England hand et by the shore
strike et when your powders runin low
if the Dons sight Devon I'll quit the port of heaven
an drum them up the channel as we drummed them long ago
Drake he's in his hammock till the great armada come
Capten art thou sleeping there below
slung atween the round shot listenin for the drum
and dreamin arl the time of Plymouth Hoe
call him on the deep sea call him on the sound
call him when ye sais to meet the foe
when the old trades plyin and the old flag flyin
they shall find him where and wakin as they found him long ago

Born in 1540, Drake was a multi-talented man who could claim to have been a privateer, politician, navigator and a naval hero. It is his naval heroics for which he is most acclaimed, taking the credit for the ultimate defeat of the Spanish Armada. On the green sward of Plymouth Hoe, Drake famously continued his game of bowls as the Spanish fleet approach – or perhaps not.

Imagine, then, this legend who stood only 5 feet 2 inches tall, with clear blue eyes and blonde hair and beard, named '*El Draque*' (the Dragon) by the Spanish. His hatred of the Spanish was kindled by the near total loss of the English fleet off Mexico, of which he had been part. Drake had been given a command, under his cousin Sir John Hawkins, and together they had been in Mexican waters buying slaves. Only two ships survived the attack, but out of it came a grudge which Drake carried for most of his career.

His greatest voyage was in 1577 when he became the first Englishman to sail round the world in an expedition funded, in secret, by Elizabeth I. His ship, the *Golden Hind*, made it safely from the Atlantic to the Pacific via the Straits of Magellan, and while voyaging north he took every opportunity to plunder the Spanish settlements of Chile and Peru. Continuing north, he claimed California for the Crown.

Instead of returning to Plymouth the way he came, where he suspected the Spanish would be waiting for him, instead he crossed the Pacific, completing his circumnavigation. His knighthood awaited him on his return in 1580.

DRAKE DEFEATS THE ARMADA

After his circumnavigation, Drake served as mayor of Plymouth for a time. He was given command of a large fleet which, in 1585, stormed Vigo and in 1587 he led the assault on Cadiz, doing huge damage to the Spanish fleet in an episode often referred to as the 'singeing of the King of Spain's beard'. This is said to have delayed the Spanish Armada's assault on England by at least a year.

When the Armada of 130 ships, including 22 galleons, finally set sail for England on 19 July, 1588, it was opposed by Drake as it approached the Channel. Famously, Drake is said to have continued his game of bowls on Plymouth Hoe while the Armada sailed into view. There are two explanations of this: either he knew the tide in Plymouth Sound was against him, and even if he had hurried, his ships would not have been able to sail. Or, it may be an entire fiction.

Either way, Drake's attack on the Armada achieved little damage, and the Spaniards sailed on in the defensive crescent formation they had adopted. Anchoring off Calais in order to take aboard their land-based soldiers for the attack on England, the Armada fell victim to the English 'fire ships' – hulks stuffed with flammable material, set alight, and allowed to drift down onto the Spaniards. As a result of this, and an attack by the Navy, the Armada fled into the North Sea returning to Spain via the north of Scotland with huge losses due to illness and starvation.

DRAKE'S PRAYER:

When thou givest to thy servants
to endeavour any great matter
Grant us also to know that it is not the beginning
but the continuing of the same unto the end
until it be thoroughly finished.

FACING PAGE: Drake's statue on Plymouth Hoe. PHOTO COURTESY OF DEVON COUNTY COUNCIL. *ABOVE:* Bow view of the reconstruction of the Golden Hind *at Brixham.* PHOTO COURTESY OF THE *GOLDEN HIND.*

The Mayflower steps. PHOTO © TIM STANGER LRPS/COAST CARDS.

■ Plymouth Dome

The Dome on Plymouth Hoe ('hoe' meaning 'high ground') brings together all of the city's maritime history in one unique setting. It celebrates the great heroes of naval battles and world exploration who have set sail from here: Drake, Cook, Frobisher, Hawkins and Raleigh. It also tells the story of the five Eddystone lighthouses and recreates the gun deck of an Elizabethan warship.

■ Mayflower Steps

The remains of old Plymouth are to be found in the Barbican district from where the Pilgrim Fathers finally departed on their Atlantic crossing of 6 November 1620. The steps down which they are said to have climbed are still there, and much visited by Americans who come to pay homage to the settlers who were inspired by their faith to voyage to the New World. Their beliefs and stated aims, in the form of a mutually agreed 'compact', formed the basis of the eventual constitution of the United States.

■ The National Marine Aquarium

Britain's first-ever educational aquarium, is to be found in Plymouth. It is now established as the premier aquarium in Britain, putting research and education before entertainment while still providing a hugely enjoyable maritime experience. The emphasis is strongly on marine science here, and the messages of conservation and sustainability are clearly voiced. This is a major, eye-opening experience.

■ Cotehele Quay

The upper reaches of the Tamar, dividing Devon from Cornwall, seem far removed from the military bustle of Plymouth. But these waterways were important trading routes in which the West Country barges operated. At Cotehele Quay (National Trust) built to service the estate of the Edgcumbe family and their medieval manor house, sits *Shamrock*, built in 1899 as a 57 foot ketch-rigged trading barge. She worked the length of the river carrying all manner of cargoes to support the local mining, quarrying and shipbuilding industries. In the early 1960s, when her working days were done, she was converted for use as a diving support vessel, and was later used in the salvage business. She has been a museum ship since the early 1970s when she was acquired by the National Trust who supervised her full restoration. A museum on the quay tells her story, and of her trading days on the River Tamar.

A seasonal ferry links the village of Calstock with Cotehele Quay using a route said to have been a ferry crossing since Saxon times.

The Shamrock *at* Cotehole Quay. PHOTO © WEST COUNTRY VIEWS.

ABOVE: Low tide at Polperro. PHOTO © WEST COUNTY VIEWS. *RIGHT: The Bodinnick ferry links Fowey to Bodinnick and makes a handy shortcut to Looe or Polperro. The house on the right is Ferryside where Daphne du Maurier lived from 1926 to 1943.* PHOTO © WWW.VIEWSOFCORNWALL.COM.

POLPERRO

From Rame Head to Land's End we are moving into the land of the small Cornish fishing villages, set behind clefts in the rocky cliffs.

For a small fishing village, Polperro has a large history told in the **Polperro Heritage Museum**. With so much of the village cloaked in tourism these days, it is difficult to imagine that here were once three fish factories working in the salting, curing and packing of pilchards caught by the local Polperro Gaffers – like the *Lady Beatrice* whose model is on display here. But given the secretive nature of this little harbour, it is hardly surprising that smuggling flourished across the Channel. It seems the local 'guernsey' sweater, known in Polperro as a 'knitfrock' was inspired by this cross-channel relationship.

FOWEY

Fowey still thrives as a commercial port engaged in the export of highly prized Cornish china clay, a business it shares with the port of Par to the west. But for all its serenity today, this was a 15th century haunt of pirates, amongst the most notorious being the Mixtow family, in particular Mark Mixtow (1400) who had a fleet of four ships, supposedly engaged in attacking the French. However, he seems to have been unable to resist any target, and only after he plundered a friendly Hanseatic ship was he called to account. His son carried on the family business and famously captured an Italian ship off the Portuguese coast, and brought it back to Fowey, where people came from miles around for a sight of it. The more daring of Fowey's sailors achieved reputations and were much sought after to fight in medieval wars. They were known as the 'Fowey Gallants'.

CHARLESTOWN

One of the few harbours in Britain (built by Smeaton, architect of the 3rd Eddystone lighthouse) where you will be greeted by the sight of the tall masts of square-rigged ships. This is no tourist enterprise, but the base for tall ships which have been specially restored, or even created, for the feature film and television industries.

This is how Charlestown would have looked when it was first established in 1790 for the export of copper and then china clay by the local landowner Charles Rashleigh, after whom the harbour is named.

Remarkably, little has changed, although nearby St Austell seems to get ever closer. It remains a true glimpse of a Georgian working harbour,

Tall ships in Charlestown harbour. PHOTO COURTESY OF WWW.VIEWSOFCORNWALL.COM.

still exporting small quantities of china clay. The **Charlestown Shipwreck and Heritage Centre** takes as its theme the shipwrecks of the Cornish coast, and the divers who explore them. There are artefacts here from 150 wrecks and the largest collection of underwater diving equipment in Britain.

MEVAGISSEY

Although tourists are the town's biggest catch these days, Mevagissey shares with many Cornish harbours long traditions of fishing and smuggling. The early 19th century smuggling trade between here and Roscoff was substantial, and those who went to their beds at night fearful that the knock on the door might be the excise man, might also have feared a visit from the press gangs sent out from Plymouth to recruit sailors.

The local sailing craft hereabouts were the 'toshers' which fished for herring, mackerel and pilchards. A principal customer for the pilchards was the Navy who christened them 'Mevagisssey Duck'. In the mid 19th century, 64 boats operated from the harbour and there are still respectable numbers of inshore craft based here. Mevagissey still operates as a fishing harbour.

Mevagissey harbour and (inset) lighthouse. PHOTOS COURTESY OF WWW.VIEWSOFCORNWALL.COM.

The **Mevagissey Museum**, housed in a boatbuilder's workshop of 1745, also reflects the agricultural hinterland, and the copper mine of 1825 which started up in the heart of the town. Also remembered is Andrew Pears, who invented the famous soap that bears his name, and lived and worked here as a barber.

Ferries run from here to Fowey, and to Charlestown in poor weather when the open sea passage to Fowey might be too rough.

FALMOUTH

When God drew the Cornish coast, surely Falmouth and the Carrick Roads were his masterpiece. Here is a vast harbour, the third largest natural harbour in the world including a major river, the Fal, running as far inland as Truro. And within the natural shelter provided by the Lizard to the West, and St Anthony's head to the east, is the town of Falmouth itself. This is where ships that had crossed half the globe, came to anchor awaiting orders.

For the protection of this important harbour stands the castles of Pendennis and St Mawes, both built on the orders of Henry VIII. Although

Falmouth harbour. PHOTO COURTESY OF WWW.VIEWSOFCORNWALL.COM.

Pendennis Castle. PHOTO COURTESY OF
WWW.VIEWSOFCORNWALL.COM.

the area of enclosed water is commonly called Falmouth harbour, in fact Falmouth is just one of several important towns and villages on the shores of the Rivers Fal and Penryn. The major deep water anchorage, to the north of the castles, is properly called Carrick Roads.

It is difficult to imagine a more perfectly placed and sheltered harbour for ships working the Atlantic, or making landfall on the English coast after a Biscay crossing. Since the 17th century it has truly been England's maritime cross roads and it was to here the news was first brought of Nelson's victory at Trafalgar, despatched by Admiral Collingwood and delivered aboard the schooner *Pickle* by Lieutenant Lapenotiere.

The Falmouth Packets

Much of Falmouth's prosperity from the 17th century through to the mid 19th century, was derived from the famous Falmouth Packets which sailed from here carrying government documents and general mail.

The first packet set sail for Coruña in Spain in 1689 when war threatened the overland route. After that they quickly became established, speeding to Europe and the West Indies. To protect the mail, the packets carried some light armour, and in their long and distinguished career often found themselves in the middle of conflicts, usually between the English and the French. Their first duty, of course, was to the mail and if it looked as though a Packet might be captured, the mail was thrown overboard.

The Packets usually carried two masts and were square-rigged, substantial ships of 200 tons, built for speed and with lengthy bowsprits carrying a substantial spread of canvas. The Packets continued till the mid 19th century, the last leaving Falmouth in 1852 when the Post Office embraced steam-driven ships and moved their base to Southampton. The legacy of the wealth brought to Falmouth by the Packets is seen in the grand houses that the Packet owners and skippers built for themselves near the Greenbank Hotel.

19th century view of the Cornish fishing fleet at Falmouth.
PHOTO COURTESY OF ANDREW CAMPBELL WWW.IMAGEDELIVERY.CO.UK.

■ Working boats of Falmouth

Still sailing, although not fully engaged in the oyster dredging for which they were built, the Falmouth Working Boats still grace the Carrick Roads. They are immediately recognised by the length of their bowsprit and the size of their gaff-rigged mainsail. A local by-law which only allows Falmouth oysters to be dredged under sail, has kept this craft alive. Few are equipped for oyster fishery these days, but when the fleet is on the move at weekly races, they remain one of the enduring maritime sights of the west country.

The Falmouth Quay Punt was a different kind of craft, less graceful perhaps, and built with a two-masted yawl rig which enabled her to jig around, waiting for incoming ships. Patience was her game. The masts were built on the short side so that when the punts came alongside the square-riggers, they would not foul each other's rigging. The quay punts provided a taxi service, taking ashore skippers and crew and returning with provisions. Not built for deep sea work, they would heave-to in the lee of the Lizard, or in the harbour approaches, waiting for business. There are no quay punts still in service, although many yachts based on their sturdy lines have been produced.

THE NATIONAL MARITIME MUSEUM – FALMOUTH

This is a breathtaking project and has won awards for its architecture and plaudits from its customers for the way the very latest techniques in museum presentation have been used to tell the maritime story. The distinctive building, with sloping roof carefully angled to match the local landscape, appears to have a misplaced lighthouse adjoining it, but this is the lookout giving views across the harbour complete with inter-active explanation. Climb down to the bottom of this tower and you are below the water, in the Tidal Zone, looking out through toughened glass, watching the marine life that drifts by and the tide as it rises and falls.

Cornish maritime history is well represented: you can hear the voices of Cornish fisherman, follow the story of the Falmouth Packets that made the town a centre of communication, and understand the workings of this maritime county, of which no part is more than 16 miles from the sea.

But this museum is much more than a collection of the 140 small craft you will find here. In Start Line and Set Sail you learn how boats are used both for work and leisure, for fishing, racing, the breaking of records, and exploration. Active workshops show how boats are built in wood, and traces their evolution.

But perhaps the most memorable part of this museum is the collection brought together under the title Flotilla and housed in an astonishing

The striking architecture of the National Maritime Museum, Cornwall. PHOTO COURTESY OF WWW.VIEWSOFCORNWALL.COM.

Falmouth harbourside. PHOTO COURTESY OF WWW.VIEWSOFCORNWALL.COM.

gallery which has been described as 'canyon-like.' There are 27 boats on display here, some suspended to give a unique view; well-designed inter-active support ensures that visitors of all ages go away with a full appreciation of what they are seeing. Amongst others, you will see a Gilbert Island out-rigger, the famous sailing canoe *Rob Roy*, scene of Victorian adventures, and the open-decked Wanderer dinghy which, remarkably, sailed to Iceland and back.

For maritime research, the growing Bartlett Library contains 10,000 reference books and a collection of Falmouth harbour records.

Outdoor exhibits vary, but the racing keelboat of the Dragon class, *Bluebottle*, owned by the Queen and once raced by Prince Philip is on display. Also, there is *Suhaili*, the 30ft ketch in which Sir Robin Knox Johnston made the world's first single-handed non-stop circumnavigation, sailing from Falmouth back to Falmouth in 1968/9.

The stated aim of this museum is to '...*promote an understanding of boats and their place in people's lives, to inspire new boat design and to promote an understanding of the maritime heritage of Cornwall'*. Few would doubt they have achieved it.

FROM FALMOUTH TO MOUNT'S BAY

In the lee of the Lizard peninsula we see a scattering of hamlets and fishing communities gaining shelter from the ever-present westerly winds. Helford River continues its link with the oyster fishery. Yachtsmen, who take the shallow channel as far as Gweek, will find oyster beds on either side of them. While nearby Falmouth represents commercial bustle, Frenchman's Creek lies as undisturbed as when Daphne du Maurier was first inspired by it. The village of Helford is the same place that it was when small craft came here to load tin.

South of the Helford River, lie the treacherous Manacle rocks, awash at high water, jagged and unforgiving. Inland, at St Keverne, the octagonal spire has served as a guiding landmark for over 350 years. 'Manacles' derives from the Cornish word *men eglos*, meaning stone church, and so a place of worship on this spot may well have provided a landmark for many years longer than the present spire. The treachery of the Manacles is underlined by the fact that 400 victims of shipwrecks are buried in this churchyard.

The Lizard and the wreckers

'Tis a bad wind that blows no good for Cornwall'

When it was first proposed in the early 17th century that a light should be established on the Lizard to provide a warning of this dangerous, rock-bound headland, the people of Cornwall were far from pleased. Shipwreck, they believed, was an unavoidable part of life for a seafaring community. And many locals survived on the income from looting ships which came to grief on their rocky shores.

Cornwall has always had an ambivalent view of shipwreck – half disaster, half blessing. The story goes that in the middle of a Cornish church service, the church doors opened and a figure entered, crying, ' a shipwreck!'. At this point, the clergyman took to the pulpit and begged his congregation not to be too hasty, and instead to give him time to remove his cloak so that he, too, could keep up with the race to be first on the scene.

It is possible that ships were sometimes guided to their doom by the exhibition of false lights; there is a widely quoted tale of the lantern that was fastened to the rear end of a cow, which was then encouraged to walk, in a confusing way, backwards and forwards along the cliff edge. Legend also has it that at Sennen Cove, just to the north of Lands End, wreckers invaded the lighthouse, kidnapped the keeper and extinguished the light. However, they had not reckoned with his young daughter who relit the tall light by standing on the family bible.

Old habits die hard: only a few years ago, a timber-carrying ship went aground on the Cornish shore spilling her load of timber. Once again the instinct rose up and soon the beach was crowded with looters, hauling away their spoils. Was wrecking ever approved of? It is true that in Cornwall's entire history, only one man has ever been found guilty of the crime.

Some of the many shipwrecks on the Cornish coast.
ABOVE: *The three-masted schooner Bessie, 4 March 1912.*
LEFT: *The Skopolos broken in two, 13 March 1980.* PHOTOS ©
RICHARD LARN. BELOW: *The Mary Barrow, driven ashore on
Porthminster Beach, 8 January 1908.* PHOTO © FRANK GIBSON.

Fishing vessels in Newlyn harbour, with St Michael's Mount in the background. PHOTO COURTESY OF WWW.VIEWSOFCORNWALL.COM.

MOUNT'S BAY

The last bay in Britain before the Atlantic is a busier place than you might imagine. This is a working coastline, with the fishing fleet at Newlyn doing as well as can be expected, given the prevailing state of the fish stocks and the burden of regulation. This was the scene of a riot in 1896 when the locals rose up against the east coast fishermen who used to come to their waters to fish on Sundays when Cornishmen stayed ashore. It took the militia to settle that one.

The large white satellite dishes on Goonhilly Down, north of the Lizard, are reminders that this was an important place in the development of transatlantic communication. The **Telegraph Museum** is at Porthcurno, and it was from the Lizard in 1901 that Marconi first made a radio link with the Isle of Wight before attempting a transatlantic transmission.

From Penzance sails the *Scillonian* – the ship which links the mainland with the Isles of Scilly, and although the town has a fine, locked harbour, it has never been a port with major commercial significance, but rather more a market town which looks to the rural hinterland for support. However, here you will find the **National Lighthouse Museum** displaying the inner workings of gas and oil lights, fog horns, buoys and all the apparatus of navigation which has been the business of Trinity House since the times of the Tudors.

The building which houses this museum formed Trinity House's buoy store, and from here repairs were carried out, and buoys replaced, throughout the west coast of England. The now listed building was first acquired in 1860 at the time of the building of the offshore lighthouse on Wolf Rock, and here granite stones were cut, prepared and stored for shipping to the construction site. The automating of lighthouses, and the use of more efficient means of providing light sources, has meant that lighthouse equipment in recent years has become redundant. Much historic equipment would have been lost had it not been collected and preserved here. The optics, the rotating prisms which concentrate a comparatively weak light into a strong flashing beam, are almost works of art. One of the largest ever constructed – for the Bishop Rock – is on display. When the keepers left and the furniture was removed from St Catherine's light (Isle of Wight), it was brought here to reconstruct a lighthouse kitchen.

A point of interest about lighthouses is that they do not actually flash. Although from a distance they might appear to flash, what you are really seeing is a narrow, revolving beam of light which crosses your field of vision. On a misty night, the concentrated rays of light can sometimes look like fingers scanning the horizon. Also, the actual light in the centre of the glass optic, or lens, can be quite small. There may only be the equivalent of five domestic bulbs of 100 watts at the heart of quite a powerful lighthouse.

A traditional toast in Cornish fishing villages:

Here's a health to the Pope,
And may he repent,
And lengthen by six months
The term of his Lent.
Its always declared
Betwixt the two poles,
There's nothing like pilchards
For saving of souls.

■ Cornwall and the pilchard

Pilchards were caught in Cornwall in huge quantities; one harbour recording a total catch of 24 million pilchards in 1907. The method used a gigantic net to surround a shoal which was then winched inshore and emptied into wicker baskets. The processing of the catch was carried out in factories ashore, the sole survivor being the **Pilchard Works** at Newlyn (a working factory and visitor centre) where pilchards are still preserved in salt in the traditional way.

Star-gazy Pie

This famous dish is a product of a Mousehole legend. One Christmas this tiny fishing village, to the south of Newlyn, found itself on the point of starvation as stormy weather had prevented the fishermen from going to sea. Selflessly, local hero Tom Bawcock braved the storm, regardless of his own safety. On his return, his little craft had to surf the waves in a storm more fierce than any in living memory. Ever since, Tom Bawcock's Eve has been celebrated in this village on the night before Christmas Eve. A dish is served which consists of a pastry crust from which peer the heads of seven different kinds of fish – representing Tom's catch. This has become the emblem of this selfless, heroic act which saved the village from starvation.

PORTHCURNO, LAND'S END

If your aim is to transmit messages across the oceans of the world by underwater cable, then it makes sense to have your sending station as close to the sea possible – hence this remarkably placed communications centre near Land's End, now the **Telegraph Museum**.

The pioneer technicians who came to this wild and rugged part of Cornwall in 1870 had little idea that they were laying the foundations for the modern internet, or that during WWII the messages they were handling would be of such strategic importance that the building was moved underground into fortified tunnels.

The first cable laid here in 1869 linked Cornwall with Bombay. Falmouth was the first choice of station, but it was thought that ships'

Inside the cable house, Porthcurno. PHOTO COURTESY OF THE TELEGRAPH MUSEUM.

Working displays. PHOTO COURTESY OF THE TELEGRAPH MUSEUM.

anchors would inevitably foul the fragile cable. Instead, the cable made its way across the sandy beach to the landing at Porthcurno where telegraph operators sat at their mahogany desks listening to the Morse code clicks. This grew to a major station and eventually 14 cables came ashore here.

Gathering the messages, which were unamplified, was no easy task. The signal had travelled 2000 miles from Newfoundland before arriving at Porthcurno and even then was only detectable with the most sensitive of magnetic needles. The operator was required to watch the movements of the needle, which corresponded to a code, and shout out the letter to someone who wrote the message down.

The telegraph station had a good run, until December 1901 when Marconi's famous three dots, sent by radio, were received in New-foundland. It was thought that cables would soon become obsolete. This proved not to be the case, and submarine cables still remain an important part of the world's communication network. Porthcurno therefore, has a distinguished place in its history.

Land's End. PHOTO COURTESY OF SOUTH-WEST TOURISM.

ISLES OF SCILLY _____

If you happen to be safely ashore in the mild weather that often shrouds these islands, then you might reasonably think yourself to be in a little bit of heaven. But if you should be at sea, uncertain of your position, with a gale blowing, these rocky outcrops form the most dangerous reef on the British coastline. They are well marked, of course, by the Bishop Rock lighthouse, but this was not built till the mid 1800s. To the east of them, in the middle of the busy shipping lane around Land's End is the Sevenstones reef, marked by what is regarded as the most exposed lightship station in the world.

Before any of these navigation aids were built, shipwreck was a common occurrence. Sir Cloudsley Shovell's fleet was wrecked here in 1707 in the worst peace-time disaster in Naval history. On Tresco, at the island's famous gardens, there is a collection of some 30 ships' figureheads, known as the **Valhalla Collection**. These have been collected from stricken merchant ships at the suggestion of the 'Lord Proprietor' of the islands, Augustus Smith, in 1840.

Figurehead from HMS Ajax. PHOTO COURTESY OF NATIONAL MARITIME MUSEUM.

■ The gigs of Scilly and Cornwall

Now a competitive sport, gig-racing has its origins in the days when pilots would wait in their gigs in the shelter of the Scilly Isles before boarding ships and bringing them safely to harbour. Scilly pilots were thought to be amongst the best in the region and their knowledge of the intricate tides around the Cornish coast was invaluable. Needless to say, it was not uncommon for the gigs to also be used to obtain salvage from wrecks. They were built for speed and swift movement through the water with the minimum of effort. Traditionally, they were built from Cornish elm, were 23 feet in length and carried 8 thwarts, or seats.

Scilly is host to the World Pilot Gig Championships which attracts entries of about 100 gigs from Faroe, Holland and Ireland, as well as Cornwall.

Portland, Plymouth Gazetteer

Museum of Net Manufacture
Bridgeacre, Uploaders, Bridport, Dorset DT6 4PF
☎ +44 (0)1308 485349
OPEN By appointment

Bridport Museum
South Street, Bridport, Dorset DT6 3NR
www.bridportmuseum.co.uk
CORRESPONDENCE TO Bridport Museum Trust, The Coach House, Gundry Lane, Bridport, Dorset DT6 3RJ
☎ +44 (0) 01308 458703
OPEN Apr–Oct: Mon–Sat 10:00–17:00

Topsham Museum
25 The Strand, Topsham, Exeter, Devon EX3 0AX
☎ +44 (0)1392 873244
www.devonmuseums.net
OPEN Mon, Wed, Sat, pm only, Easter–Oct; also Sun Jun–Sept

Teignmouth & Shaldon Museum and Historical Society
29 French Street, Teignmouth, Devon TQ14 8ST
☎ +44 (0)1626 777041; (862265: Curator AH)
www.devonmuseums.net
OPEN Daily

Brixham Heritage Museum
The Old Police Station, Bolton Cross, Brixham, Devon TQ5 8LZ
☎ +44 (0)1803 856267
www.brixhamheritage.org.uk
OPEN Feb–Easter: weekdays 10.00–13.00. Easter–Oct: Mon–Fri 10.00–17.00, Sat 10.00–13.00

Dartmouth Museum
The Butterwalk, Dartmouth, Devon TQ6 9PZ
☎ +44 (0)1803 832923
www.devonmuseums.net
OPEN Mon–Sat. Apr–end Oct: 11:00–16:30; winter: 12:00–15:00

Britannia Royal Naval College
Dartmouth, Devon TQ6 0HJ
☎ +44 (0)1803 834224 (tours); 677787 (GV); 677233/677247 (Museum)
www.royal-navy.mod.uk/static/pages/1949.html
OPEN BA only. Guided tours via Dartmouth Tourist Office, or GV BA

Lulworth Cove, Dorset.
© DORSET COUNTY COUNCIL.

Salcombe Maritime Museum
Old Town Hall, Market Street, Salcombe, Devon TQ8 8DE
☎ +44 (0)1548 843080
www.salcombeinformation.co.uk/active.htm
OPEN Daily, Easter–31 Oct

Overbecks Museum and Garden
Sharpitor, Salcombe, Devon TQ8 8LW
☎ +44 (0)1548 842893
www.devon-calling.com/nt/overbecks.htm
OPEN Sun–Fri, Apr–Jun; daily in Aug; Sun–Thur Sept & Oct

Ship model from Dartmouth Museum. © DARTMOUTH MUSEUM.

Plymouth Naval Base Visitor Centre
(Incorporating the Plymouth Naval Base Museum) HM Naval Base, South Yard, Devonport, Plymouth, Devon PL2 2BG
☎ +44 (0)1752 554200
www.royal-navy.mod.uk/static/pages/5300.html
OPEN GV (BA): telephone to arrange guided tour of Base & South Yard

Fishing boats in Dartmouth harbour. © DEVON COUNTY COUNCIL.

Smeaton's Tower
The Hoe, Plymouth, Devon
Correspondence to: City of
Plymouth Museums & Art
Gallery, Plymouth Dome,
The Hoe, Plymouth, Devon
PL1 2NZ (☎ 01752-603300)
☎ +44 (0)1752 600608,
668000
FAX +44 (0)1752 256361
www.plymouthdome.info
/index.cfm?fsa=dspsmeaton
OPEN Daily in summer. Enquire
about winter opening

Plymouth City Museum and Art Gallery
Drake Circus, Plymouth,
Devon PL4 8AJ
☎ +44 (0)1752 304774
www.plymouthmuseum.
gov.uk
OPEN Tue–Sat, also BH Mon

Plymouth National Marine Aquarium
Fishquay, The Barbican,
Plymouth, Devon PL4 0LH
☎ +44 (0)1752 600301
www.national-aquarium.
co. uk
OPEN Daily (except Christmas
Day)

Cotehele Quay Museum
Cotehele Quay, St Dominick,
Saltash, Cornwall PL12 6TA
☎ +44 (0)1579 350830.
www.nmm.ac.uk
OPEN Daily, Apr–Oct
Educational programme
anytime BA

Shipwreck and Heritage Centre
Quay Road, Charlestown, St
Austell, Cornwall PL25 3NJ
☎ +44 (0)1726 69897
www.shipwreckcharlestown.
com
OPEN Daily, 1 Mar–31 Oct

Mevagissey Folk Museum
East Quay, Inner Harbour,
Mevagissey, Cornwall
☎ +44 (0)1726 843568
www.mevagissey.net/
museum.htm
OPEN Daily, Easter–Oct

National Maritime Museum Cornwall
Discovery Quay, Falmouth,
Cornwall TR11 3QY
☎ +44 (0)1326 313388
www.nmmc.co.uk
OPEN Daily, from 10:00

Trinity House National Lighthouse Museum
Wharf Road, Penzance,
Cornwall
☎ +44 (0)1736 360077
www.lighthousecentre.
org.uk
OPEN Daily, Easter–Oct;
evenings BA

Museum of Submarine Telegraphy
Porthcurno (near Land's End)
Cornwall
☎ +44 (0)1736 810966
www.porthcurno.org.uk
OPEN Sun–Fri + BH Sats;
Apr–2 Nov (daily July &
Aug). Sun, Mon winter

Valhalla Collection
Valhalla, the Ships'
Figurehead Collection,
Tresco Estate,
Isles of Scilly
☎ +44 (0)1720 422849
FAX +44 (0)1720 422807
OPEN Daily from 10:00
ADMISSION £8.50 adults,
under 14s free (includes
entrance to the Tropical
Gardens)

Helford River, Cornwall.
© SOUTH-WEST TOURISM.

BA: By arrangement
BH: Bank holiday
GV: Group visits

Ferry across the Mersey. PHOTO COURTESY OF THE MERSEY PARTNERSHIP (TMP) WWW.VISITLIVERPOOL.COM.

LUNDY,
IRISH SEA

**From Land's End to Solway Firth
including the Isle of Man**

- Padstow ■ Bude
- Appledore and Bideford
- Ilfracombe ■ Watchet
- Bristol ■ Monmouth
- Tenby ■ Milford Haven
- Cardigan Bay
- Birkenhead ■ Liverpool
- Lytham ■ Morecombe
- Fleetwood
- Barrow-in-Furness
- Whitehaven ■ Maryport
- Isle of Man

Bedruthan Steps on the North Cornish coast. PHOTO © WWW.VIEWSOFCORNWALL.COM.

Sea area 'Lundy', known as the Bristol Channel, has also been called the 'Wrong Channel' due to the deceptive way a ship might think itself sailing the length of the south coast of England, when it was really heading for the dead end past Bristol. The tidal range here is enormous – amongst the largest to be found anywhere in the world. This creates the famous Severn Bore as the incoming tide effectively tries to overtake itself, creating a moving wall of water in the process.

For ships entering the Bristol Channel in the days of less precise navigation, the room for error was small, the shelter sparse, especially on the iron-bound northern coasts of Cornwall and Devon which has no harbour of refuge.

Two of Britain's major harbours are found in these waters, at Bristol and Liverpool, and much of Britain's maritime trading history with the Americas and Ireland was conducted from here. The major port of Milford Haven is of modern importance, being a deep water harbour which can safely house massive crude oil carriers.

> *'From Padstow Point to Lundy Light*
> *Is a sailor's grave by day or night'* (TRAD)

THE CORNISH COAST

None of the coastline from Cape Cornwall to Hartland Point affords much shelter for the hard-pressed mariner. St Ives, although an inspiration for artists and a delight to stroll through on a fine Cornish day, is exposed and provides only moderate shelter for the small, inshore fishing fleet. Hayle was once the busiest port in Cornwall in the late 18th century, engaged in the export of tin, copper and coal and from where a packet steamer to Bristol operated in the 1830s. Industrial decline meant inevitable maritime decline.

Newquay has reinvented for itself the maritime leisure industry centred around the Atlantic surf. But this was once an important centre from which local ships traded with America, and where fishing, smuggling and mineral exports were part of a thriving trade. The Huer's House, or fishermen's watch tower, reminds you that on this northern Cornish coast the pilchard was of such significance that it was worth posting a lookout – the huer – to watch the seas for signs of a shoal. As a result of one man's watchfulness, a single catch in the 1860s was large enough to fill 1,000 carts and provide the fishermen with the modern equivalent of a lottery win.

PADSTOW

Padstow has been a fishing port since the 6th century after St Petroc crossed the sea from Wales and founded a monastery. **The Padstow Museum**, just yards from the harbour, tells the vivid maritime history of the town which was at its peak in the 19th century; the harbour was developed, the piers improved, and shipyards, which launched 29 ships in the 1860s, provided employment for the town. The museum houses a collection of traditional boat-building tools.

Padstow was also the scene of large-scale emigration in the 19th century when both the major local industries of mining and farming became depressed. Ships left from here bound for Quebec, the emigrants having to supply

Padstow harbour. PHOTO © WWW.VIEWSOFCORNWALL.COM.

their own food for the crossing. The ships returned from Canada loaded with timber which fed the shipyards. The coming of iron ships, however, was bad news for the timber craftsmen of Padstow, and fishing again became important, as the town became a base for North Sea trawlers passing through these waters.

The entrance to Padstow harbour requires sailors to pass over the most menacingly named sandbanks to be found anywhere in Britain – the Doom Bar.

THE BUDE CANAL

The maritime history of this town, told in the **Bude Stratton Museum**, is centred around an audacious attempt to cross from the Bristol Channel to the English Channel by canal along a route starting at Bude then via the Tamar to Plymouth 90 miles away. It wasn't intended to be merely a trading route: the beach sands at Bude were particularly rich in lime, and the canal would be a convenient way of transporting the sands inland to provide valuable fertiliser for the poor, acidic soils of inland Cornwall.

Of course, such a canal met with considerable geographical difficulties: instead of locks it was intended to build inclines up which barges, or tub boats, would be hauled. The canal only reached as far as Launceston, and the hugely complex inclined planes provided frequent breakdowns. The railway arrived in 1898, and although the harbour was used for some sea trade, it became difficult to navigate and ships took their business elsewhere. The canal is now a haven for pleasure craft.

Sea lock at the end of Bude canal. PHOTO COURTESY OF VIEWSOFCORNWALL.COM.

The Rev Hawker of Morwenstow

The village of Morwenstow, between Bude and Hartland Point, provides one of the least attractive prospects in Britain – to the stranded seafarer. The beauty of the village gives no hint of the treacherous coastal cliffs, and the peace of the wooded valleys gives no clue that an endless succession of ships have been dashed on these unforgiving shores. The wrecks, as elsewhere in Cornwall, were always a mixed blessing because the looting provided a valuable income for the hard-pressed coastal community.

But the vicar of Morwenstow, the Reverend Robert Stephen Hawker (1830–1875) took it as his Christian duty to recover sailors' bodies, and give them a Christian burial even at some risk to his own life. He was a true eccentric who once teased his parishioners by dressing as a mermaid and sitting on an offshore rock. When a crowd gathered, he stood up to reveal his true identity, and then sang the National Anthem. He is also credited with the invention of the harvest festival tradition and wrote 'The Song of the Western Men' which has become a Cornish anthem.

THE SONG OF THE WESTERN MEN

A good sword and a trusty hand!
A merry heart and true!
King James's men shall understand
What Cornish lads can do.

And have they fix'd the where and when?
And shall Trelawny die?
Here's twenty thousand Cornish men
Will know the reason why!

Out spake their captain brave and bold,
A merry wight was he:
"If London Tower were Michael's hold,
We'll set Trelawny free!

"We'll cross the Tamar, land to land,
The Severn is no stay,
With 'one and all,' and hand in hand,
And who shall bid us nay?

"And when we come to London Wall,
A pleasant sight to view,
Come forth! come forth, ye cowards all,
Here's men as good as you!

"Trelawny he's in keep and hold,
Trelawny he may die;
But here's twenty thousand Cornish bold,
Will know the reason why!"

Hartland Point. PHOTO COURTESY OF WEST COUNTRY VIEWS.

HARTLAND POINT AND HARTLAND QUAY

The Romans called the severe headland of Hartland Point '*the promontory of Hercules*'. Any ships that was stranded here faced certain destruction. It was somewhat defiant, then, of three of England's most famous navigators – Sir Francis Drake, Sir Walter Raleigh, and Sir John Hawkins, to finance the building of a harbour at Hartland Quay, to the south of the headland in order to provide some refuge on this inhospitable coastline.

The **Hartland Quay Museum** is located in the upper rooms of what were once the thriving harbour buildings, used by coastguards and dock workers when this was a thriving port. The museum admits to being small, but is packed, inevitably, with the tales of local shipwrecks, and the story of the disappearance of the quay in a gale in 1887.

APPLEDORE AND BIDEFORD

At Appledore you find a marine industry which has neither slipped into history, nor survives solely to feed the tourism. This may have been a fishing village since Anglo-Saxon times, granted freedom by Elizabeth I for the part it played in defeating the Spanish armada, but today it boasts the largest covered shipbuilding yard (at the time of its opening) in Europe. At Appledore Shipbuilders, they build bulk carriers, supply-vessels, and ocean survey ships to the highest of modern standards. They also built a full sized replica of a Roman galley, and a replica of Sir Francis Drake's *Golden Hind*.

The North Devon Maritime Museum, in a fine listed building, is packed with ship models, and tales of local wreck and rescue. This museum is run by the energetic North Devon Museum Trust who have received many awards for their work. This is also an important resource centre for written archive material and photographic collections. Most recent addition is an Appledore Salmon Boat. These were traditionally burnt on the death of their owner, but this one has survived and is now being restored by a museum volunteer who remembers building it as an apprentice in 1948.

Bideford Quay. PHOTO COURTESY OF WEST COUNTRY VIEWS.

Further along the banks of the River Torridge lies Bideford. Occasionally used by small coasters, this port was built in the 17th century to maintain an import trade in wool between England and Spain. A plaque in the parish church celebrates the life of Sir Richard Grenville who died in 1591 from wounds received after a battle with 15 Spanish galleons off the Azores. This episode was the inspiration for Tennyson's poem, *The Revenge.*

THE REVENGE

At Flores in the Azores Sir Richard Grenville lay,
And a pinnace, like a fluttered bird, came flying from far away:
"Spanish ships of war at sea! we have sighted fifty-three!"
Then sware Lord Thomas Howard: "Fore God I am no coward;
But I cannot meet them here, for my ships are out of gear,
And the half my men are sick. I must fly, but follow quick.
We are six ships of the line; can we fight with fifty-three?"

Then spake Sir Richard Grenville: "I know you are no coward;
You fly them for a moment to fight with them again.
But I've ninety men and more that are lying sick ashore.
I should count myself the coward if I left them, my Lord Howard,
To these Inquisition dogs and the devildoms of Spain."

The SV Kathleen and May. PHOTO COURTESY OF WWW.KATHLEEN-AND-MAY.CO.UK.

■ The SV *Kathleen and May*

This unique three-masted sailing schooner was the very last of the sailing merchant schooners to be registered in Britain. After a career spent largely trading across the Irish Sea, she retired in 1960 and was laid up on the River Torridge. Only after her discovery by the Duke of Edinburgh did a full restoration take place. She has since been in display in London, at St Katherine's Dock, but Bideford is now her home.

The Paintings of Reuben Chappell

Chappell (1870–1940) divided his time between Goole in Yorkshire and Par in Cornwall, specialising in ship portraiture. His paintings were usually of smaller ships, drawn with great accuracy and without missing a single detail; they often sailed on a similarly coloured sea with a glimpse of land in the distance, and another ship on the horizon. Two important collections of his work are held in north Devon: one at the Commodore Hotel in Instow, the other at the Brampton Parish Council Offices where enquires should be directed to the Parish clerk.

Ilfracombe harbour. PHOTO © WEST COUNTRY VIEWS.

ILFRACOMBE

The Victorians turned this town into a resort, but the protection provided by the cliffs have made this a useful little harbour for generations of fishermen, and those who were later engaged in the 'tripper trade' between north Devon and Wales. This is also the closest mainland harbour to the offshore island of Lundy. From here the 'Lundy Packets' regularly sailed carrying mail and supplies to the small community. The **Ilfracombe Museum**, housed in the former laundry of the splendid Ilfracombe Hotel, describes itself as *'a cross between an Edwardian collector's study and granny's attic'*. Most recently opened is the Lundy Island Room.

WATCHET

At Watchet, they celebrate the 'flattie', a remarkable local craft which was built in many shapes and sizes but all based on a fundamental design of a small, double-ended boat with no keel. One hundred years ago, fleets of flatties operated from the Somerset shores, but only one

This is the 'flattie', built in the 1930s, that initiated the museum. Watchet enthusiasts renovated it and sailed it at the Festival of the Sea, Bristol in 1996. PHOTO COURTESY OF WATCHET BOAT MUSEUM.

original survives in sailing condition and is in the care of the Friends of the Flatners, and on display at the **Watchet Boat Museum**.

To be a true flatner, the boat needs to have been built to a precise specification. For a start, it must carry a spritsail rig, rather uncommon in English waters although used on a grander scale by the Thames barges. These boats had no keels and used a centreboard, although some early craft may have used leeboards. The flatties were clinker built, generally using nine-inch planks.

Like so many of the traditional craft of Britain, the flatner was ideally suited for the waters in which it was to sail: the double ends made it useful in the steep seas of the Bristol Channel when trying to make headway against them. The shallow draft gave easy beach launching in a region where a huge tidal range gave rise to many drying harbours. The lightness of the boats helped in poor breezes.

The flatners, came in three 'styles': turf boats which carried peat from the Somerset levels to local markets where they operated more like a barge; the River Boats were about 20 feet long and were used for fishing, particularly for salmon. The sea boats were the largest at 23 feet; they carried a jib and a longer rudder, and worked the breadth of the Bristol Channel carrying both coal and sheep from Wales.

The first flatners were used on the Somerset levels to carry peat and withies to market.

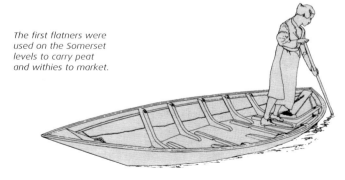

BRISTOL

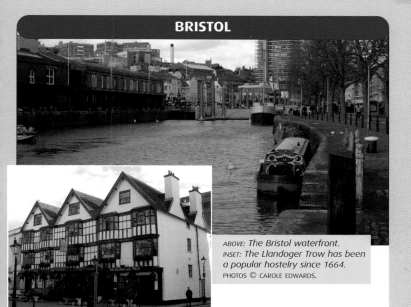

ABOVE: *The Bristol waterfront.*
INSET: *The Llandoger Trow has been a popular hostelry since 1664.*
PHOTOS © CAROLE EDWARDS.

The city is hardly well situated to become one of the major ports of Britain – once the third largest town in England in the 14th century after London and York. It stands six miles from the sea, although a long haul is then still necessary before reaching open waters. The Avon is a hugely tidal river, and before the provision of a 'floating dock' in 1809, the tide caused a distinct shortage of water at Bristol for much of the working day. None of these disadvantages were shared by Liverpool, and the two ports have often been engaged in fierce competition for business, particularly in the slave trade era.

The Bristol waterfront has been used as a setting by many writers of maritime fiction: a fine, half-timbered inn standing in King Street, the Llandoger Trow, is said to be the 'Spyglass Inn' in Robert Louis Stevenson's *Treasure Island*, and the *Hispaniola* set sail from the quayside a few yards from the inn. Also, it may have been where Daniel Defoe met Alexander Selkirk – the castaway whose story was to form the basis of *Robinson Crusoe*. The Llandoger Trow, which gives the inn its name, is the name of a coastal craft, once common off the shores of Wales.

■ The Voyage of John Cabot

A major boost to Bristol's fortunes was provided in 1497 by John Cabot, a Venetian navigator who, like so many merchants at the time, was seeking new and quicker ways to trade with the Far East. Such voyages of exploration needed sponsorship, and Cabot's first thought was to turn to Spain. But the voyage of Christopher Columbus to the West Indies in 1492 (then believed to be part of Asia) meant the Spaniards had little inclination towards more exploration, for they thought they had found their route to the Orient.

Replica of the Matthew.
PHOTO © PAUL FRANKS.

The English crown and the Bristol merchants were keener on supporting Cabot, and in 1496, King Henry VII issued orders to Cabot to sail '*to discover and investigate, whatsoever islands, countries, regions or provinces of heathens and infidels, in whatsoever part of the world placed, which before this time were unknown to all Christians.*' After an initial voyage in 1496, during which he was forced to return to Bristol, he sailed in 1497 aboard the *Matthew* and 35 days later raised the English flag on an unknown land claiming it to be his New Found Land.

A replica of Cabot's ship *Matthew* celebrated the 500th anniversary of his voyage in 1997 by crossing the Atlantic to Newfoundland. She is a now a familiar sight in Bristol, where she was built, and people can book voyages aboard her along the west coast of Britain.

■ Isambard Kingdom Brunel

The influence left on Bristol by this 19th century engineering genius is remarkable. He called his Clifton Suspension Bridge his 'first love and darling', having been only 25 when he won the competition to design it. It was not completed, however, until five years after his death.

Brunel's work on the Floating Harbour undoubtedly added to the city's prosperity. The uncontrolled rise and fall of tide here caused huge stress to ships

Brunel. PHOTO © NATIONAL MARITIME MUSEUM.

The Clifton Bridge. PHOTO © CAROLE EDWARDS.

moored in Bristol as, twice a day, their hulls came to rest of the bed of the river. The expression, '*ship shape and Bristol fashion*' describes a ship able to take this punishment to its structure. The damming of the river enabled ships to remain afloat, but did not provide any way in which foul, sewage-infested water could escape. Brunel was approached for a solution, and in 1832 he designed a series of sluices called the Underfall. A Brunel-designed dredger, or 'dragboat' worked alongside these to remove the silt. A similar craft, the *Bertha*, built by Brunel, is thought to be the oldest existing steam-driven ship in the world.

At the **Bristol Industrial Museum** you are presented with a working picture of Bristol and its docks far removed from the romance of Cabot and distant waters. This is the industrial face of Bristol and the Museum is located in an old transit shed by the floating dock. There are 700 exhibits here and the slave trade, conducted through this harbour between Britain, Africa and the Caribbean is described (see also Liverpool). But in this museum, which one visitor said was 'the best kept secret in Bristol', there are also five dockside Fairburn Steam cranes, a steam railway and three historic vessels.

The steam tug *Mayflower* (1861), the motor tug *John King* (1935), and the fire-float *Pyronaut* (1934) are the workhorses of this harbour, and while having none of the pedigree of *Matthew* or SS *Great Britain*, they have every reason to be proud of the contribution they have made to Bristol's maritime importance. They are on display here.

SS *Great Britain*

Of all Brunel's gifts to Bristol, the SS *Great Britain* is possibly the most impressive of all. Every ship since her launch has been influenced by her: she is the grand-mummy of them all. After she was launched in 1843, the ideas about how ships should be built and propelled changed forever.

Amazingly, until 1970 she had been discarded and left to rot in the Falkland Islands. Had she eventually succumbed to rust and waves we would have lost the world's first iron-hulled, screw driven, steam powered passenger liner – the largest ship of her day. She broke barriers to world travel, proved new ways of ship construction. She is an impressive example from the golden age of Victorian engineering.

Like many such ground-breaking ideas, this ship was a scientific marvel if something of a commercial failure. She was originally conceived as a paddle steamer, but the new technology of screw propulsion was gaining ground and her engines were modified to drive a massive 16 foot iron propeller. At 100 feet longer than her rivals, she was expected to carry 250 passengers and 130 crew.

Only three years after launching, passengers were in short supply, and after running aground in Dundrum Bay in Northern Ireland, her engines were severely damaged. Under new ownership she was revitalised, rebuilt, and did brisk trade taking emigrants to Australia to pursue the gold rush. She was much modified with a new engine, changes to her superstructure, and a new rig. Later, she was to serve as a troop ship taking 45,000 British and French soldiers to the Crimea in 1854. Amazingly, in the late 1870s, she was deemed no longer fit to carry passengers and her engines were removed and replaced with a tried and tested three-masted sailing rig. The most innovative engine-driven ship of all time, had been robbed of her pride.

Launch of the SS Great Britain *in 1843.* PHOTO COURTESY OF SS GREAT BRITAIN TRUST.

SS *Great Britain*

After a rough trip around Cape Horn carrying Welsh coal to San Francisco, she returned to the Falklands where she was sold as a hulk and used as a coal barge. There she remained in a rotting state until rescue came in 1970. In her career which spanned 45 years, she sailed a million miles and was once described as the 'greyhound of the seas'. She is now at rest in the dry dock in which she was built.

SS Great Britain, *in Bristol dry dock*. PHOTO COURTESY OF SS GREAT BRITAIN TRUST.

The Industrial Museum.
PHOTO © PAUL FRANKS.

The **Bristol Maritime Heritage Centre** is next to the SS *Great Britain*, and the *Matthew* (when in harbour) acts as a gateway for visitors to these two ships. The museum stands on the site of Hill's old shipyard and many of the exhibits relate to the ships which were built here arranged around the hull of a Brunel-designed dredger *BD6* – now used as a cinema – which had a long working life and was used in Bristol as recently as the 1950s. Before Hill, the shipyard was owned by James Hillhouse who engaged in building ships for the slave trade. He was also a major investor in slaving and left £30,000 on his death, making him more than a millionaire by modern standards. He was also engaged in the building of small warships for the Royal Navy and on display here is a reconstruction of such a vessel.

The Bristol Channel pilot cutter

These were the monarchs of the Western Approaches, built to be at sea in any weather, and operated from all the major harbours. Scilly had its own fleet, given its favourable position.

The pilot cutter was a stoutly built craft, usually around 40 feet, but cutters as large as 60 feet long were built. They were gaffed-rigged and designed for speed. Pilotage was a competitive business where the first man on board got the lucrative job. And since they were never built to carry cargo, they were built around the needs of the crews. This created a ship that was comfortable at sea and is the reason that they have survived as yachts. The intrepid sailor and mountaineer, Bill Tilman, valued their sturdiness and speed. The design has proved enduring and many modern replicas have been built. The pilots themselves were considered a race apart; fiercely proud, competitive and often a law unto themselves.

Aerial views of the waterfront and marina. PHOTOS © CAROLE EDWARDS.

© NATIONAL MARITIME MUSEUM.
Captain Horatio Nelson.

MONMOUTH – The Nelson Museum

Horatio Nelson may have been born in Norfolk, made his name at Trafalgar, and been buried in St Paul's Cathedral, but in the unlikely setting of this border town of Monmouth you find a remarkable collection representing his life and loves. The collection was started by Lady Llangattock, a member of the local Rolls family which became half of the Rolls-Royce partnership.

This is regarded as one of the major Nelson collections in Britain. Ignoring Nelson's glass eye (admitted by the museum to be just one of many fakes) there is remarkable written material, much of it personal, including Lady Nelson's last letter to her husband pleading with him to return to her from Emma Hamilton. However, given the prose which Nelson lavished on Emma, it is clear that Lady Nelson was engaged in a lost cause:

'*My Dearest Emma, your letter of yesterday naturally called forth all those finer feelings of the Soul which none but those who regard each other as you & I can ever evince. Although I am not able to write so much and so forcibly mark my feelings as you can yet I am sure I feel all the affection which is possible for man to feel towards woman and such a Woman.*' – Nelson writing in July 1801.

Not all the letters here are love letters – there is correspondence between Nelson, Hardy, and Collingwood which together give remarkable insights. Nelson's fighting sword is also on display here.

THE MARITIME HISTORY OF SOUTH WALES

Opening in 2005 is the **National Waterfront Museum** combining the collections housed in the former **Swansea Maritime Museum** and at Cardiff.

Coal has been the major influence on the maritime centres along this stretch of coast from Cardiff to Milford Haven. The industrial boom brought about by the use of steam meant that the particular brand of coal found in the South Wales coal fields, known as 'steam coal' for the amount of heat it produced, was in huge demand. Until then, the harbours of Newport, Cardiff and Swansea had been of little importance other than to local fishermen and traders – these were never major maritime centres, like Bristol or Falmouth.

Tugs and cranes at Swansea. PHOTO © PHOTOLIBRARY WALES.

The expansion of the coal trade took place in the first two decades of the 1800s when investors saw a huge opportunity to expand Cardiff docks to accommodate ships of increasing size. In 1839 the Marquis of Bute linked the docks to the pitheads and ironworks by a direct rail link, bringing further expansion, until at the end of the 19th century, it could claim to be one of premier coal ports of the world.

The town of Barry was created entirely to service the needs of the coal industry, and after the construction of a £2 million harbour it also broke records in coal exporting as the village population swelled from just 87 people to 13,000 in a handful of years. Swansea was also shaken to its roots by the coal trade. Before the industrial revolution it had been a quiet little harbour on the River Tawe; but copper smelting, zinc and tin plate works, as well as coal, turned a rural coastal community into a vast industrial landscape within 50 years.

But the boom evaporated almost as fast as it had it appeared, and after WWII, there was a rapid industrial decline along this entire coast. The themes here now are of regeneration, and restoration.

Tenby in 1586. IMAGE COURTESY OF TENBY MUSEUM AND ART GALLERY.

TENBY

As far removed from the Welsh industrial landscape as it is possible to be, Tenby has Georgian and Regency buildings overlooking one of the prettiest harbours on the west coast.

The town's commanding position over Carmarthen Bay made it an ideal location for a protective castle, built in the 12th century, but which fell to Cromwell in 1644 after a fierce battle and attack from both land and sea. The **Tenby Museum and Art Gallery** is housed in the castle's remains. The museum has strong links with the Tenby lifeboat, which is well represented here, also piracy which appears to have been a favoured local pastime.

MILFORD HAVEN

There appears to be no decline in the fortunes of Milford Haven as a port. With a clear entrance facing the deep waters of the Atlantic, this has been a major terminal for long-distance oil carriers of a size which would not find a berth anywhere else in Britain.

Milford Haven may claim a maritime history longer than any other, for it is believed that stone used in the building of Stonehenge were transported from here. Leaping forward a few thousand years, we find the establishment of a port here, as recognised by Parliament, in 1790.

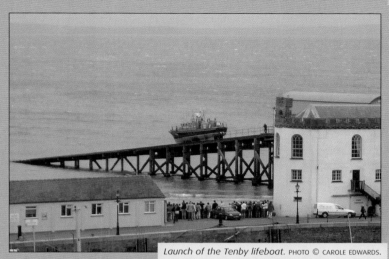

Launch of the Tenby lifeboat. PHOTO © CAROLE EDWARDS.

Following a rapid expansion, it was declared by Nelson, on a visit in 1802, to be 'one of the finest harbours' he had ever seen. Much of its success was based on the encouragement of the Quaker whalers of Nantucket to settle here in 1793. The whalers brought with them the valuable whale oil which was then in great demand to light the streets of London, and this led to what is known as Milford Haven's first oil boom. The Quakers, incidentally, brought with them an expertise in municipal planning which led to the town being built on an American grid system.

Together with a naval dockyard here, and a growing passenger trade with Ireland and the United States, the town maintained its prosperity after the whaling trade declined.

As the fishing went into steep decline, Milford Haven found that its lucky streak had not deserted it. Throughout the 1960s there was determined building of oil terminals, leading to Milford Haven's second oil age. World economics change, and the oil industry is often the first to feel it, so the most recent of Milford's oil ages may be coming to a close.

The **Milford Haven Museum**, housed in a former whale oil store, tells the story of the golden ages of this town from whale oil to mineral oil.

A pirate's tale

There has never been a more successful pirate in history than John Roberts, known as Black Bart, who was born in 1682 in the village of Little Newcastle, not far from the coastal town of Fishguard. Remarkably, his career lasted only four years during which he captured over 400 ships and, at his death, his personal fortune was $80 million (at today's rates).

There were few more gentlemanly or devout pirates than Black Bart. He encouraged the saying of prayers on his ships, and forbade drinking and gambling. His preferred refreshment was tea. Unmistakeable in his crimson waistcoat and breeches, complete with hat and red feather and diamond cross which he wore round his neck, he embarked on an unprecedented assault on the West Indies in 1720, capturing more than a hundred ships. He hanged one island governor who tried to stop him. From here he sailed for Africa and made money selling slaves from the ships he captured. His career ended off the coast of (modern) Gabon where HMS *Swallow*, under the command of Challoner Ogle, caught up with him. In the fight that followed, Black Bart was shot and his body immediately thrown overboard at his own request.

THE ARTICLES
These were to be signed by every man joining one of Black Bart's pirate ships. If only all shipowners in history had such a moral code!

- Every man shall have an equal vote in affairs of moment.
- None shall game for money either with dice or cards.
- The lights and candles should be put out at eight at night, and if any of the crew desire to drink after that hour they shall sit upon the open deck without lights.
- Each man shall keep his piece, cutlass and pistols at all times clean and ready for action.
- No boy or woman to be allowed amongst them. If any man shall be found seducing any of the latter sex and carrying her to sea in disguise he shall suffer death.
- None shall strike another on board the ship, but every man's quarrel shall be ended on shore by sword or pistol.
- Every man who shall become a cripple or lose a limb in the service shall have 800 pieces of eight from the common stock and for lesser hurts proportionately.
- The musicians shall have rest on the Sabbath Day only by right. On all other days by favour only.

The Smalls lighthouse

This lighthouse, 13 miles off the Welsh mainland was first lit in 1776. It protects shipping from a cruel, rocky shoal which stands dangerously in the way of ships working the Irish Sea, especially if they are bound for the Bristol Channel.

This story may be responsible for the long-standing rule that no light shall have less than three keepers. In the late 18th century, one of its keepers, Thomas Griffiths, died while a storm raged around the lighthouse. His only companion was fearful that he may be accused of the man's murder, as there was no proof that Griffiths had died of natural causes. In order to preserve the evidence, the keeper decided to build a coffin from wood scavenged from the light's interior fittings. This coffin he lashed to the outside of the lantern so that when the tender next called, the body was there for all to see and examine. It turned out that the next relief was not able to

Smalls lighthouse. PHOTO COURTESY OF CORPORATION OF TRINITY HOUSE

take place till three weeks later, by which time, it is said, the keeper had gone mad because the light repeatedly cast eerie shadows of the crude coffin. So that no single keeper may be accused of another's murder, with no witnesses to prove it one way or the other, it was then decided that all lighthouses should have three men on station.

CARDIGAN BAY

There is a legend which says that Cardigan Bay was once dry land and within its confines were no less than 16 cities. Much of the land, however, was below sea level and was kept dry by dykes, ditches and sluice gates. In a moment of madness, the drunken son of the King of South Wales, Siethennin, in AD440, opened the sluice gates to flood the land which was never seen again.

If true, Siethennin, in a single action, created a magnificent bay of sandy beaches, and small tidal harbours. It has not been a coastline which has worked its way much into maritime history; rather it has got on with the job of coastal trading, sometimes to Ireland, and occasionally across wider oceans carrying emigrants. The shallow, drying harbours were never a great asset. However, the export of Welsh slate kept a maritime tradition alive, and it was only with the coming of steam-driven ships requiring deep harbours with good access to coal supplies, that the towns of Cardigan and Aberystwyth became once again harbours mainly for the local fishing fleets. Aberystwyth, however, remains the finest seaside resort in the whole of West Wales and its **Ceredigion Museum**, while mainly a folk museum of the lives and traditions of west Wales, represents local maritime history through paintings, photographs and models.

Tucked neatly into the protective arm of the Lleyn Peninsula, and in the shadow of Snowdonia, is Porthmadog where the **Maritime Museum** on the old slate quay tells the story of the ships that worked from here, carrying exports of slate originating from the quarries at Blaenau

The National Coracle Centre

PHOTO COURTESY OF THE NATIONAL CORACLE CENTRE.

Coracles have been in use in British waters, since Roman times, and are seen in varying forms around the world, but they have their strongest associations with Wales, hence the National Coracle Centre at Newcastle Emlyn, Carmarthenshire.

There seem to be as many different styles of coracle as there are rivers in Wales, but essentially a coracle consisted of a basketwork frame over which was stretched, originally, animal skin and nowadays waterproofed calico. The propulsion is by paddling, although there is probably more to this than meets the eye – it would be very easy to paddle round in circles. In fact, fishermen usually work their coracles from the bow, holding the paddle in one hand and making a figure of eight through the water with the blade. If the fishing net needs to be handled as well, there is a one-handed technique which achieves a similar effect. A fisherman might paddle upstream for 10 miles before casting his nets and drifting down again with the flow. While the construction might appear to be simple, this is deceptive and the coracle builders who regularly give displays here prove that the bending of the willow or ash to the required shape calls for an instinctive understanding of the way wood can be worked.

Coracles have had many uses over the centuries, not only as fishing boats but as ferries across rivers. They are said to have been used by Wellington during his Indian campaigns when the ease that one could be carried on a man's back added to the coracle's versatility. Recent restrictions on salmon and trout fishing in the Welsh rivers specifically excluded the coracle fishermen on account of their historic importance and benign fishing methods.

Barmouth, one of the many small harbours in Cardigan Bay. PHOTO © MARGARET BRAIN.

Ffestiniog. This was a major shipbuilding centre, prized for its workmanship and the speed of its schooners.

Although the harbours of Gwynned are small, in their heyday they were bustling ports and the three-masted schooners in which Porthmadog specialised – known as Western Ocean Yachts – were regular visitors to all parts of the world, not just carrying slate but joining the salt fish trade with Newfoundland.

The **Lleyn Historical and Maritime Museum**, housed in the Old Church, once the site of a 6th century Celtic church, uses photographs and paintings to recreate the maritime atmosphere of this once bustling collection of harbours around the Lleyn Peninsula.

Of all the towns of North Wales, only Holyhead has been of enduring maritime significance, managing to ride the ebbs and flows of this region's seafaring fortunes – the **Holyhead Maritime Museum** is housed in the oldest lifeboat house in Wales. Together with the **Seawatch Centre** at Moelfre they provide a picture of the proud seafaring heritage of Anglesey. Holyhead is the island's largest town and thanks to the huge breakwater built over a

Statue of Richard Evans, coxwain, at the Seawatch Centre, Moelfre. PHOTO © MARGARET BRAIN.

Anglesey Sea Terminal, Amlwch. PHOTO © MARGARET BRAIN.

century ago, it has one of the most protected harbours on this coast. This has encouraged the traffic across the Irish Sea both in passengers and containers. Despite being described by the Admiralty in 1748 as being '*no more than a cove between two rocks*', the port of Amlwch grew to become the most important in Wales, drawing its prosperity from the copper industry and also from ship repair work as a result of the many wrecks on this lethal coastline. The remains of the 19th century shipyards can be seen, and a heritage trail leads round this small and picturesque port. A **Heritage Centre** has been established in one of the town's old sail lofts.

The Lleyn peninsula from Llandanwg beach. PHOTO © MARGARET BRAIN.

HISTORIC WARSHIPS AT BIRKENHEAD ────────

It is often the case that although tomorrow's history is within our reach, we easily let it go. This was certainly the case with warships that fought in the Falklands War of 1982. Without the foresight of a group of enthusiasts, these significant ships in our naval history might have been lost forever. It is worth remembering that of all the 900 Royal Navy ships that fought in WWII, only two survive.

Of course, not every ship that floated is worthy of preservation, but the collection at Birkenhead contains four craft of undoubted significance.

HMS *Plymouth* was hit four times during the Falklands conflict. Despite a raging fire, the casualties were light. Most significant, perhaps, is that she led the invasion fleet into San Carlos Water, known as 'Bomb Alley'. In her wardroom, the eventual surrender of South Georgia by the Argentinians was signed. Launched in 1961, she was the last of the Type 12 anti-submarine frigates of the Rothesay class.

HMS *Onyx* played a game less of combat and more of subterfuge. As the only non-nuclear submarine to take part, she was able to work close to the shore and much of her work involved landing special forces from the 20 men of the SAS and Special Boat Squadrons. This was no luxurious billet – she was often so crowded that she became known as 'the sardine's revenge'.

HMS *Bronington* may not have seen as much action as the other ships here, but her name is probably the best known. This was the ship on which HRH the Prince of Wales took command in 1976 as part of his naval training. She also has the distinction of being the last wooden warship to be built for the Navy. After her commissioning, minesweepers were built out of glassfibre materials, like yachts. *Bronington* was built in 1953, one of the Ton class of minesweepers which

HMS *Bronington*. PHOTO COURTESY OF THE WARSHIP PRESERVATION TRUST.

were engaged as much in patrol work as the sweeping of mines. They became known as the 'police cars' of the Navy for their ability to sort out problems quickly and efficiently.

U534 was a German submarine built in 1942, and the most mysterious of exhibits here. As the order was given by Nazi command for all German submarines to surrender, the young captain of *U534* ignored the order and sailed towards Norway. She was soon sunk by bombers of RAF Coastal Command. The young men who manned her managed to escape in what has become one of the legendary submarine escapes of all time. The unanswered question is why did her commander refuse to obey his order to surrender? Some suggest she was bound for South America taking prominent Nazis into exile. Another theory is that she was laden with treasure to fund the Nazis who had already fled. The raising of her was controversial, but since no members of her crew had died on board, the wreck did not have the protection of being an official war grave. She was eventually lifted in 1993, the bill paid by a Danish publisher, It was thought that since the Mersey was the departure point for the Atlantic convoys, so often the target of *U534*, this should be her final resting place. She sits, incidentally, close to where the world's first mechanically powered submarine, the *Resurgam*, was built.

U534. PHOTO COURTESY OF THE WARSHIP PRESERVATION TRUST.

MARITIME MERSEYSIDE

Had it not been for the meanderings of the River Dee, and the consequent silting which forced the decline of Chester as a port, Liverpool may never have grown to become one of the world's major ports in the days when international trade was conducted by sea. Cotton, tobacco and timber from all corners of the Empire came through Liverpool making it the second largest city in Britain by 1850. The merchants built imposing dockside and warehouses in classically inspired architecture and in the houses they built for themselves, the traders betrayed their

The restored Albert Dock, Liverpool. PHOTO © CAROLE EDWARDS.

true wealth. The fact that not far in the hinterland was poverty, crime and destitution did not matter much to them – it merely added even more spice to that rich mix which came to be known as 'Liverpudlian'.

In 1880, the dockside stretched for seven miles. Liverpool ships arrived here carrying forty per cent of the entire world's trade. It was the most prosperous port in the world. But it will be remembered not for the vastness of its material trade, but for the way in which Liverpool became the place of embarkation for human souls on a vast scale. This was England's back door through which millions have left, often of their own accord, but sometimes with little choice.

The **Merseyside Maritime Museum**, to be found on the revitalised Albert Dock, has become one of Britain's major museums. In a complex covering seven acres, every aspect of Liverpool's history, from slavery through luxury liners to the Battle of the Atlantic, is represented. This is also the home of the **Customs and Excise National Musuem**, and taken with the historic ships afloat in nearby docks (and the Tate Gallery) this is a place to linger.

Anchor outside the Maritime Museum.
PHOTO COURTESY OF THE MERSEY PARTNERSHIP
(TMP) WWW.VISITLIVERPOOL.COM.

The Maritime Museum, Liverpool. PHOTO © CAROLE EDWARDS.

The museum is a fine distillation of what seafaring has meant to Britain, and you will leave with more than just an understanding of Liverpool's importance. You will learn of the life of a seafarer, the marine environment and the effects that ships have on it; the contrasting squalor of the slave ships compared to luxury liners who made this their first European port of call. Taken together with the ships afloat, and the stunning atmosphere of this revitalised dockland setting, a visit here is a complete maritime education.

The Liverpool slave trade

London and Bristol had a head start on Liverpool, but by 1750 this was the undisputed capital of the world's slave trade. You were as likely to find on sale in the waterside chandlers the apparatus of slavery, such a leg-irons, as you were rope and cordage. Few who lived in Britain and enjoyed such imports as molasses, sugar, rum, tobacco and rice, knew that the ships which brought them to Liverpool were returning to the Americas packed with slaves.

The slave trade was hugely convenient, and benefited all sides – providing you weren't one of the slaves. They were often captured from African leaders who were keen to barter for textiles, alcohol or guns. After sailing back to Liverpool, they were loaded onto ships recently arrived from America which had off-loaded their cargoes. On arrival in America – assuming they survived the journey in the appalling conditions to which they were condemned – the slaves were put to work producing the goods which the slave ships carried back to Liverpool. It was such a profitable way of trading that it was not until 1807 that slavery was abolished by law, although illegal trading doubtless continued after that.

■ The emigrant trade

No sooner was the despicable slave trade in decline, than began the voluntary export of people from Liverpool. It became a gateway to a new world and a new life for over nine million people between 1830 and 1930. Liverpool had established a reputation throughout Europe and people, often destitute, travelled by sea to Hull, then crossing England to Liverpool where the emigrant ships waited, bound for America or Australia. As the maritime museum's display shows, they were allowed little baggage, often just a wooden chest with minimal possessions. They may not have found a berth straight away and endured the squalid conditions of the Liverpool boarding houses (reconstructed here). Once at sea, things hardly improved, and in crowded conditions disease was common. Not until WWI did the emigrant trade decline when the United States and Canada started to close their doors.

The Battle of the Atlantic

Liverpool was one of the most frequent destinations in WW2 for the Atlantic convoys which carried vital supplies of food and munitions from the United States. Often under attack from fleets of German U-boats, the Merchant Navy suffered heavy losses including 30,000 men and 2000 ships. The battle against the U-boats was conducted from Liverpool employing new techniques such as the rapidly developing radar, and Asdic for underwater detection. The Battle of the Atlantic was not only the longest campaign of WWII, it was arguably the most vital. The **Western Approaches Museum**, beneath Rumford Street in Liverpool, paints a picture of the onshore activities in ensuring the safety of the Atlantic convoys. Here, a reconstruction of the offices, control rooms and command HQ, alongside a depiction of the working lives of the Wrens and WAAFs who worked here, add to the full picture of Liverpool's part in this long-running battle of WWII.

LYTHAM

The old lifeboat house.
PHOTO © DOROTHY MOIR.

The **Lytham Lifeboat Museum** is housed in the old lifeboat house, and tells the story of Lytham St Anne's lifeboats since 1851. However, the role of the Lytham lifeboat in the worst disaster in RNLI history is the most dramatic of the tales told here.

On 9 December 1886, a German barque, the *Mexico* sent out a distress call having grounded off Southport. Three lifeboats launched despite atrocious weather – the Southport boat *Eliza Fernley*, the St Anne's lifeboat, *Laura Janet* and the Lytham boat, *Charles Biggs*. The Southport boat may have been the first to reach the wreck, having been launched off the beach close to where the *Mexico* ran aground, but as she approached the wreck she was overturned in huge seas. Two of her crew decided to swim to shore and were the only survivors, although some were washed ashore and later died. It became clear as more bodies were washed up, that the *Laura Janet* had also been lost, together with her entire crew. Out of 44 men involved in the rescue, 27 died.

The Lytham lifeboat, *Charles Biggs*, managed to reach the *Mexico*, and rescued all of her 12-man crew.

MORECAMBE BAY

Stretching from Fleetwood to Barrow in Furness, this second largest bay in Britain, after the Wash, is both a curious and treacherous place. It is mostly shallow, which, together with a large tidal range means the the tide goes out a long way – as far as ten miles. Equally, it returns with great speed to trap those who have failed to make it to the shore in time. It is possible to walk across Morecambe Bay but it would be extremely foolish to attempt it alone, even if armed with maps and guide books. The banks and quicksands shift and no chart is reliable for long. Instead, a guided walk with the Queen's Guide to the Sands, Cedric Robinson, is a much safer bet. This official post was first created in 1536 and remains in the gift of the Duchy of Lancaster. Only a fisherman of Cedric Robinson's experience – he has been doing this for 40 years – has the knowledge to

Small craft at low tide in Morecambe Bay. PHOTO COURTESY OF PETER WAKELY/ENGLISH NATURE.

guide you safely across the bay, providing you obey the signals he gives you with his whistle and shepherd's crook. The journey from Arnside to Grange-over-Sands is approximately six miles, taking about three hours to walk. Be prepared to wade in places, and keep at the back of your mind that the incoming tides hasten across the sands faster than a man can run.

■ Morecambe Bay Fisheries

Fishing has always been an important industry here, but you didn't always need a boat to ensure a good catch. The cocklers traditionally worked on foot, armed with spades and forks, accepting the dangers of this place in return for a living. The shrimp fishers used a push net, attached to a wooden frame, and walked through the water netting their catch. For fish such as salmon and sea trout, nets known as 'haaf-nets' were attached to large wooden frames; these were held in the water by the fishermen, trapping the fish as they swam into them. Whammel netting was another method, using a huge net paid out from the stern of a whammel boat which made its way across the bay as the tide ebbed, leaving the net behind.

The most unlikely method of fishing, which would have brought you up short if you'd seen it, was 'cart-shanking'. This was common in northern parts of the bay: a shrimp net, attached to a large beam, was fixed to a cart which was pulled through the water by a cart-horse, sometimes well up to its flanks. Tractors later took over the haulage. The history of fishing in Morecambe Bay, as well as the story of the mid 18th century heyday of Lancaster as a port, is told in the **Lancaster Maritime Museum**. Once a busy trading port until silting of the entrance forced the construction of canals, there was much traffic between here and the West Indies. It is difficult to imagine now, but the level of trade here was once eclipsed only by London, Bristol and Liverpool.

FLEETWOOD

The fishing business of Fleetwood has always been far removed from the inshore work of the Morecambe Bay fishery. From Fleetwood, steam trawlers joined the fleets from Hull and Grimsby to fish the distant northern waters off the Faroes and Iceland. Now a museum ship, the 615 ton fishing vessel *Jacinta*, which can be seen in the fish dock, if not away for repairs, is a reminder of what was once the main business of Fleetwood. This vessel holds the British record for wet-fish landing and now provides visitors with a stark reminder that the achieving of such a catch is a harsh business conducted in a less than amiable environment.

But Fleetwood is more than just a 'fish town'. The **Fleetwood Museum** also tells the idealistic story of the creation of this town, part of the dream of Sir Peter Hesketh (born 1801) to build a resort and seaport on his own land. In order to achieve what he hoped might be a 'perfect' trading community, complete with direct railway line to London Euston, he hired the architect Decimus Burton who was later to design much of the layout of London's Hyde Park, and the triumphal arch at Hyde Park Corner.

Steam trawlers at Fleetwood. PHOTO © PETER BRADY,
COURTESY OF WWW.MARINE-HERITAGE.CONNECTFREE.CO.UK

The Fisherman's Friend

This remarkable lozenge, known and enjoyed the world over, was invented in Fleetwood, where it is still produced by the same family firm. One of the early residents of the newly established town was a pharmacist, James Lofthouse. His speciality was a menthol based 'tonic' which he bottled and labelled as the 'Fishermen's Friend'. This was widely sought by the fishing community to ward off the cold. But it was not until Lofthouse managed to create a lozenge to the same recipe that his product achieved wide recognition; visitors to nearby Blackpool spread the word that this 'sweet' really could ward off the cold – the fishermen said so!

Fleetwood thrived in Victorian times, both as a resort and a departure point for pleasure steamers to the Isle of Man. Decimus Burton was given a free hand in designing the town, hence the remarkable Pharos Lighthouse: 90 feet high with a 13-mile range, one of three lights which guide ships safely into Fleetwood. The Pharos was unashamedly based on the design of the Pharos light built by Ptolemy in 280BC on an island off Alexandria, in north Africa. Just one more of Fleetwood's architectural quirks.

BARROW-IN-FURNESS

As in Fleetwood, a great deal of idealism was brought to the building of Barrow-in-Furness. As the town developed around the steelworks and shipyards, the houses for the workers were built along wide, tree-lined streets. Later, as suburbs started to develop, these were laid out as a 'garden city'. This is in contrast to the conditions endured by the early workers who came to Barrow when the first railway arrived, bringing new prosperity – the 3000 workers found themselves confined to a mere three hundred wooden huts.

The **Dock Museum**, a stunning modern development built over an

A stunning contemporary building houses the Barrow Dock Museum. PHOTO COURTESY OF THE DOCK MUSEUM.

A sailing vessel on display. PHOTO COURTESY OF THE DOCK MUSEUM.

original Victorian dry dock, tells how Barrow evolved from a tiny hamlet, around Furness Abbey into a major world shipbuilding centre. Here they have built ships for the Royal Navy since 1852 when warships were ironclads, to modern state-of-the-art fighting vessels. This remains the principal ship building port in Britain, and a major iron and steel centre; much of its prosperity coming from the Vickers shipyard, now GEC Marine. The important Vickers Photographic Archive of rare and evocative glass negatives is held by the museum.

WHITEHAVEN

More town planning was practiced at Whitehaven, which can boast of being the first deliberately planned town in Britain since the Middle Ages, and its outline is still apparent.

This harbour's prosperity was built on 17th century exports of coal to Ireland from nearby mines, particularly the town's Haig colliery which runs under the sea. This required a considerable fleet of ships, and in the summer months, when coal was less in demand, these traded as far as America, making Whitehaven into a thriving port dealing in sugar, rum and, inevitably, slaves.

In what might be mistaken for a lighthouse by the harbour, the **Beacon Museum** tells the story of the influence of the land-owning Lowther family. There is a collection of scrimshaw and much interactive material and displays of social and maritime history.

■ When the Americans attacked Whitehaven

Although it seems unlikely, this port was once of such a size that an attack was mounted on it in 1778 during the American War of Independence. The assault was led by John Paul Jones who is remembered in America as the 'father' of their Navy, but in England was better known as something of a pirate. John Paul (the Jones was his own addition) was born in Scotland but served a seaman's apprenticeship in Whitehaven, becoming a master after taking command of a slave ship on which the captain and mate had

Fishing boat in front of the Beacon Museum. PHOTO COURTESY OF COPELAND BOROUGH COUNCIL.

died of fever. His flaw was his temper, and after killing the ringleader of a mutiny in the West Indies, he fled to Virginia and took up residence.

With the seeds of the American Revolution already sown, Jones joined the newly formed Navy and quickly rose through the ranks and

Whitehaven marina at sunset. PHOTO COURTESY OF THE COPELAND BOROUGH COUNCIL.

supervised an expansion of the Navy from a handful of ships into a small fleet. After attacks on the French off Brest, he sailed for his old haunt of Whitehaven intending to capture the two forts which guarded the harbour. Two boats set off, one to capture each fort, and although the one under Jones' command was successful, the crew of the other had decided to make for the nearest inn. So he set fire to some colliers moored in the harbour, and retreated unhurt.

Whitehaven remains the only English port ever to have been invaded by the Americans, and it is said to be the very last port to be attacked in WWI when a German U-boat found its way into the harbour.

MARYPORT

Again, an elegant town with a grid-based pattern of streets, and a port where at one time a million tons of cargo left every year including Cumbrian coal. The **Maryport Maritime Museum** claims to hold the sea chest of Fletcher Christian, the mate on HMS *Bounty* and leader of the infamous maritime mutiny against Captain Bligh.

Also at Maryport, the **Maryport Steamships Museum** which has in its care the Scottish oil-fired steam tug *Flying Buzzard*, and the former Navy victualling ship *VIC96*.

The Maritime Museum, Maryport. PHOTO © JULIAN THURGOOD.

THE ISLE OF MAN

This small island set in the middle of the Irish sea is self-governing – its ancient parliament has met regularly for a thousand years, making it the oldest established governing body in the world.

With no part of the island far from the sea, the place has been dominated by its maritime traditions. Fine Viking boats have been unearthed here, but the main theme has been one of fishing and exploitation of the sea to support a fragile island economy. Seabirds were once a common dish here; seaweed was the fertilizer of choice on many of the farms. In the 19th century, a quarter of the population was engaged in one way or another with the fishing trade, sometimes ashore in curing sheds or net repairing.

One of the exciting displays at the House of Mannanan. PHOTO COURTESY OF THE MANX NATIONAL HERITAGE LIBRARY.

The **House of Manannan**, at Peel, gives a flavour of the Viking and Celtic influences on the Manx seamen. Manannan is the island's great mythological sea god who, it is said, would always protect the island from its enemies by clouding it in mist should it ever come under attack. This museum, in his honour, is a fine building, partly contained in the old Peel railway station. The star of its shop must be the replica Norse longship which was built in Norway and sailed to Peel in 1979 to celebrate the millennium of the island's parliament. Also remembered is Sir William Hillary (1771–1847) who, in 1824, appealed to the British nation for the setting up of a '*royal institution for the preservation of life from shipwreck*', which became the modern RNLI.

The Nautical Museum, beside Castletown harbour.
PHOTO COURTESY OF THE MANX NATIONAL HERITAGE LIBRARY.

The **Nautical Museum** at Castletown came into being after a remarkable discovery which was made in 1935. The Quayle family had always been a distinguished Manx family throughout the 18th century. History had recorded George Quayle as a loyal servant of the island, working in trade and commerce, and involving himself with the government of the island. But the discoveries of 1935 revealed him in a different light.

Adjacent to the Quayle family home was an unknown vault, and when opened it was found to contain an entire 18th century schooner-rigged armed yacht, the *Peggy*. Some years later, when the yacht had been given to the Manx Museum trustees, the boathouse opened to the public as the **Nautical Museum**.

The discovery of the yacht caused sufficient excitement, but further investigation showed Quayle to be a man of broad talents. In his workshop he had constructed his own telescope, and had drawn up plans for an invasion barge which could carry 30,000 troops to France to fight Napoleon. The building of the boathouse absorbed a large part of his creative energies. He enjoyed trap doors, secret exits, and had built himself a cabin room above the boat cellar which was a perfect replica of the stern cabin of a naval warship of the Nelson era.

The *Peggy* confined herself to a little trade with English ports, but never on a huge scale. However, Quayle insisted that his yacht was armed with cannon in case he stumbled across 'marauders' in the Irish Sea.

Lundy, Irish Sea Gazetteer

Padstow Museum
The Institute, Market Place, Padstow, Cornwall.
NB: museum is moving from its current home in summer 2005
☎ +44 (0)1841 532470
www.cornish-links.co.uk/
museums.htm
OPEN Mon–Fri, Easter–Oct

Bude-Stratton Museum
The Wharf, Bude, Cornwall EX23 8AG
☎ +44 (0)1288 353576
www.budemuseum.org.uk
OPEN Daily, Easter–Sept, Sun & Thurs in Oct

Hartland Quay Museum
Hartland Quay, Hartland, Bideford, N. Devon EX39 6DU
☎ +44 (0)1288 331353
www.devonheritage.com/
hartland/museum.htm
OPEN Daily, Easter week. Daily Spring BH–30 Sept

Burton Art Gallery and Museum
Kingsley Road, Bideford, Devon EX39 2QQ
☎ +44 (0)1237 471455
www.devonmuseums.net
OPEN Tue–Sun also BH Mon

North Devon Museum Trust
Odun House, Odun Road, Appledore, Bideford, N. Devon EX39 1PT
☎ +44 (0)1237 422064
www.devonmuseums.net
OPEN Daily, Easter–31 Oct, pm. Also open am, Mon–Fri, May–Sept

Ilfracombe Museum
Wilder Road, Ilfracombe, North Devon EX34 8AF
☎ +44 (0)1271 863541
www.devonmuseums.net
OPEN Daily, Easter–Oct; Mon–Fri am, Nov–Mar

Watchet Boat Museum
Harbour Road, Watchet, Somerset (opposite the railway station)
☎ +44 (0)1984 633117
www.wbm.org.uk
OPEN Tues–Thurs, Sat & Sun (14.00–16.00), BH, Easter–end Sept, or BA

The SS Great Britain
Great Western Dock, Gas Ferry Road, Bristol.
☎ +44 (0)117 926 0680
www.ss-great-britain.com
OPEN Daily except Christmas
A reconstruction programme has been taking place on SS Great Britain. Completion due summer 2005

Bristol Industrial Museum
Princes Wharf, Prince Street, City Docks, Bristol BS1 4RN
☎ +44 (0)117 9251470
www.bristol-city.gov.uk/
mus/bim.htm
OPEN April–Oct: Sat–Wed; Winter: Sat & Sun only

Bristol Maritime Heritage Centre
Wapping Wharf, Gasferry Road, Bristol BS1 6TY
☎ +44 (0)117 926 0680
OPEN Daily except over Christmas

The Nelson Museum
New Market Hall, Priory Street, Monmouth, NP25 3XA, Wales
☎ +44 (0)1600 710630
www.monmouth.org.uk/
nelson.htm
OPEN Mon–Sat (incl. BH) 1000–1300, 1400–1700, Sun 1400–1500

Replica of The Matthew *at Bristol.* © CAROLE EDWARDS.

Lifeboat Museum, Barmouth.
© MARGARET BRAIN.

Tenby Museum and Art Gallery
Castle Hill, Tenby,
Pembrokeshire, Wales
SA70 7BP
☎ +44 (0)1834 842809
www.tenbymuseum.
free-online.co.uk
OPEN Daily 10:00–17:00,
1 Apr–1 Nov; Mon–Fri in winter

Milford Haven Museum
The Old Custom House, Sybil Way, The Docks, Milford Haven, Pembrokeshire, South Wales SA73 3AF
☎ +44 (0)1646 694496
www.pembrokeshirecoast.
org.uk
OPEN Daily, Easter–Oct;
GV BA

National Coracle Centre
Cenarth Falls, Newcastle Emlyn, Carmarthenshire SA38 9JL, Wales
☎ +44 (0)1239 710980
www.aboutbritain.com/
NationalCoracleCentre.htm
OPEN Sun–Fri, Easter–end Oct, or BA

Barmouth RNLI Museum
RNLI Boathouse,
The Promenade, Barmouth, Gwynedd, Wales
LL42 1NF
www.lokalink.co.uk/
lifeboat_museum/1_1.htm
OPEN Daily, Easter Sat–end Sept, or BA

Barmouth Sailors' Institute, Ty Gwyn and Ty Crwn
Quayside, Barmouth, Gwynedd, North Wales.
☎ +44 (0)1341 241333
www.barmouth-wales.
co.uk/history.html
OPEN Usually Mon-Sat, May-Sept, but enquire about details

Ceredigion Museum
Coliseum, Terrace Road, Aberystwyth, Ceredigion SY23 2AQ, Wales
☎ +44 (0)1970 633087, 633088
www.ceredigion.gov.uk/
coliseum
OPEN Mon–Sat 10:00-17:00.
Also Sun during school holidays

Porthmadog Maritime Museum
Oakley Wharf No. 1, Porthmadog, Gwynedd, Wales
☎ +44 (0)1766 513736, 512864
www.worldwidewales.tv/
index2.php?mid=204
OPEN Daily in Easter week, and between May BH to 30 Sept, or BA

Lleyn Historical and Maritime Museum
Old St Mary's Church, Church Street, Nefyn, Gwynedd, N Wales
☎ +44 (0)1758 720270
www.penllyn.com/1/Hanes/
MORWROL.HTML
OPEN Daily from early-July to mid-Sept

Amlwch Port Heritage Centre
The Sail Loft, Amlwch, Anglesey.
Tel +44(0)1407 832277
www.copperkingdom.co.uk
OPEN Easter to Oct: 1
0:30-17:00

Holyhead Maritime Museum
Newry Beach, Holyhead, Isle of Anglesey/Ynys Mon, North Wales
☎ +44 (0)1407 769745
www.geocities.com/
dickburnell
OPEN Tues–Sun (pm only), Easter–autumn

Historic Warships at Birkenhead
The Warship Preservation Trust, East Float, Dock Road, Birkenhead CH41 1DJ
☎ +44 (0)151 650 1573
www.warships.freeserve.co.uk
OPEN Apr–Aug, Mon–Sun 10:00–17:00; Sep–Mar Mon–Sun 10:00–16:00

Merseyside Maritime Museum
Albert Dock, Liverpool, Merseyside L3 4AA
☎ +44 (0) 151 207 0001
www.liverpoolmuseums.org.
uk/maritime
OPEN Daily, 10:00–17:00 except Christmas & New Year

HM Customs and Excise Museum
Albert Dock, Liverpool
L3 4AQ
☎ +44 (0)151 478 4499
www.liverpoolmuseums.org.
uk/customs
OPEN Daily, 10:00–17:00 except Christmas & New Year

Lifeboat Herbert Leigh. © THE DOCK MUSEUM.

Western Approaches Museum
1–3 Rumford Street,
Liverpool L2 8SZ
☎ +44 (0)151 227 2008
www.subbrit.org.uk/rsg/
places.html
OPEN Mon–Thurs & Sat,
Mar–Oct

Lytham Lifeboat Museum
East Beach, Lytham,
Lancashire FY8
☎ +44 (0)1253 730155
www.legendol.freeserve.
co.uk/museum.html
OPEN Tue, Thurs, Sat & Sun,
May BH–Sept. Also Wed pm
in July & Aug

Lancaster Maritime Museum
Custom House, St George's
Quay, Lancaster, Lancashire
LA1 1RB
☎ +44 (0)1524 382264
www.canaljunction.
com/iwhn
OPEN Daily, Easter–Oct:
11:00–17:00; 12:30–16:00 in
winter. GV BA

Fleetwood Museum
Queens Terrace, Fleetwood,
Lancashire FY7 6BT (Part of
the Museum of Lancashire,
County Museums Service)
☎ +44 (0)1253 876621
www.nettingthebay.org.uk
OPEN Daily, Apr–early Nov
(Mon–Sat 10:00–16:00, Sun
13:00–16:00)

The Dock Museum
North Road, Barrow-in-
Furness, Cumbria LA14 2PW
☎ +44 (0)1229 894444
www.dockmuseum.org.uk
OPEN Tues–Sun + BH Mon,
Easter–Oct; Wed–Sun,
Nov–Easter
ADMISSION Free

The Beacon
West Strand, Whitehaven,
Cumbria CA28 7LY
☎ +44 (0)1946 592302
www.copelandbc.gov.uk/
thebeacon/default.htm
OPEN Tues–Sun. Also BH
Mon in July & Aug

Maryport Maritime Museum
1 Senhouse Street, Shipping
Brow, Maryport, Cumbria
CA15 6AB
☎ +44 (0)1900 813738
www.visitcumbria.com/wc/
marymar.htm
OPEN Daily, Easter–end Sept;
enquire for winter opening

Maryport Steamships Museum
Elizabeth Dock, South
Quay, Maryport,
Cumbria CA15 8AB
☎ +44 (0)1900 815954
OPEN Daily, Easter–Oct (check
by phone before visiting)

House of Manannan
East Quay, Peel, Isle of Man
☎ +44 (0)1624 648000
www.gov.im/mnh
OPEN Daily, 10:00–17:00

The Nautical Museum
Castletown, Isle of Man
☎ +44 (0)1624 648000
www.gov.im/mnh
OPEN Daily 10:00–17:00,
Easter–Oct

BA: By arrangement
BH: Bank holiday
GV: Group visits

Cloch lighthouse, Clyde estuary. PHOTO COURTESY OF THE GREATER GLASGOW AND CLYDE VALLEY TOURIST BOARD.

MALIN, HEBRIDES

From Solway Firth to Cape Wrath

Girvan ■ Irvine ■ Saltcoats ■ Campbeltown ■ Inverary
Greenock ■ Glasgow ■ Clydebank ■ Dumbarton
The Hebrides

Girvan harbour with Arran in the background. PHOTO © UNDISCOVERED SCOTLAND.

It is difficult to believe that the short length of coastline that stretches from the North Channel to Cape Wrath was once home to both the largest maritime industrial site in Britain: the Clyde, and some of the smallest and remotest maritime communities.

The Clyde, of course, dominates, and its contribution to British maritime history since the first establishment of shipyards is considerable: more ships were built here than at any other place in the world, all stamped with the hallmark of indisputable quality – Clydebuilt.

GIRVAN

The **McKechnie Institute** in its octagonal tower of 1888 stands at Girvan, famous for record catches of whiting. Built by a local philanthropist, Thomas McKechnie, it was once described as, '*every evening the place is all but crowded with labouring men, fishermen, tradesmen and others.*' It maintains its community use and houses a collection of maritime memorabilia from both Girvan and Ailsa Craig, the most impressive landmark in the Firth of Clyde. This

The McKechnie Institute. PHOTO © UNDISCOVERED SCOTLAND.

granite island, rising to 1,100 feet is the plug of an ancient volcano and the granite from which it is made was once used to craft the best curling stones. With 10,000 breeding pairs each year, this is one of the largest gannetries in Scotland.

IRVINE

Scotland has three important museums with a maritime theme and the one at Irvine is designated as the national collection (see also **Clydebuilt** and **Denny Ship Model Tank**).

Irvine was once the main port for the growing city of Glasgow before the dredging of the Clyde in the 18th century. The harbour mouth was made difficult by a shifting sand bar where the flow of river water met the sea. In order that ships' captains would know the all-important depth of water over the bar, the Pilot House was built. It employed an automatic apparatus designed by Martin Boyd, an early 20th century harbour master, and from this tall, white-painted tower the depths were signalled to approaching ships.

The **Scottish Maritime Museum** is housed in what was once part of the Linthouse Shipyard, in particular the **Linthouse Engine Shop** which was scheduled for demolition until its historical importance was appreciated. This is now the biggest historical building in the UK, with 35 massive iron pillars supporting a roof consisting of 26,000 sq ft of glass. Here they practiced the mammoth art of building Victorian steam engines in this typical heavy engineering workshop. You will see here

The Linthouse Engine Shop at Girvan. PHOTO © UNDISCOVERED SCOTLAND.

Vessels moored at the Maritime Museum pontoons. PHOTO © UNDISCOVERED SCOTLAND.

anchors, chain and moorings which were typical iron products. It must also be remembered that much of the shipbuilding prosperity was built on the backs of the shipyard workers who rarely shared in the corporate wealth. The Shipyard Workers Tenement Flat, reconstructed here as it would have appeared in the 1920s, is a reminder of what, for many families, was a poor living. In the depression of the 1930s, shipyard workers' wages could sometimes be halved without notice. For many, the luxury of an inside toilet did not arrive until the 1950s.

■ The ships at Irvine

Not all of the museum's collections of ships afloat can be boarded, but at least one is open every day. Nevertheless, this is an important collection, and sight of it is sufficient to satisfy the curiosity of anyone wanting to understand more of the maritime history of the Scottish coast.

Katie is a small fishing boat of 1937, complete with fish hold and small wheelhouse, first owned by a Skye fishermen. She is typical of the inshore fishing boats of these waters, although in her lifetime she has served as a naval supply vessel, and a yacht.

Pleasure boating is represented by *Vagrant*, a small racing yacht designed by William Fife whose family of boat builders were considered the best in Victorian and Edwardian times. The beautiful *Corola* is believed to be the oldest sea-going steam yacht in the world and was rescued from a breaker's yard in 1970. She was built in 1898 by Scott and Sons, at

Bowling in Dunbartonshire, for their weekend pleasure trips around the Hebrides. Working craft are represented by the *Spartan* of 1942, originally a naval inshore craft during WWII, working as a supply vessel. *Garnock* was the very last tug owned and operated by the Irvine Harbour Company. Her working life was brought to a dramatic end in 1984 when engaged in the (legal) dumping of substandard explosive. No sooner had a load been jettisoned than it blew up! *Garnock* was never the same again.

The engine shed and museum reception.
PHOTO © UNDISCOVERED SCOTLAND.

SALTCOATS

The industrial face of the Clyde remains well hidden as you travel the Ayrshire coastline, often low and sandy, famous for its golf courses, beaches and the mildness of its climate. The **North Ayrshire Museum**, at Saltcoats, has many maritime exhibits: ship models, bells, photographs and a model of Ardrossen harbour. Two major ferry companies were once based here: the Burns Laird Line and the Hogath line which sailed between Ardrossan and Belfast. Their archives are kept in the museum.

However, the most famous resident of Saltcoats may have been the redoubtable Betsy Miller who became the first woman to be registered as a sea captain in 1847. Born in 1792 to a shipping family, she spent her childhood aboard her father's ship. It was assumed, however, that Betsy would take up office duties eventually, which she did. The premature death of her brother gave her the opportunity to take command of the family ship, the *Clytus*, arguing 'who knows her better than I do?'

Betsy Miller. COURTESY OF SALTCOATS COUNTY COUNCIL.

The Clyde Puffer

'I prize the little lighters – carriers of coal and coastal merchandise, whose broad uplifting bows, squat funnels, thick short masts and derrick mass so often in a figure that recalls old galleys on Celtic tombs.'

Neil Munro, 1907.

The Puffer remains much loved, and fondly remembered by those who recall the working days of these coasters. But it was the author Neil Munro who penned the stories of the *Vital Spark* and its hapless skipper, Para Handy, who turned the Clyde Puffer into an object of international affection.

The Puffers were designed to thread the waterways between mainland Scotland, the offshore islands, and the inland waterways such as the Forth and Clyde canal. They were built for versatility, and their design enabled them to carry 100 tons of cargo which could be delivered ashore by her own gear, needing no crane onshore. Many islands had no deep water harbours, so it was also a requirement that a Puffer should be able to take the ground, sit upright, and allow the unloading to continue. For this reason, they were box-like underwater, and less attractive when unladen. The length of them, at 66 feet, was determined by the length of the shortest canal lock they were likely to negotiate, which was 70 feet. Not all Puffers were built to precisely the same design – whether the ship was intended for inshore or offshore work determined her final build.

Their name came from the days of the early ships which used non-condensing steam engines where the exhaust was diverted into the funnel. This gave the distinctive 'puffer' sound.

There were few jobs in these waters for which a Puffer could not be used. They were to be found carrying coal to island communities, carting livestock, sand dredging, and hauling barley to distilleries.

The Puffer *Eilean Eisdeal*, built in Hull in 1944 and one of the last puffers to be built, was refitted in 2001. She now sails from the pier at Inverary.

Puffer VIC 32, maintained by the Puffer Preservation Trust, steaming through the Crinan Canal. PHOTO COURTESY OF THE PUFFER PRESERVATION TRUST. www.savethepuffer.co.uk

The *Clytus* carried coal from Saltcoats to Dublin for many years, Betsy took command of the 14-man crew. She did not retire till the age of 70. On one trip, when trouble loomed and stranding on the Ayrshire coast looked inevitable, she insisted on going below to change her clothes with the words, '*Lads, I'll gang below and put on a clean sark, for I wid like to be flung up on the sawns kin of decent. Irvine folk are nasty, noticin' buddies.*' In the event, the ship was saved, the crew claiming that Betsy's change of 'sark' had brought them good fortune.

CAMPBELTOWN

If the journey to the **Campbeltown Museum** seems a lengthy one, then you will not be surprised to know that Campbeltown is the furthest town from any other town on the British mainland. No surprise, then, that this is a maritime community where the coming and going of the ferries, and the fishing fleets are the main traffic here.

Mostly devoted to the non-maritime history of the town and the social history of Kintyre, the museum also tells the story of the fishing fleets, and remembers the days when this town boasted no less than 31 distilleries.

Lifeboats in Campbeltown harbour.
PHOTO © UNDISCOVERED SCOTLAND.

INVERARY – The Artic Penguin Maritime Heritage Centre

Despite the name, this is no wildlife centre. Alongside the Inverary Quay you will find this three-masted schooner, the *Artic Penguin*, built in 1911. She is a fine example of a riveted iron ship, and a contemporary of the *Titanic*. The romance of the sea is evoked through the carvings on whale-teeth and walrus tusk of many a salty adventure, while the story of grittier business of the Highland Clearances is also told. There is archive film of the history of the Clyde, and artefacts raised from the *Lusitania*.

GREENOCK

Home to some of Scotland's finest art, the **McLean Museum and Art Gallery** at Greenock, also tells the story of the Clyde shipbuilders, and remembers Greenock-born James Watt, pioneer steam engineer. Watt, born in 1736, repaired ships' instruments in his father's workshop, employing talents which he later took to London where he served an apprenticeship. Watt was asked to carry out repairs to a Newcomen steam engine and his interest was aroused in this branch of engineering, realising the weaknesses in the way the engine had been designed. In 1783, James Watt established for the first time the term 'horse-power' by which the 'strength' of an engine might be measured.

GLASGOW – The Clydebuilt Maritime Museum

This award-winning museum brings the latest technology to telling the story of the River Clyde, and the days when the word 'Clydebuilt' was an international mark of respect. The *QE2* and *Queen Mary* were built on the Clyde, along with many vessels long-forgotten. 2,000 ships were built here during WWII and the launching of new vessels, or ships in for repair, was a common sight.

A dockside scene at Clydebuilt. PHOTO COURTESY OF THE GREATER GLASGOW AND CLYDE VALLEY TOURIST BOARD.

Until the 19th century, the Clyde was a trading river, well positioned for use by ships crossing the Atlantic to the Americas or Indies. The major imports were sugar, rum and tobacco and, on the backs of these goods, great fortunes were made by Glasgow merchants, in particular the 'Tobacco Lords' who built substantial houses in the city to celebrate their wealth. However, with the arrival of the Industrial Revolution, and the discovery of nearby coal and iron ore deposits, the Clyde embraced heavy industry and became legendary in the building of steam engines and ships. Labour was in plentiful supply, and cheap, and with the widening and deepening of the Clyde in the early

SV Glenlee. PHOTO COURTESY OF THE GREATER GLASGOW AND CLYDE VALLEY TOURIST BOARD.

1900s, the growth was rapid. Having built 69,000 tons of ships in 1862, this rose to 750,000 at the outbreak of WWI. It was then one of the world's major industrial sites.

Of all the sailing ships built on the Clyde, only five remain and the three-masted barque, SV *Glenlee*, probably represents the peak of sailing ship design. She is now designated **The Tall Ship at Glasgow Harbour**, and can be found at Yorkhill Quay, Glasgow.

Launched in 1896, her kind was soon to be eclipsed by steam, but *Glenlee* managed four circumnavigations of the world, including 15 passages round the dreaded Cape Horn, before her last voyage in 1919. By then she had completed 5,000 days at sea.

Restoration commenced in 1993 after her rescue by the Spanish navy who found her sunk in Seville after vandalism. Riggers from around the world came to Glasgow to take part in the re-stepping of the masts, bringing with them their expertise gleaned from working on the other Clydebuilt sailing ships around the world. Apart from the impressive sight of this vessel, there are also interactive displays recalling the great days of trading under sail.

The names, Harland and Wolff, John Brown and Alexander Stephens have now gone; reminders of a time when the song of the Clyde was

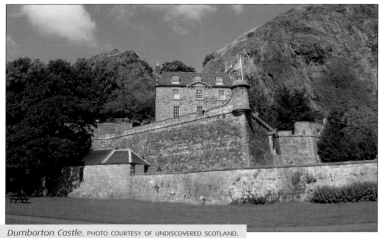

Dumbarton Castle. PHOTO COURTESY OF UNDISCOVERED SCOTLAND.

the chiming of the hammer on the red hot iron rivet. (For the social and industrial history of the Clyde, see also the **Clydebank Museum**, located in the Town Hall at Clydebank, near the shipyards which gave the Clyde its reputation).

DUMBARTON – the Denny Ship Model Experimental Tank

Victorian ship designers soon learnt that the only certain way to test ships for speed and seaworthiness (before so much as a plate was laid) was to test a model of the ship in a tank. The world's first tank was the Denny Tank, at Dumbarton, built in 1882 and was the length of a football pitch. The clay moulding beds, in which designers would make casts of their ships for testing, are still preserved. Named after the William Denny shipyard, it is still used for assessing designs.

Dumbarton itself has no small place is maritime history. For centuries it was the lowest fordable point on the Clyde; it is said to have the longest recorded history of any British stronghold, and has been home to many castles. More recently, the *Cutty Sark* was launched here in 1869. Also here is the MV *Kyles*, the oldest Clydebuilt vessel afloat in Britain which is open for viewing.

THE HEBRIDES

Three museums reflect the maritime history and traditions of the Hebrides. They are to be found at Port Charlotte on Islay, at Hynish on Tiree (the Skerryvore Museum) and at Stornoway on Lewis (the Museum Nan Eilean)

■ Islay

The **Museum of Islay Life**, housed in the former Free Church, contains a large collection relating to the archaeology of the island, and reflects changing island life through reconstructed rooms including a Victorian farmhouse and a croft. History lies richly on this island – there have been Mesolithic, Neolithic and Bronze Age finds, as well as early Christian churches and medieval gravestones. The museum's library has over a thousand books relating to island life. Maritime activity here is largely inshore fishing, although the museum displays artefacts from Armada ships wrecked on these shores.

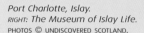

Port Charlotte, Islay.
RIGHT: The Museum of Islay Life.
PHOTOS © UNDISCOVERED SCOTLAND.

■ Tiree

The **Skerryvore Museum**, Tiree, tells the story of the building of the Skerryvore Light which stands 12 miles southwest of the island, and can be seen with a telescope. The museum is housed within the old signal tower, restored by the Hebridean Trust. This spiral staircased tower claims to be '*the smallest museum in the world*'.

Skerryvore Lighthouse has been described as '*the most beautiful lighthouse in the world*', and it is certainly the tallest in Scotland, the product of the fertile engineering mind of master marine engineer, Alan Stevenson, the uncle of Robert Louis Stevenson. It took 150 men 6 years to construct this light on a rocky reef which is often awash.

■ Lewis

The **Museum Nan Eilean**, in Stornoway, was the first fully professional museum to be established in the Western isles. In a theme that has recurred in so many ports and harbours of the British coastline, the maritime memory here is of the great days of the herring boom: huge fleets took mammoth catches which were handled by small migrating armies ashore. Displays of photographs show herring packing on the quay taking place on a scale unimaginable today. With its proximity to the open Atlantic, the story is told of the part the island played in the whaling trade.

Stornoway harbour is quieter today. PHOTO © UNDISCOVERED SCOTLAND.
INSET: A Scottish trawlerman. PHOTO COURTESY OF SHETLAND MUSEUM.

Malin, Hebrides Gazetteer

McKechnie Institute
Dalrymple Street, Girvan,
South Ayrshire KA26 9AE,
Scotland
☎ +44 (0)1465 713643
www.south-ayrshire.gov.uk/
galleries/mckechnie.htm
OPEN Tues–Sat

Scottish Maritime Museum
Harbourside, Irvine,
North Ayrshire, KA12 8QE,
Scotland
☎ +44 (0)1294 278283
www.scottishmaritime
museum.org
OPEN Daily: 10:00–17:00.

North Ayrshire Museum
Manse Street, Kirkgate,
Saltcoats, North Ayrshire
KA21 5AA, Scotland
☎ +44 (0)1294 464174
www.visitsaltcoats.com/
museum.html
OPEN Mon, Tue, Thu–Sat,
10:00–13:00 & 14:00–17:00

**Denny Ship Model
Experimental Tank**
Castle Stret, Dumbarton,
G82 1QS
☎ +441389 743093
www.scottishmaritime
museum.org/dumbart.htm
OPEN Mon–Sat 10.00–16.00
(ex Christmas and N Year)

**The Tall Ship at Glasgow
Harbour**
Yorkhill Quay, 100 Stobcross
Road, Glasgow G3 0QQ,
Scotland
☎ +44 (0)141 339 0631
www.glenlee.co.uk
OPEN Daily

**Clydebuilt Maritime
Museum**
Braehead Shopping Centre,
Kings Inch Road, Glasgow
G51 4BN, Scotland.
☎ +44 (0)141 886 1013
www.scottishmaritime
museum.org/glasgow.htm
OPEN Daily

**The Artic Penguin
Maritime Heritage Centre**
The Pier, Inveraray,
Argyll PA32 8UY, Scotland.
☎ +44 (0)1499 302213
www.visitworthy.co.uk/
SM_maritime1.htm
OPEN Daily

Clydebank Museum
Town Hall, Dumbarton Road,
Clydebank,
West Dunbartonshire
G81 1UE, Scotland
☎ +44 (0)1389 738702
www.scottishmuseums.org.
uk/museums
OPEN Mon–Sat (pm only on
Mon, Wed, Thurs & Fri)

**McLean Museum and Art
Gallery**
15 Kelly Street, Greenock,
Inverclyde PA16 8JX
(Renfrewshire) Scotland
☎ +44 (0)1475 715624
www.glasgowgalleries.co.uk
/mclean.htm

OPEN Mon–Sat, except BH &
local public holidays.
Evening GV BA

Campbeltown Museum
Public Library & Museum,
Hall St, Campbeltown,
Kintyre, Argyll & Bute,
Scotland
☎ +44 (0)1586 552366/67
OPEN Tues–Sat (Confirm as
times vary)

Museum of Islay Life
Port Charlotte, Isle of Islay,
Argyll & Bute, Scotland
PA48 7UN
☎ +44 (0)1496 850358
www.islaymuseum.
freeserve.co.uk
OPEN Daily, Easter–31 Oct;
Sun pm in winter, or BA

Skerryvore Museum
Hynish, Isle of Tiree,
Argyll & Bute, Scotland
☎ +44 (0)18792 220606
www.hynishcentre.co.uk/
thingstodo.htm
OPEN Enquire as renovation
work may be in progress

Museum Nan Eilean
Francis Street, Stornoway,
Isle of Lewis, Western Isles
HS1 2NF
☎ +44 (0)1851 709266
www.w-isles.gov.uk/
museum.htm
OPEN Mon–Sat, Apr–Sept;
Tues–Sat in winter

**BA: By arrangement
BH: Bank holiday
GV: Group visits**

Puffer Vic 32.
© PUFFER PRESERVATION TRUST.

INDEX